**W9-DDI-021**

# British History in Perspective
General Editor: Jeremy Black

PUBLISHED TITLES

*Titles continued overleaf*

Please note that a sister series, *Social History in Perspective*, is now available. It covers the key topics in social, cultural and religious history.

**British History in Perspective
Series Standing Order**
ISBN 0–333–71356–7 hardcover
ISBN 0–333–69331–0 paperback
(*outside North America only*)

You can receive future titles in this series as they are published by placing a standing order. Please contact your bookseller or, in case of difficulty, write to us at the address below with your name and address, the title of the series and one or both of the ISBNs quoted above.

Customer Services Department, Macmillan Distribution Ltd
Houndmills, Basingstoke, Hampshire RG21 6XS, England

# BRITAIN AND THE COLD WAR, 1945–1991

Sean Greenwood

# #4198199H

First published in Great Britain 2000 by
**MACMILLAN PRESS LTD**
Houndmills, Basingstoke, Hampshire RG21 6XS and London
Companies and representatives throughout the world

A catalogue record for this book is available from the British Library.

ISBN 0–333–67617–3 hardcover
ISBN 0–333–67618–1 paperback

First published in the United States of America 2000 by
**ST. MARTIN'S PRESS, INC.,**
Scholarly and Reference Division,
175 Fifth Avenue, New York, N.Y. 10010

ISBN 0–312–22858–9

Library of Congress Cataloging-in-Publication Data
Greenwood, Sean, 1944–
Britain and the cold war, 1945–1991 / Sean Greenwood.
p.   cm. — (British history in perspective)
Includes bibliographical references (p.    ) and index.
ISBN 0–312–22858–9 (cloth)
1. Great Britain—Foreign relations—1945–   2. Cold War.
I. Title.   II. Series.
DA588.G74   1999 2000
327.41—dc21                                             99–42655
                                                        CIP

This book is printed on paper suitable for recycling and made from fully managed and sustained forest sources.

10   9   8   7   6   5   4   3   2   1
09   08   07   06   05   04   03   02   01   00

Printed in Hong Kong

To S. P. R. Attlee

# CONTENTS

# GLOSSARY

| | |
|---|---|
| ACC | Allied Control Council |
| AIOC | Anglo-Iranian Oil Company |
| ANF | Atlantic Nuclear Force |
| CFM | Council of Foreign Ministers |
| CIA | Central Intelligence Agency |
| CND | Campaign for Nuclear Disarmament |
| CoS | Chiefs of Staff |
| CSCE | Conference on Security and Co-operation in Europe |
| EC | European Community |
| EDC | European Defence Community |
| EEC | European Economic Community |
| ERP | European Recovery Programme |
| FCO | Foreign and Commonwealth Office |
| FRG | Federal Republic of Germany |
| FTA | Free Trade Area |
| GDR | German Democratic Republic |
| ICBM | Inter-Continental Ballistic Missile |
| INF | Intermediate Nuclear Force |
| IRBM | Intermediate Range Ballistic Missile |
| IRD | Information Research Department |
| JIC | Joint Intelligence Committee |
| MEC | Middle East Command |
| MEDO | Middle East Defence Organisation |
| MIRV | Multiple Independently Targetable Re-entry Vehicle |
| MLF | Multilateral Force |
| NATO | North Atlantic Treaty Organisation |
| NPT | Non-Proliferation Treaty |
| NSC | National Security Council |
| PRC | People's Republic of China |
| PUSC | Permanent Under-Secretary's Committee |
| PUSD | Permanent Under-Secretary's Department |
| RIO | Regional Information Office |
| SALT | Strategic Arms Limitation Treaty/Talks |
| SDI | Strategic Defence Initiative |
| SEATO | South East Asia Treaty Organisation |
| UK | United Kingdom |
| UN | United Nations |
| US | United States |
| USSR | Union of Soviet Socialist Republics |
| WEU | Western European Union |

# INTRODUCTION

It is important to face some of the historiographical issues associated with any study of the Cold War head on from the start. One overarching problem is how to decide when a conflict, which involved no declaration of war and no direct military activity between the major participants, has actually started. The honest answer is: with some difficulty. It is a puzzle which has absorbed scholars ever since they first began to tackle the contest as a historical question and continues to divide them. One historian, for instance, has offered the warning that 'it would be a great mistake to try and write a history of the cold war which began in 1945', the implication being that the phenomenon had origins reaching much further back.[1] This is, of course, undeniable. But where should an investigation of origins open; 1941, 1939, 1917? The consequence of a historian adhering strictly to Maitland's principle that History is 'a seamless web' might easily be that we end up, as A. J. P Taylor once proposed, in 410 AD. The decision to settle on 1945 as the point of departure for this investigation is based to an extent upon the prosaic factor of restricted space. The author also happens to believe that it is perfectly reasonable to begin a detailed examination of the Cold War, as opposed to its pre-history, in that year. Not only had the period of acute tension and animosity threatening a general clash of arms between the major Communist and non-Communist Powers – what is usually taken to be the Cold War – not yet achieved its fully developed form, it remained beyond the horizons of any of the future opponents. Indeed, the earliest, and not very widely supported date for the beginning of the Cold War is early 1946.

There is also a problem of definition. It has been argued that the simple description above represents a rather narrow reading of what the Cold War was about – that in other words, the received compre-

1

hension is essentially a misapprehension. This alternative version asserts that to contemporary British policy-formers, the Cold War was not synonymous with Soviet-Western relations, but was viewed more broadly as 'all measures short of international armed conflict' – which they naturally wished to deter – and included propaganda and subversion to fight and win the contest. There is nothing novel in this, except that this interpretation goes on to suggest that the creation of regional defence systems such as the North Atlantic Treaty Organisation were more or less arms in this propaganda war and had principally a political as opposed to a military objective. One of these political aims, it is suggested, 'was to convince the inhabitants of a region that they were facing a military threat from the Soviet Union rather than a political and ideological challenge which military and political elites saw as more real and more dangerous'.[2] There is a difficulty with this picture. Preserving what they had – in Britain's case, in the face of an evaporating world influence – did indeed condition the Western Powers to act in the way that they did and to favour a world order based on the *status quo*. But the implication that the threat was a construction – almost a virtual projection exaggerated by sophisticates to frighten the primitives and to serve their own purposes – goes against the evidence that the USSR was increasingly judged in all the Western capitals to be a real and substantial danger. Certainly attempts to fight a political Cold War, including the use of covert methods, were energetically pursued. Yet these were tributary activities flowing from the main stream of the perceived necessity for containing alliances and military preparedness, which enabled other means of Cold War fighting to be engaged with some confidence that hot war, was unlikely to occur except by accident. It is to these more traditional, perhaps pedestrian, aspects of the Cold War that this study has given emphasis.

Increasingly, such defensive structures were assembled within the context of a struggle engaged between, as they were termed almost throughout, the Superpowers. Indeed, from what might be called its mature phase, the mid-1950s onwards, the Cold War was predominantly a Soviet-American affair. It would be perverse to suggest otherwise and the mainstream of historiography of this episode accurately reflects this fact. Why then a study of Britain and the Cold War? Several answers may be given. By the end of the 1970s attention was being drawn to the narrow focus of early histories of the period, assembled almost entirely by American historians researching into mainly American archives. These, whilst offering stimulating and valuable new perspectives on aspects of postwar East-West confrontation, were essentially exercises in the history of American diplomacy and as studies of the totality of the Cold War were, therefore, narrow and inevitably incomplete. One result of this American-centredness was that Britain's part in a sequence of events which has dominated international relations in the second half of the twentieth century seemed at times to be relegated to little more than that of a bit player. The giant figure of Winston Churchill coining the most evocative metaphor of the period in his 'Iron Curtain' speech at Fulton, Missouri, in March 1946, was seldom omitted from these accounts. Ernest Bevin also usually achieved honourable mention, as a sort of working class *alter ego* of Churchill supposedly carrying the baton of Churchillian foresightedness to the North Atlantic Treaty in 1949 before exhaustedly passing it to the safe hands of the United States. Beyond that? Not much. From the 1970s, the progressive availability of British official records and subsequent pleas by some European historians for the 'depolarisation' of Cold War history acted as a significant corrective to this asymmetrical depiction so that by the end of the 1980s what might be termed a British school of Cold War historians had begun to emerge, working largely from British archives and setting their findings against the work in the United States which continued to flourish.[3] Since then, however, concerns that the particular focus of these British studies might end up presenting as lop-sided a picture as those they were trying to adjust have been overtaken by the impact of the important release of archival material from the repositories of the former Soviet Union and some of its satellites. This has had the result of tilting attention back to the activities of the Superpowers (though China does now get more of a look in) and, once again, there is the danger of the British role in the Cold War being marginalised.

What was this role? In a very general sense, the 'polarised' version of the Cold War is correct. For 35 of the 45 years or so of Cold War, it was the Superpowers who made the running. Britain's greatest contribution was to the origins of the Cold War up until around 1955. From then, the struggle was increasingly operated by the designs and desires of the White House and the Kremlin. But Britain's part in the early Cold War years not only helped give shape to the conflict, it also at times gave it impetus. The exposed position of Britain and its global possessions which engendered a heightened sense of anxiety drove them towards what was to be called containment before this had become settled policy in the United States and even to precipitate action before the purposes of the Soviet Union had been finely discerned. At the same time, Britain's own intentions were more complex than is sometimes portrayed. For instance, the once received wisdom that America was cleverly enticed by Britain into protecting Western Europe from Soviet Communism between 1945 and 1949 has effectively been exposed as a myth. Moreover, British input to the Cold War did not cease after 1949 and for another 20 years or so their influence was such that British policy-makers were sometimes able to angle the direction of the contest in significant ways. The pulse of British influence was to become more feeble after 1956, and more so after 1968, but was to persist in the face of continuing economic debilitation and the rise of rival centres of authority in Western Europe until the final days of the Cold War.

As the latter might suggest, an examination of Britain and the Cold War is an important aspect of Britain's own recent history and a fragment of the lengthy story of British postwar decline. That this descent seemed less precipitous post-Second World War than should have been the case by any measure of economic or military strength owes a good deal to the frequent correspondence of interests between Britain and the United States and much of what follows is necessarily an investigation of the peaks and troughs in that relationship. This is unavoidable. American power rapidly made the USA a leading contestant in the Cold War and, despite their attempts sometimes to evade this fact, qualified the responses of the British. Though this author has consciously tried to avoid adding to the list of specific inquiries into the Anglo-American partnership, any attempt to construct an account of Britain's part in the Cold War which ignores this central reference point would be akin to writing about Dr Watson without Sherlock Holmes. Yet Britain's own performance in the Cold War has an intricate significance influencing the pattern that that conflict was to adopt, but also conditioning, the way in which the British saw themselves in the second half of the twentieth century. And although the eclipse in British ability to modify the behaviour of the two major participants in the Cold War did not occur with the rapidity that trans-Atlantic accounts have usually inferred, the process of decline itself is undeniable. This descent has dictated the shape of this book. So too has the availability of detailed historical analysis under the restrictions of the 'Thirty Year Rule'. Like the efforts of an increasingly insolvent housepainter, the labourer's brush is more abundantly laden at the beginning than at the end of the edifice. But then, origins are frequently more convoluted than conclusions and, in this context at least, Bevin was more significant than Thatcher.

I welcome the chance at this point to acknowledge the assistance of my two friends and colleagues, James Ellison of Queen Mary and Westfield College, University of London and Kevin Ruane of Canterbury Christ Church University College. In particular, Kevin's astonishing generosity made my understanding and therefore, it is hoped, this book the richer. The brunt of the necessary obsession was taken soothingly by my wife Deborah and it is with much love that I dedicate this book to her.

# 1

## COMBAT RECONNAISSANCE, 1945–46

Wherever the start of the Cold War is pinpointed, the fact remains that the alliance which had worked to defeat the Axis Powers had, within only five years of the end of the Second World War, been reconfigured into a new source of international tension. It should not, however, be inferred from this sharp descent that this rift was either generally expected or desirable to British policy-makers. Quite the opposite. The optimistic assumption, particularly in the Foreign Office, was that the wartime partnership would iron out the issues which came between them and continue as a force for stability in peacetime. The experience of the first half of the twentieth century stimulated many in Whitehall to concentrate attention rather on German capacity for revival as the most likely source of future problems. Linked to this, Britain's plainly reduced position in the world relative to her wartime partners and the need to prevent the resurgence of an aggressive Germany encouraged the view that the survival of the alliance would provide a hedge both against British weakness and any revival of German strength. Thus the trend of British policy in 1945 was towards international co-operation, not East-West confrontation. As early as 1942, the War Cabinet had accepted a Foreign Office draft for a postwar World Organisation on the basis that this body would act as the general guarantor of peace and also the conduit for continued co-operation between Britain, the United States and the Soviet Union, the calculation being that mere association with such powerful allies would, of itself, bolster Britain's own shrinking position as a state of the first rank.[1] Anthony Eden, the Foreign Secretary, put it succinctly to the War Cabinet near the end of that year: 'we can only hope to play our part either as a European Power or as a World Power if we ourselves form part of a wider organisation.'[2]

This desire to institutionalise the wartime alliance and project it into the future was, inevitably, not without its problems and much Foreign Office time during the war was given up to deciphering how this ideal might be achieved. Wartime disagreements over the post-war shape of Poland and the independence of the Baltic States provided particular instances of a more general anxiety about future Soviet activity. As for the political contours of the rest of Eastern Europe, the British had demonstrated little sustained interest in it other than to dream up various unrealistic confederal schemes which, in any case, conflicted with the overall Allied strategy that the Red Army would be first on the scene to 'liberate' these nations. The exception was Greece. The requirement to shield the Straits and cover Britain's passage across the Mediterranean towards Suez made it essential to the British that Greece should escape inclusion in a Soviet sphere. This was made abundantly clear to Stalin by Churchill when he visited him in Moscow in October 1944 and when the infamous note known as the 'percentages agreement' was ticked. Indeed, the consistency of the British position over Eastern Europe meant that Stalin could be excused for deciphering this as a signal that, so long as he restrained himself over Greece, the remainder of Eastern Europe was more or less his. The same message was reinforced at the Big Three conference at Yalta in February 1945. The territorial settlement of Poland was essentially in Stalin's favour and the Declaration on Liberated Europe with its sentiments of free elections for the Eastern European states could be dismissed as eyewash. This anyway was how Stalin chose to interpret it. His pressure on Poland, Bulgaria and Rumania immediately post-Yalta to install governments sympathetic to the Soviet Union was an amalgam of a dictator's heavy-handedness and the demeanour of a legitimate seigneur among his vassals. Churchill, nevertheless, was genuinely shocked and before long was importuning Roosevelt's successor to be firm with Stalin. As it was not the line the Prime Minister had himself taken thus far over Eastern Europe Truman's decision to stonewall his British ally was understandable. By the time Hitler's Germany had collapsed the majority of states in Eastern Europe had therefore fallen and, despite intermittent and ineffective pressure from the Western Powers over the next two years, were to stay under the sway of the Soviet Empire. In Stalin's eyes, of course, they were not the first victims of the Cold War but rather the legitimate booty of the Second World War.

But the British, especially Eden and his advisers in the Foreign Office, had concerns too over the reliability of the United States *vis à*

*vis* their most pressing concern, a future German resurgence. The
Americans, it was felt, 'are likely to be quitters' and that 'if our policy
has been such as to alienate Soviet Russia we may be left again with
Germany alone'.[3] If, therefore, the Americans chose to return to a
policy of isolationism, Britain would need to fall back upon her 20
year alliance with the Soviet Union. This nervousness over the future
direction of American policy accounts for some of the passivity towards looming Soviet control over Eastern Europe – though there
was little, in any case, that the British could practically do to prevent
it. It also went some way towards producing, by the end of 1944, a
further permutation to the insurance policy of the World Organisation. This was the so-called Western bloc which envisaged a grouping
of Western European states acting under British leadership. Part of
the thinking behind this proposed mirror-image of the Soviet bloc,
which was plainly taking shape in Eastern Europe, was that it would
make up a second half of an encircling barrier to contain Germany. It
might also, it was thought, serve to consolidate the association with
the USSR. The Foreign Office view was that after the war, the Russians 'will take a very tough line with Germany and may do many
things there which will cause offence to worthy people in this country
and the United States', but that 'we should be unwise to falter in our
support of Russia for such reasons, since it could only react to the
advantage of Germany and a cooling-off of our relations with Russia.'[4] The best-case scenario for the future, so far as the British were
concerned, was spelled out in a House of Commons statement in late
1944 following Eden's return from the Dumbarton Oaks conference
where the framework of the World Organisation (or United Nations
as it was soon called) had been set up. This ran:

> To put the matter in a nutshell, we must, if we can, have some World
> Organisation embracing the bulk of the nations and eventually,
> perhaps, all nations. We must, in any case, preserve and reinforce
> our alliance with the Soviet Union and our fraternal association
> with the United States. And finally we must, if we can, have the
> closest possible defence arrangements with France and with the
> smaller nations of Western Europe. These will be the three pillars
> of our post-war foreign policy.[5]

Thus, as the European war drew to a close, a Soviet bloc in Eastern
Europe continued to be judged as not detrimental to Britain's princi-

pal interests. Although Russian military strength and ideological pretensions could not help but be a worrying mixture to the British, and especially so the further west the Red Army penetrated, such anxieties were spasmodic. Churchill's gloom over Stalin's high-handedness in Eastern Europe after Yalta was not fully contagious and it was still possible in the summer of 1945 for the Moscow Embassy to discount uncomfortable aspects of Soviet behaviour along the lines that, 'Russia today is rejoicing in all the emotions and impulses of very early manhood and spring from a new sense of boundless strength and from the giddiness of success. It is immense fun to her to tell herself that she has become great and that there is little or nothing to stop her making her greatness felt.'[6] It was not always easy to sustain so genial a view. Three days before setting out for the final wartime Big Three Conference at Potsdam, Eden confided in Churchill to finding the 'world outlook gloomy and signs of Russian penetration everywhere'. This temporary bout of melancholy did not, however, inhibit his ability on the same day to 'entirely endorse' a Foreign Office assertion that 'we must base our foreign policy on the principle of co-operation between the three World Powers. In order to strengthen our position in this combination we ought to enrole the Dominions and especially France not to mention the lesser Western European Powers, as collaborators with us in this tripartite system.'[7]

Churchill's mistrust of the Soviet Union tended to run deeper than that of the Foreign Office. At his meeting with Stalin in October 1944 Churchill had felt able to reassure him that 'it was no part of British policy to grudge Soviet Russia access to warm water ports and to the great oceans and seas of the world ... [the British] no longer followed the policy of Disreali or Lord Curzon.'[8] But, as Potsdam approached in the summer of 1945, the Prime Minister was clearly working to stiffen the stance of the Americans towards the Russians. Even so, his attitude to the Soviet Union continued to oscillate. As one biographer has noted, 'as long as he remained Prime Minister, and even afterwards, Churchill's moods of belligerency would be accompanied by a wistful belief that if only he and Stalin could get together, everything would be all right.'[9] Somewhat later, in 1948 his, by then not infrequent boast, of 'how much he had foreseen what might happen after the war and how anxious he had been to go in from the South in order to prevent the Russians spreading themselves so far across Europe', came to the ears of his old political associate, Lord Halifax with a new twist. 'I might even have turned the Germans on them!', he was reported to have declared. Mildly shocked, Halifax found 'it hard to believe that [Churchill] really said this and it is one of those things, I suppose, that must never see the light. But as a bit of history it is very entertaining.'[10] Later still, in 1954, Churchill was to cause a furore in the Commons when he hinted more publicly that this had been his intention. We now know that in May 1945, he had indeed ordered the drawing up of a military contingency plan, codenamed 'Unthinkable', which envisaged the use of British and American forces supplemented with the remnants of Hitler's *Wehrmacht* should the Red Army's sweep across northern Europe fail to come to a halt.[11] As it turned out, the British Chiefs of Staff (CoS) rejected 'Unthinkable' on the basis that the West was outnumbered on the ground by Soviet forces and because of likely lack of American enthusiasm.

The Prime Minister might reasonably have expected greater support from his military advisers than he was given, for the domain of the most consistent doubts about the postwar attitude of the Soviet Union was not Churchill's memoranda, but the reports of the CoS. A coincidence of opinion between the military and the diplomats on the need for some form of British-led Western European group after the war existed, but this was about as far as agreement went. The Service Chiefs viewed the Soviet Union rather than Germany as Britain's most likely future enemy, were 'profoundly sceptical' of the practicality of the United Nations Organisation, and exhibited even less faith than the Foreign Office in American reliability.[12] They believed that the proposed Western bloc would provide some security against the Soviet Union, especially if Germany was brought into such a defensive system. 'In fact,' the CoS insisted, 'Germany would be the key to the security of these Islands in the future and, however unpalatable the fact might be there might well come a time when we should have to rely on her assistance against a hostile Russia.'[13] The kind of thinking which was beginning to gain favour amongst the Chiefs of Staff during 1944 was spelled out in Cabinet committee by the Secretary of State for War, Sir James Grigg. In his opinion:

Russia would do whatever she liked in Europe east of Berlin, and would squeeze out all the small countries in Eastern Europe except for her own satellites. Russia would get there first and we should have no say in what she did. The United States was interested only in places of economic and commercial importance to her ... At the same time she was going to see that our export trade did not revive and that the British Empire was weakened politically as much as possible. It was therefore time for us to realise that the Tripartite Alliance was a chimera, not only as regards Germany, but also in relation to a World Organisation ... [He] suggested that on the long view, it would be no bad thing if Germany should suffer so greatly from very rough Russian treatment that a purged Germany might turn towards association with Western Europe rather than east-wards.[14]

This was a 'grotesque' vista to officials in the Foreign Office, who vigorously condemned any idea of the inclusion of Germany in a Western bloc. In their view, 'the adoption (in the advance of any need to do so) of a policy of building up our enemies so as to be able to defeat our allies would seem ... to derive from some kind of suicidal mania.'[15] A policy of reviving Germany would merely precipitate an obvious reaction from the USSR and with the Americans 'frightened right out of any participation in a World Organisation'.[16] Of course, the Chiefs were professionally obliged to provide for Britain's security and the simple fact that Hitler was vanquished and Stalin victorious encouraged a sort of time-lapse to a pre-1907 world, where Britain staunchly withstood the press of Russia's masses on the Khyber Pass and in the Straits. In this mind-set, the Anglo-Soviet alliance was an aberration and the sheer size and the military and industrial potential of the Soviet Union alarmed the military experts in a way that the actual strength of the USA did not. The military planners were also inclined to believe that one lesson of the 1930s was that too much faith had been placed in the League of Nations and too little attention given, until almost too late, to coping with a Power bent upon aggression.

The Foreign Office looked to recent history too, though they seized upon a different lesson. This was that Germany, unless confined by a tight ring of neighbouring states, could soon revive to cause further serious mischief. There was little conflict of opinion within the Foreign Office over the vital support Moscow could provide in preventing this, but there were differing views over how this assistance might be won. Christopher Warner, the Head of the Northern Department, before long a hard-liner on Russia, initially went in for rather cosy imagery. 'I am as convinced as ever I was', he wrote to the British Ambassador in Moscow, 'that the Russians want to be reasonable, but influential, members of the club, even though they think some of the rules are damned silly and want to change them. They *are* members now but are not allowed into some of the rooms and I'm worried that they may get fed up with waiting and being mucked about and may go off and start another club of their own.'[17] By contrast, Gladwyn Jebb, of the Economic and Reconstruction Department, favoured a more tough-minded approach. 'Buttering up the Russians ... is no good,' he told Hugh Dalton, wartime President of the Board of Trade. 'The only result is that they despise you.'[18] What is clear is that the assertion that there was an 'inflexibility and single-mindedness assumed of Soviet policy by the Foreign Office' does not stand up to close inspection.[19] As late as October 1945, even a supposed hardbitten Russophobe such as Sir Orme Sargent 'personally believed that the Russians still want to co-operate with the Western countries' and that difficulties with them was explicable 'by the wholly understandable desire of the Russians to drive hard bargains whilst their military strength in Europe was still strong'.[20]

In retrospect, Foreign Office aspirations – that the USA could be persuaded to help in the task of European peacekeeping (which hardly anyone other than Churchill really expected and even he had told Stalin that he 'did not think that the Americans would stay very long [in occupied Germany]')[21] and that British and Soviet objectives were essentially compatible – might seem particularly frail constructions. But what we now know of Soviet postwar planning suggests that at least one strand of this optimism was not entirely unfounded. The Soviet intention was ruthlessly to exploit Germany for purposes of their own reconstruction. This, it was judged, would best be done through co-operation with the Allies, maintaining a united Germany and without promoting social revolution. Indeed, Russian planning exhibited little interest in fostering revolutionary change in postwar Europe which, it was considered, would induce a deterioration in inter-Allied relations. One Soviet exercise in prognostication suggested that relations between Britain and the USA were likely to become more abrasive because of capitalist competition. This would impel the British to reach an understanding with the Soviet Union which could result in the creation of an Eastern European bloc under Soviet leadership, a Western bloc formed by the British, and a neutral bloc, including Germany, between the two.[22] Such projections, unknown of course to Whitehall, were not inconsonant with paths of thought being pursued by the Foreign Office. Even without access to this thinking, Foreign Office officials felt that the consequence of accepting the forecasts of the CoS, the revival of Germany, was both repugnant and the seed of a self-fulfilling prophecy of Soviet antagonism. Given Britain's weakness, officials in the Foreign Office had little choice other than to hold to their faith and to dismiss the Chiefs' opinions as 'anti-Russian extravagances'. As Clark and Wheeler point out, by the end of the war 'concern about the Soviet Union had already become part of the fabric of [British] post-war security' and that the Anglo-Soviet Alliance 'was not strong enough to bear the burden of post-war settlement but not sufficiently adversarial to be abandoned altogether'.[23] For the time being, the Chiefs and the Foreign Office seem to have reached something of a compromise, with the former agreeing 'to restrict to the narrowest possible limits discussions and circulation of papers in which the hypothesis of Russia as a possible enemy was mentioned'.[24]

As well as being hampered at the tail end of the war by hostility from the Foreign Office, the CoS found themselves in the early months of peace fettered by a reduced resource provision for their military projections. After the summer of 1945, the incoming Labour Government supervised the running down of arms production and the demobilisation of the armed forces.[25] This had a lot to do with the new government's perceived need for economies. But ideological motives were also at work. Many prominent members of the new Labour Cabinet brought with them to office vague, but determined views that a system of international relations based on 'spheres of influence', the 'balance of power' and inter-state rivalry had proved a disaster and that some new form of co-operative approach through a World Organisation had to be found.[26] This was a perspective sharpened by the advent of the atom bomb. No one felt this more keenly than the new Prime Minister, Clement Attlee. For Attlee: 'the coming of the atom bomb means that we have got to consider from a new angle most of the problems of foreign policy and defence and that many principles hitherto accepted as axiomatic will have to be amended or discarded.'[27] Unless war was now banished from human society, he wrote to President Truman in September 1945, 'I ought to direct all our people to live like troglodytes underground as being the only hope of survival, and that by no means certain.'[28] In similar vein, Stafford Cripps, Labour's President of the Board of Trade, had asserted during the recent General Election campaign that 'we must all get out of our minds any idea that the World Organisation and world co-operation are Utopian ideas which are not practical. They are indeed the only really practical ideas in the light of the existence of the atomic bomb.'[29] For a short time, and against the advice of both the CoS and the Foreign Office (who were at one at least on this), such thinking supported an inclination within the Labour Cabinet to mark the dawning new age of peace by sharing atomic secrets with the Soviets whilst seeking international forms of control of atomic weapons.[30]

This 'internationalism' was not simply the quirky baggage of British socialism. Churchill's Coalition had also publicly encouraged notions of a better postwar world via endorsement of the idealism of the Atlantic Charter, the Declaration on Liberated Europe and the World Organisation which, to those looking on from beyond the negotiating tables, appeared to be subscribed to by both the United States and the USSR. Also, as we have seen, permanent advisers on foreign policy held to the view that continued co-operation between the Allies was both practicable and best. What was rapidly to confound these rosy hopes and draw both the Labour Government and its foreign specialists closer towards the more dismal views of the CoS was a blizzard of disquieting international developments extending in an arc from Teheran to Paris during the first year of the new government.

A depressing indication of what was to come was provided by the Council of Foreign Ministers (CFM). This was the setting for the first postwar gathering of the victorious Powers which met in London in September 1945 as part of an agreed series of conferences, to be held in the Allied capitals and prepare the ground for peace treaties with the defeated Axis states. The London CFM broke up in October without settling anything. Even before the CFM gathered, Ernest Bevin, the new Foreign Secretary, was already apprehensive over prospects of Soviet influence extending to Greece, where tensions between monarchists and Communists were moving towards civil war, and he was predisposed to resist this. His belief, as he told the Defence Committee of the Cabinet six months later, was that the loss of British influence in Greece would cause British authority in southern Europe, the Mediterranean and the Middle East to fall like dominoes and 'if we move out of the Mediterranean, Russia will move in'.[31] A proposal at the CFM from Molotov, the Soviet Foreign Minister, for a Russian trusteeship of an ex-Italian colony in North Africa which would, in Bevin's view, 'come across the lifeline of the British Empire' added to British pessimism.[32] Bevin's adoption of a negotiating stance which resembled an attempt to wring a pay increase from resisting bosses was not conducive to a harmonious settlement, particularly as Molotov relished the unyielding role which the Foreign Secretary had assigned him. The proceedings of the CFM, indeed, gives us a snapshot of the style and positions of the representatives of the victors in the brief months between peace and Cold War; Bevin alternating between pleas to the Russians for a frank 'cards on the table' approach and a gauchely belligerent demeanour; James Byrnes, the American Secretary of State, exuding deviousness in his desire to wrap up a deal which would settle his reputation as a peacemaker at home; and Molotov relying on technicalities to press for Soviet gains whenever he observed the lack of unity of purpose between the two Western negotiators. Though it was a discouraging overture to those in London who hoped to base world peace and British interests on postwar Allied collaboration, optimism was not lightly abandoned. After the London CFM had drawn to its desultory conclusion, opinion in the Foreign Office was that 'the Russians are being slow and cautious in all questions of international collaboration, but they have not decided to be uniformly obstructive ... They place their short term selfish interests above the less certain long term advantages of collaboration. But they are quite willing to collaborate when it pays.'[33] On his return from another three-Power meeting in Moscow in January 1946, Bevin was inclined to believe that the terrible devastation he had witnessed in the Soviet Union accounted for its behaviour in Eastern Europe and suggested to the Cabinet that some public acknowledgement of Soviet economic difficulties might ease relations between the two countries.[34]

The early months of 1946 saw more disquieting developments. To a backdrop of Soviet diplomatic pressure on Turkey to revise the Montreux Convention governing passage of warships through the Straits (which they believed they had already been tacitly promised by their Allies), a demand for a Soviet base on the Straits and territorial claims in north-eastern Turkey, Stalin also created what amounted to a war scare over Iran. Russian failure to meet an agreed withdrawal from a joint wartime Allied occupation of the country, the fomenting of a breakaway nationalist movement in Iranian Azerbaijan via the Moscow-backed Tudeh party and the reinforcement of the Soviet military presence there in March 1946 convinced Bevin that 'this means war'.[35] He urged a group of influential Americans that it was 'vital to stand up to Russia ... Appeasement must be avoided at all costs ... So he begged America to weigh the importance of opposing the present designs on Persia.'[36] Something like a firm front was, in fact, agreed between London and Washington and this, coupled with Stalin's sense of caution, brought an end to the pressure on Ankara and Teheran and international tension dissolved. In the meantime, however, the first meeting of the United Nations Security Council in January – the focus of those who held 'internationalist' hopes – was sullied by accusation and counter-accusation by the Soviet and British representatives of interference in, respectively, Iran and in Greece.

At precisely the same time as these disconcerting events were unfolding, the Soviet threat seemed to surface much nearer to Britain. The swing to Communism in the democratic states of Western Europe was a matter for general concern, given the links between the indigenous Communist parties and Moscow. Nowhere, however, was this more disconcerting in early 1946 than in France. Here, the Communists had the greatest proportion of the vote, but lacking a majority, were forced to work with the Socialists and the Christian Democrats. This uneasy arrangement seemed to be made workable only by the strong hand of Charles de Gaulle. De Gaulle himself seems to have been a victim of this view of his own indispensability and, at the end of January 1946, in an attempt to sway the decision over the constitution of the Fourth Republic, he decided to resign. This turn of events was viewed in London as potentially calamitous and, for a time, Bevin was sure that France would descend into civil war with a Communist France as the probable outcome. Gloom was followed by the even gloomier with reports filtering through from Germany during February of a forced merger between the Social Democratic Party and the Moscow-controlled Communist Party in the Soviet Zone of occupation. This proved, in the long run, to be the most significant development of all because it seemed to presage a one-party state in Soviet-controlled Germany which could be used as the base for the communisation of the whole of the state. This fear of a Sovietised Germany was to provide, amidst a myriad of other problems, the most important single factor in the deterioration of relations between London and Moscow.

A greater readiness to accept that the USSR presented a more imminent security risk in those quarters which up to now had been resistant to this view becomes clearly discernible in the early part of 1946. One indication of this was the evaporation of an initial willingness demonstrated by some members of the Labour Cabinet to share atomic secrets with the Russians. There was some sensitivity on the British side to the possibility that some explanation for increased East-

West tension might be placed at the door of the atomic bomb. As the Soviets had not been informed before the bomb was used on Japan, they might easily assume that the two Western Powers had plans for future atomic co-operation with one another. This, it was recognised, was bound to make the Russians nervous and might incline them towards intransigence in negotiation simply to demonstrate that they were not to be overawed by the new weapon. But the dismal experience of the London CFM turned Attlee and Bevin away from such solicitude. High expectations of a continuation of wartime Anglo-American atomic co-operation, which had been promised to Churchill and appeared to have been reiterated to Attlee, did, however, survive. These, along with the broader prospects of international control, were to be dashed in August 1946, when the Truman Administration passed the McMahon Act legislating for life imprisonment or the death penalty for anyone passing atomic information to a foreign state. Meanwhile, the Labour Government had already decided in late 1945 to create Britain's own atomic production plants. Even so and despite pressure, for example from the CoS, that the product should be atom bombs as well as peaceful atomic technology, no formal decision was taken – and then only by a small Cabinet subcommittee – to produce a British bomb until January 1947. Status, frustration over the American *volt face* and the leverage the bomb would provide in Washington were all ingredients in this final decision. So too was deteriorating relations with the Soviets. It has been argued that fear of Russia was a spur from the start and that 'it was the prospect of being confronted with an atomic-armed USSR in the future which was the principal calculation underlying British attraction to atomic weapons in 1945, and it was from such a projected strategic environment that early British ideas of nuclear deterrence were to develop.'[37] What seems clear is that an already existing momentum for the development of Britain's own atomic bomb was now accelerated out of apprehension of a threat which Soviet atomic weapons might pose to Britain in five or six years' time.

The change of emphasis amongst the Government's diplomatic advisers was rather more marked. Neither the conviction that Russian tactics were purposely aimed at embarrassing Britain as the weaker of the two Anglo-Saxon States nor the dispiriting episode of the London CFM had, at the end of 1945, prevented officials from hanging on to the belief that 'the Soviet Government wish to collaborate with the Western Powers in the post-war problems.'[38] But by the spring of 1946, events had caused opinion to stiffen into an assumption that Britain was faced with an ideologically motivated opponent whose objectives were only limited by its current military and economic capacity to achieve them. A clear example of this abrupt transformation is provided by the advice of Frank Roberts who, from January 1946, was British Chargé d'Affaires in Moscow. At the end of October 1945, Roberts considered it 'a mistake to look only for sinister motives behind Soviet policy.'[39] Four months on, in a series of despatches to London influenced by his opposite number in Moscow, George Kennan, whose recent 'Long Telegram' had sounded alarm bells in Washington over the Kremlin's far-reaching objectives and the implied incompatibility between the Soviet system and the West, Roberts was stressing 'the ever-increasing emphasis laid here upon Marxist-Leninist ideology as the basis for Soviet internal and foreign policy' that 'Soviet security has become hard to distinguish from Soviet imperialism and it is becoming uncertain whether there is, in fact, any limit to Soviet expansion.' Though they might quibble over the detail in his exegesis, Roberts's colleagues in Whitehall did not dispute the central message and had themselves already arrived at similar conclusions.[40] Roberts's assessment was particularly valuable to London because of the dearth of information of what was going on in the USSR. The Joint Intelligence Committee (JIC) of the Chiefs Of Staff, at that point the core body of British intelligence appraisal, admitted: 'we have practically no direct intelligence, of a detailed factual or statistical nature, on conditions in the different parts of the Soviet Union, and none at all on the intentions, immediate or ultimate, of the Russian leaders.' In the JIC's estimation, which Roberts was to reinforce, Soviet policy had recently shifted from one of collaboration with the West to 'a policy of opportunism to extend her influence wherever possible without provoking a major war' at least until the completion of the first postwar Five Year Plan had begun to restore the losses incurred in the recent war.[41] In April, and in the light of these uncomfortable predictions, the Foreign Office set up a Russia Committee which was intended systematically to analyse Soviet intentions and draw up the appropriate responses based on 'the fact ... that Russian aggressiveness threatens British interests all over the world'.[42]

The disquieting events of early 1946 propelled the Foreign Office towards the doleful view of the Soviet Union which the CoS had held for some time and the general optimism amongst officials which had survived the war gave way to a more morbid tendency to assume the worst. This, as suggested, was not always the product of a rational process and with imperfect intelligence on Soviet intentions and activity, British policy at this point was frequently based less on solid information than on guesswork. Material from the archives of the former Soviet Union and its satellites indicates that pessimism may have set in too soon. Riding high on the jubilation of victory, Stalin appears to have been still willing to pursue Soviet objectives within the context of the Big Three and was being prompted by his leading foreign policy specialists to do so. The errors of these advisers were to assume that an Anglo-American dispute was more likely than a Soviet-American and, more significantly, that the West would accept the creation of a Soviet sphere of influence and so cause Stalin to push beyond the bounds of Western tolerance. Stalin, however, does not seem to have been convinced of an impending clash between the Western Powers. In November 1945 he warned the Polish leadership that 'the English and the Americans ... are closely connected to each other' and that their intelligence services were spreading the view that East-West conflict was imminent simply to gain diplomatic advantages. 'I am', he nevertheless asserted, 'completely certain that there will be no war, it is rubbish. They are not capable of waging war against us. Their armies have been disarmed by agitation for peace and will not raise their weapons against us. War is not decided by atomic bombs, but by armies.'[43] In another sense, the glum views percolating in the Foreign Office were quite legitimate. It seems clear that Stalin's moderate approach in the short term served much more ideologically driven long-term objectives. 'Whether in thirty years or so [the Western Powers] want to have another war', he went on to say to the Poles, 'is another issue.' He remained the cautious revolutionary, convinced of an inevitable show-down with capitalism, though recognising that the Soviet Union was too exhausted to promote this for some time. Pressure at perceived weak points in areas outside the existing Soviet sphere were designed as early probes in an eventual bid for more unlimited expansion. The concomitant stiffening of the Western attitude towards the Soviet Union appears to have taken an over-confident Stalin by surprise.[44] Soviet troops were withdrawn from Iran because, as he told the Azerbaijani Communists whom he had recently been urging on, their presence now 'undercut the foundations of our liberationist policies in Europe and Asia'.

A crucial effect of the bleak outlook from London in the early months of 1946 was that British policy in their zone in occupied Germany now began to be eased into reverse. This was a decisive development. In a sense, the political history of Europe since 1871 has been the history of attempts by Germany's neighbours to confine this powerful economic and geostrategical entity, which straddles the centre of Europe, within acceptable bounds. It was the second attempt within a generation to do so which had produced the alliance against Hitler and the costs of previous failures to contain Germany were at the forefront of the minds of all the victors in 1945. At the same time, the fragility of the friendship between the two European allies committed to the defeat of fascist Germany meant that neither could view with equanimity the prospect of a revived Germany in league with the other. This was, and continued to be, the nightmare of the CoS. As already noted, a *leitmotif* of much British thinking at the end of the war was that Germany must, once and for all, be kept in check, that this was a common purpose between the United Kingdom and the USSR and that the pursuance of this objective would be the bond which kept the two wartime allies in a partnership for peace. As Attlee put it in the, already difficult, summer of 1945 when the Russians were consolidating their hold on Eastern Europe, 'I think we must at all costs avoid trying to seek a cure by building up Germany or by forming blocs aimed at Russia ... Any suspicion – and the Russians are not slow to form suspicions – that we are trying to deal softly with the Germans, or to build her up, would be such an obvious threat to Russia that we could thereby harden the present Soviet Government's attitude in Eastern Europe and help to give actual shape to our fears.'[45]

There remains some debate over how, why and exactly when this principle came to be discarded. What is certain is that within a year of Attlee's warning, the British had begun to contemplate 'dealing softly with the Germans'. Economics played an important part in pushing them forward. On top of their own domestic economic difficulties, the British found themselves, by the end of 1945, having to divert scarce financial and food resources to prevent their occupation zone in north-west Germany from complete collapse. The root cause was the havoc caused by war upon a defeated population. But the British were, to a degree, the cause of their own misfortune. It was they who had insisted on occupying the most industrialised, and therefore most ravaged, area of Germany and they who had helped draw up the Potsdam Agreement in 1945, which they rapidly came to see as a legal bind that both prevented them from taking effective remedial action in Germany and gave advantage to the Russians.

The Potsdam Agreement, it has been stated, 'was incomplete, unrealistic and ambiguous'.[46] With hindsight it certainly has the hallmark of a doomed arrangement. But in the summer of 1945, it could easily appear as a reasonable, if flawed, attempt to resolve differing Allied perceptions as to how the defeated state should be treated whilst avoiding the errors of the 1919 settlement. Specifically, Potsdam tried to ensure the permanent subjugation of the Germans, that Germany should pay significant reparation for the damage done by the Nazis – principally to the Soviet Union – and that the cost of occupation should fall on the occupied rather than the occupiers. Until a central government acceptable to the Allies was set up, Germany was to remain temporarily divided into four zones of occupation. In the meantime, Germany's economic performance was to be throttle-controlled so that its economic strength did not exceed that of its neighbours and, to try to ensure that the Germans paid their own way without external assistance, reparation from plant and machinery was to be allocated from Germany's residual industrial capability.

What those who had drafted the Potsdam Agreement preferred to sweep under the carpet was the potential for serious dispute over how much industrial material was necessary for the Germans to stand on their own feet, and therefore what proportion of their industrial capacity would be available for reparation payments. In a short space of time, the British were at loggerheads with the Russians over this with the former demanding that a greater amount of Germany's productive potential be immune from allocation for reparation – in order to free Britain of the need to make up the deficit – and with the Soviet Union interested in seeing the greatest amount possible earmarked for reparation. The importance of this central and incompatible issue as a force which helped thrust the two Powers towards confrontation cannot be doubted. But the economic differences between the two were only pressed to complete irresolution because each drew a political inference from them. For the Russians, this was the suspicion that the British position seemed to have changed since the Potsdam Conference and now implied a desire to rebuild Germany, probably to be used against the Soviet Union. The British stance, which *had* altered, sprang from the fear that material conditions in the British Zone were so depressed that Communism would take a hold there – a worry heightened by intelligence that the Russians seemed intent upon organising their own zone as a possible base for the communisation of the rest of Germany. Though British anxieties were overstated, they need to be seen in their context.[47] These were not entirely rational times and with Soviet pressure detectable in a swathe from Persia to Paris, it is not hard to understand why London might have exaggerated western Germany as a potential seedbed of Bolshevism. When the Russian's premised their demand for reparation on a lower level of steel production in Germany than Britain thought essential, it brought together British worries about the cost of their zone and about Soviet intentions. As Bevin expressed it, 'it is difficult to see what the Russians are after by adopting this attitude unless it were to make the standard of living in West Germany so low that Communist influence would rapidly spread over it.'[48]

The complex turn of events which took place in occupied Germany during 1946 are worth summarising before examining the British part in them in detail. During the early months of the year, disagreements between the occupying Powers over the letter of the Potsdam clauses relating to Germany, particularly over reparation payments, mounted, culminating in May in the decision of General Clay, the military governor of the US Zone, to suspend the allocation of surplus economic resources for reparation in his zone. The victors' failure to resolve their differences and the Potsdam Agreement's legislation for unanimity within the Allied Control Council (ACC) for Germany had produced deadlock by the summer. In an attempt to cut across these disputes and to implement the Potsdam concept of an economically unified Germany, the American Secretary of State, James Byrnes, on 11 July offered to fuse the US Zone of occupation in Germany with any other occupation zone. The British, eager to reduce their costs in Germany, were the only occupying Power to accept the US proposal and contributed towards the creation of an Anglo-American Bizone which was set up the following year. This was ultimately to lead to the creation of two separate German states.

This sketch of events requires important qualifications. Clay's reparation halt and Byrnes's call for zonal fusion were important milestones towards the division of Germany, though they tend to suggest a higher American profile in the beginnings of this process than was actually the case. Although attitudes amongst some US policymakers did begin to harden at this time, American opinion in general lagged behind a British perception of a need for a new approach to Germany which began to assert itself in the spring of 1946.[49] At the same time, the severe implications of a shift in German policy for

Anglo-Soviet relations and for the future of Germany and Europe injected occasional irresolution into British actions, which meant that a divided Germany did not become a fixed policy until the end of that year. Put another way, though they recognised that the logic of a reassessment of their position in Germany was likely to bring about a split along the western boundary of the Soviet Zone occasionally gave pause to British policy-makers, it did not, as we shall see, fundamentally sway them from their new course. It is possible, indeed, to go further than this and suggest that British determination to use the industrial potential of their occupation zone, principally the Ruhr, for the recuperation of the West, whilst simultaneously resisting Russian claims on this capacity, made East-West confrontation difficult to avoid.

The Ruhr, the single most important industrial region in Germany, was the central issue for Bevin. This area represented not only his concerns about Germany's political future, but also, for a time, it was where his hopes for the rehabilitation of the shattered economies of the Western European democracies were concentrated. His concern fanned his determination either to prevent the area from again becoming a German arsenal, or of affording a foothold in the West for the Russians. His hope made him sympathetic to a possibility, pressed most energetically by the French from the summer of 1944, of removing the Ruhr from Germany and setting up an international regime to govern the industries of the region. At the end of 1945 he informed his Cabinet colleagues that he was 'seeking a middle course' in Germany by listening to French proposals for an international regime in the Ruhr whilst trying to allay Soviet fears that he intended to build up the war potential of the area against them.[50] The fact is, however, that Bevin had set his mind against the Soviets playing anything other than a marginal role in the operation of the Ruhr industries from the start. His preference was to keep them out of the Ruhr altogether. He expressly told the French and the Belgians that 'it was a mistake to refer to the "internationalisation" of the Ruhr since this implied Russian participation. He thought it important that the Ruhr should come within the orbit of the Western European countries and that it should be linked up closely with their economies and made to serve the common good.'[51] This was a dangerous notion. Everyone knew that the Russians expected to share in the governing of the Ruhr. This was, indeed, the very reason why Bevin wanted to head them off. Both Churchill and Eden had led Stalin to believe that they favoured international control of the Ruhr after the war and both strongly implied that they envisaged Soviet participation.[52] Bevin may not have known this, but he was well aware that to set up a special regime in the Ruhr without the agreement of all the occupying Powers would be a clear breach of the Potsdam Accords. As his experts in the Foreign Office were to point out to him as his views on the future of the region matured, to leave the Soviet Union out of any scheme for the control of the Ruhr 'would be in contravention of Potsdam and lead to a head on clash with the Russians ... This clash may be inevitable, but if we do put forward a new scheme now and exclude the Russians the clash will be precipitated.'[53]

Debates on the future of the Ruhr which took place inside the Foreign Office need to be seen alongside the unravelling of the Potsdam agreements on Germany in the early months of 1946. Inter-Allied administrative bodies for Germany, conceived as a means by which the vanquished state would function as an economic unit before the creation of a federal government, were never set up. The French, who had a zone of occupation but had not been at the Potsdam Conference and therefore did not feel bound by the decisions made there, used this circumstance as an excuse to block joint administrations as a bargaining tool to obtain one of their major foreign political objectives – the separation of the Ruhr and the Rhineland from Germany. In this way an already evident tendency for the occupation zones to assume the shape of autonomous units was reinforced. More significantly, the ACC in Berlin, whose task it was to decide on the level of industry necessary for Germany to pay its own way before allocations for reparation could be made, soon reached an impasse. This was pivotal. It reflected the different perceptions over the treatment of Germany which had been glossed over at Potsdam and supplied a new source of suspicion between each of the occupying Powers. As already noted, it was the British position which had changed since Potsdam. Having insisted on occupying the north-west industrial region of Germany, the British discovered that their inheritance was largely a bomb-shattered ruin with a demoralised, ill-housed and half-starving population. With 70 per cent of the zone's food having to be imported, the British were faced with the prospect of spending millions of scarce dollars annually in order to prevent complete collapse. Logically enough, the British in the ACC pressed for the retention of a high level of industrial resources in Germany so that the Germans might begin to support themselves. However, this ran head-on into the Soviet counter-proposal, initially supported by the United States, for a low-level of resource being allowed the Germans on the equally logical ground that the more Germany was permitted to retain, the less there would be available for reparation.

As already noted, Bevin's concern with the basic cost of occupation was unquestionably a key consideration in preventing him from going along with the Russians. In February 1946, he warned the Cabinet of 'a serious risk that German production would be reduced to a level which would impose a continuing charge on the taxpayer in respect of essential imports into the British Zone.'[54] One solution to this seemed to be to support the French view on separation of the Ruhr from Germany. This might allow Britain to escape from the log-jam in the ACC and deal with the principal industries in their own zone as they saw fit. It was soon rejected, partly on the, perhaps obvious, ground that a British zone denuded of the resources of the Ruhr was unlikely to resolve Britain's economic difficulties in Germany, but also, as Bevin revealingly pointed out to the French Foreign Minister, 'if we were to take away the Ruhr it would probably mean that the Soviets would colonise the rest of Germany.'[55] This political concern was increasingly emphasised as the justification for a shift of policy in Germany towards retaining the Ruhr in Germany, using the region to revive the economy of the British Zone and hence as a bulwark against advancing Communism. It was a new perspective which was shared by others. The Head of the German Department in the Foreign Office accepted that 'the real weakness of our position lies ... in Potsdam and its aftermath. As a result we find ourselves aiding and abetting the disintegration of Germany's social structure ... Potsdam, in fact, will complete the ruin of every class which might be on our side.'[56] Oliver Harvey, Assistant Under-Secretary at the Foreign Office, returned from a visit to the British Zone in March in a deeply dejected state by what he had seen. 'If we can get Western Germany past the world food and economic crisis and put her on the way to economic recovery and readjustment before we withdraw our military government,' he judged, 'we might effect lasting work. If we go, leaving only the army of occupation in strategic areas, or if we allow premature centralisation, while famine and economic chaos remain, I doubt if the German democratic parties can stand for one moment against totalitarianism.'[57] The Head of the Supply and Relief Department also asserted that 'if we allow Germany to starve and continue with idle factories we can, I think, reckon on a large increase in Communist support and consequently for a movement for a link up with the Russian zone in a matter of months.'[58]

Sustained by such opinions, Bevin took up a suggestion first made by John Hynd, a junior minister with responsibility for Britain's occupied territories. Hynd was convinced too that 'Russian policy was clearly to destroy industry in the west of Germany and to build it up in the east.' He wanted the Germans themselves to be put in charge of the industries of the Ruhr even if this contravened Potsdam and 'amounted to the partition of Germany.'[59] With the help of his experts, Bevin refined Hynd's proposal to include the setting up of a new provincial authority within the British Zone as a preliminary to the inauguration of a German-run corporation which would rehabilitate the economy of the Ruhr. For Bevin, a signal advantage of this scheme was that it envisaged international participation in the running of the Ruhr only after quadripartite control of Germany had come to an end. In other words, it would put off Russian involvement in the region for the foreseeable future. The new proposal was laid before the Cabinet on the basis that it 'faced the fact that Europe was now being divided into two spheres of influence and it would give us an opportunity to prove that we could build up in western Germany, under a democratic system, an efficient industrial organisation which challenged comparison with that which was being created under a different system in east Germany.' To add force to his argument, Bevin drew attention to a recent statement by the CoS that 'policy towards Germany should be guided by the consideration that Russia is our most likely potential enemy and is a more serious enemy than a revived Germany.'[60]

On 3 May Bevin informed the Cabinet that the Russians intended to thrust into the Western zones with the newly formed Socialist Unity party as the spearhead, that the Soviets 'had established themselves in their own zone, are making a strong bid to capture Berlin for the Communists and are preparing to launch out on a more forward policy in the West.' This information came via a convoluted route from Marshal Zhukov, the Russian commander of the Soviet Zone, through George Kennan, the American Chargé in Moscow, and then passed on to London by Roberts and may have been intended as a signal to the West from the now out-of-favour Zhukov of a Soviet change of policy in Germany.[61] It may be true that Bevin's exposition to his colleagues lacked clarity and 'tended to veer from one possible line to another'.[62] Yet there can be no mistaking that its thrust was weighted towards convincing his colleagues that a divided Germany was now likely and its key message was that Russia now presented a greater danger than a revived Germany.

The Cabinet, however, remained unconvinced. Bevin showed hesitancy too, no doubt because the ramifications of what he now contemplated, even in the electric climate of spring 1946, gave pause for thought.[63] It was possible to rationalise a more vigorous British stance in Germany as no more than a bargaining position – 'that we should not offer to the Russians in West Germany any greater facilities than they might be prepared to give us in East Germany i.e. participation in the industrial area of Saxony' – as a means of opening up the Soviet Zone to the West. This was precisely the position that Bevin adopted during the CFM which met in Paris throughout the summer. But he did not need his Permanent Under Secretary to tell him that what was on offer was an unequal swap which the Russians would not entertain.[64] There was now something of a hiatus. The logic of Bevin's stance over the Ruhr was an eventual showdown. At the same time, a reluctance finally to rupture relations with the Russians, a need to convince others – his Cabinet colleagues, the Dominions' Prime Ministers and the United States – and, perhaps, himself that it was not he, but Russia, who was reneging on Potsdam, held him back.

Though Bevin was clearly wary of moving without the, still uncertain, support of the United States, this does not mean, as has been suggested, that he anticipated at this stage an Anglo-American *partnership* over German policy.[65] Despite a growing coincidence of views between his own and those now being expressed by American officials in the State Department and the Moscow Embassy, he showed little inclination to rush to co-ordinate his stance with that of the USA. Rather the opposite. He was unsure of the reliability of the Americans and preferred to find Britain's own solutions to the German problem. Each of the major American initiatives on Germany during the spring and summer of 1946 – General Clay's decision to halt the dismantling of industrial plant for reparation, and Byrnes's offer to fuse the US Zone with any of the others – was originally viewed with scepticism. The dismantling halt was judged potentially more damaging to Western European industrial recovery than harmful to the Russians. As for a zonal merger, Bevin was 'most anxious in dealing with the Americans lest they should suddenly change their minds and leave him in the lurch'. His instinct to act without them was rein-

forced by a frame of mind which 'understood how we could reorgan-
ise the British zone by itself in such a way as to balance exports and
imports, but he could not see so clearly how this could be done with
the two zones together' and he had to be persuaded by his advisers
before eventually picking up the American offer.[66]

Once negotiations between the British and the Americans for the
fusion of their occupation zones had started in the summer of 1946
(inevitably the Soviets did not take up Byrnes's proposal, nor did the
French) both parties publicly denied that this implied the end of German unity. The Americans may well have been sincere and have
considered that the combined Anglo-American Zones could be a building block towards an eventual Western-oriented single Germany. There
are signs that Bevin toyed with this possibility – a sort of reversal of
the magnetic pull which he believed the Russians were counting on.[67]
But this route, if he ever really took it seriously, was not his preferred
option for long. From first being apprised of Byrnes's offer in July
Bevin had recognised that bizonal fusion was likely to be an irretriev-
able act of division and that what he was opting for was a fractured
Germany. Moreover, his uncompromising stance on the Ruhr – 'the
most important single problem affecting our position in Germany' –
militated against any *rapprochement* with Moscow over Germany.[68] His
increasingly inflexible position is indicated by his laying down in
October of deliberately unacceptable conditions for unity, including
that the Russians be asked to share the burden of the financial deficit
in the two Western Zones.[69] By the end of 1946, the concern in Whitehall was that, having completed the stripping of their own zone, the
Russians would now seek economic union with Western Germany. As
the Soviet Zone was now judged 'a liability rather than an asset if
united with the Western zones', it was agreed that this should be resisted and that if the Americans, as was suspected, should be tempted
to come to terms with the Russians, 'we should do our best to dis-
suade them.'[70]

If, as has been suggested, 'it is too strong to speak of a change in
British policy towards the unification of Germany in spring 1946'[71]
what may reasonably be asserted is that the transition from collaboration to animosity and from unity to division represents a continuum
based upon Bevin's unswerving determination to ring-fence the Ruhr
from any significant Soviet presence, and on his search for a more
vigorous approach to the German problem which had its origins in
the early months of that year. By the end of 1946, a noticeable switch

in emphasis had taken place from stressing political to economic circumstances as justification for British actions in Germany. This did not mean that fears of Communist infiltration had ceased to be a major spur to action. By emphasising economic issues, Bevin may have helped to clinch the approval of a Cabinet which had little taste for altercation with the Russians and was more exercised by the debilitating impact of the German occupation on the British economy. Economic arguments also had the asset of offering more concrete evidence for planting responsibility for division squarely on the Russians. This is where Bevin had always intended it should lay. In May he had warned the Cabinet that 'if there is to be break [over Germany] the Russians must be seen to be responsible for it.'[72] In fact, for Bevin, the future of the Ruhr, Communist penetration of Western Germany and the economic condition of the British Zone were inseparable issues and he continued to believe, as he told Attlee in the spring of 1947, that 'it was quite clear what the Russians are after, namely, to get into the Ruhr, to make our zone impossible to work and to create a disturbance so as to get a grip on that great area.'[73]

Was Bevin right to base his policy in Germany on the premise of preventing an eventual Soviet take-over? According to East German sources, in June 1945 Stalin instructed the Communists in the Soviet Zone to begin to secure a dominant position there as part of a push for a united Germany under Communist influence. This, as we have seen, ties in with information supplied to the Foreign Office by the Moscow Embassy and, if true, validates the fears of those who were alarmed at the implications of the forced merger between the Social Democrats and the Communists in the Russian Zone. However, these sources – as does material from the Kremlin archives – also point other ways. More damning to British policy in Germany, it may be that Stalin had opted for unity and co-operation with his occupying partners as the most realistic way of keeping Germany in check and with socialism in Germany as no more than a foggy, distant ambition. In this scenario, Stalin's willingness to compromise, particularly in order to obtain reparation, could not be discounted and the British determination upon a final split in Germany, made in advance of the Americans, made them the front-runners in prematurely inducing the Cold War. It is also possible that Stalin's attitude towards Germany was more schizophrenic. With half of the great prize in his hands, he was unable to decide whether to neutralise or to communise it.[74] Perhaps Bevin sensed this. As late as May 1946, in an admission that also mirrored his own zig-zag policy, he stated that he was still unsure whether Moscow had opted for a united or dismembered Germany. The fact is that, no matter how accurate their speculation may or may not have been, the Foreign Secretary and his advisers were formulating policy largely on assumptions about what Soviet intentions in Germany might be rather than on firm fact. When they sought hard evidence that the Russians were acting illegally in their zone in order to justify changes in the status of the Ruhr, this proved difficult to find. The contention, for instance, that the Soviets were reusing plant removed as reparation from Western Germany in the Eastern Zone was supported on the flimsy ground that 'there was no confirmation that this was happening but it was thoroughly in line with Russian policy.'[75] Nor were the British themselves beyond stretching the strict letter of the law over unilateral removal of reparation from their own zone because, it was speciously argued, 'we were surely entitled to some consideration in view of our sacrifices.'[76]

The supreme significance of the German Question, the imperfections of the arrangements for Allied control and the darkening international atmosphere in which the latter were set meant that both British and Russians behaved with a mixture of wariness and prudence. In the end, it was Bevin who stole the march on Stalin in Germany by acting on the reasonable assumption that, as one official was later to express it, 'even if Russian world domination can be discounted [the] bear will certainly not resist pushing [its] paw into soft places.'[77] Looking back, it is possible to see that the divergence over Germany which emerged in 1946 provided the first major battleground in the Cold War. But Bevin did not see it this way. Colliding with his suspicions of the Soviets and adding to his caution were anti-German prejudices which made him haver over where the real future threat lay. As he admitted to Sir Brian Robertson, the British Military Governor in Germany – 'I tries 'ard, Brian, but I 'ates them.'[78] Thus, in early 1947 and with the Anglo-American zonal fusion agreement now in force, he remained unsure whether the main threat to European peace came from the Soviets or a revived Germany. He continued to fear that 'the Germans were much more dangerous than the Russians' and that it was 'of the utmost importance that the Four [Occupying] Powers should pursue a common policy towards Germany who still constituted the biggest menace to peace in Europe.'[79]

Moreover, the Foreign Secretary was not prepared to relinquish hope of East-West agreement as readily as the military Chiefs or many of his own diplomatic advisers. There are misleading signs that this was the case; his assertive determination at the London CFM to delineate Britain's own sphere in the Mediterranean presented with shop-steward style pugnacity; his sometimes intemperate reactions to events in Iran and in France, as well as his attitude to Soviet participation in the control of the Rhur. What we are faced with in examining British actions during the first 18 months after the end of hostilities in Europe is, in fact, something rather more complex than a simple assertion that the British were in the lead in provoking the Cold War. Though there were dangers to be faced and interests to be protected, Labour Government policy was some way off from viewing friction between the Powers as being spread out on all fronts. Contests could be compartmentalised. Toughness in Germany was intended to make the Soviets back off, exactly as firmness in the eastern Mediterranean and the Middle East had done. In the summer of 1945 Bevin had warned colleagues that:

> if the Russian challenge to our position in Greece and Turkey is successfully countered in its early stages, it is probable that the Soviet Government will not persevere in their present policy. But if they are successful in Greece, Turkey will be the next to go and an assault on our position in the Middle East would soon follow. The one thing which might encourage them to persevere in their present course would be for us to weaken in our determination to preserve Greece.[80]

Increasingly, as it had been for some time for the CoS, the analogue was the appeasement of the 1930s. With no certainty that the Soviets either had a blueprint for expansion or were implacably hostile to Britain, what seemed to be at stake was not a wholesale fracture of relations between the Communist and non-Communist worlds, but rather the need to settle, through affirmative assertion of their interests, specific points of friction until some general *modus vivendi* could be arrived at.

These attempts to plug a leaky dike were not always logically pursued and were arguably at their most irrational in Germany where, until very recently, a policy of constraint had been accepted as an important bonding force in Anglo-Soviet relations and where German division was frequently acknowledged as implying a fissure across Europe. But it was an inconsistency born of the still nebulous form of the challenge that Britain was facing. This helps explain the stuttering rather than linear progress which characterised Britain's drift towards Cold War. A halting pattern of hopeful sparring is evident throughout this period and survived as the Labour Government's political strategy at least two years after taking office. In a telling conversation with the Foreign Secretary during the Paris CFM in September 1946, Harold Nicolson noted that Bevin:

> is on the whole optimistic. He says this: 'Now look 'ere, 'arold, when I took this job on I knew it wouldn't be a daisy. In fact, no Foreign Secretary has had to keep so many plates in the air at the same time. But what I said to my colleagues at the time was this: "I'll take on the job. But don't expect results before three years." Now it's patience you want in this sort of thing. I'm not going to throw my weight about 'ere in Paris. I'm going to sit sturdy 'ere and 'elp.'[81]

There were other brakes upon all-out altercation. One was the 'internationalist' approach to world affairs which remained in evidence in the Cabinet until at least the end of 1946. A second was the notion of the Third Force. Bevin, as we shall see, was the principal exponent of the latter whilst the greatest champion of 'internationalism' in the government was Attlee. 'During the formative period of the cold war', it has been pointed out, 'Attlee was a committed internationalist, actively opposed to a military strategy based on the traditional imperial pattern ... and open-minded about the nature and aims of Soviet foreign policy.'[82] This was bound to produce a clash between the Prime Minister and his more hawkish CoS. The Chiefs' rule of thumb that the USSR should be assumed potentially hostile had, by early 1946, led them to the view that Britain's position in the eastern Mediterranean and the Middle East was vital either as a deterrent to Soviet aggression by providing bases for potential air strikes against the industrial areas of the southern USSR or as strategic outposts should war come. Attlee, admitting uncertainty over the Soviets' intentions, favoured British disengagement from the Middle East and preferred the settlement of disputes by negotiation, preferably through the United Nations. In September 1945, when Russian demands for the revision of the Montreux Convention and claims on the ex-Italian colonies were troubling Bevin, the CoS were 'shaken' by the Prime Minister's assertion that if the United Nations Organisation 'is a reality, it does not matter who holds Cyrenaica or Somalia or controls the Suez Canal.'[83]

Though his faith in the United Nations sometimes flagged, Attlee
had a bank of other arguments to which he had recourse throughout
1946 in order to counter what he called the 'strategy of despair' of
the CoS. In his view, the Middle Eastern states could not be defended, to try to do so would be an intolerable drain on British resources
and might, in any case be taken by the Soviet Union as aggressive
and produce the adventurism it was intended to prevent. Instead of
facing points of friction head-on, he advocated abandoning the British role in the Mediterranean and Middle East, constructing a
defensive parameter across Africa between Lagos and Kenya leaving,
what a Cabinet colleague called, 'a wide glacis of desert and Arabs
between ourselves and the Russians.'[84] Attlee believed that the Government 'should seek to come to an agreement with the USSR after
consideration with Stalin of all our points of conflict' before commit-
ting itself to the strategy advocated by the CoS.[85]

This non-confrontational thesis received support from inside the
Cabinet and also from the military expert, Basil Liddell Hart. Given
his reputation for robustness, Bevin's response is interestingly irreso-
lute. As on particular occasions over Germany, he remained nervous
of too sweepingly strident a response to the Russians. One of the first
acts of the Foreign Office's Russia Committee, which had been set up
in the spring of 1946 and was now packed with born-again hard-liners such as Christopher Warner, was to urge with the fervour of the
newly converted that the government mount an 'all-out offensive' programme of political warfare against the Soviet Union to include
widespread propaganda and possibly also wartime style undercover
sabotage raids into the Communist sphere.[86] Iran, the centre of the
recent crisis, was seen as a prime target for what the Committee had
in mind. Bevin showed no inclination to do this and 'held to heel a
Russia Committee straining at the leash'.[87] Yet officials persisted and
gathered sufficient evidence of Soviet inspired anti-British propaganda
in the Middle East eventually to persuade Bevin to go along with
them. It may be, as Raymond Smith suggests, that it was a combination of this pressure and the CoS's worries about the British position
in the Middle East which prompted Bevin in January 1947 to come
out decisively against Attlee's proposals for, what the Foreign Office
dismissively termed an 'Alice in Wonderland', neutral area.[88] Bevin
had also demonstrated for some time a concern for Britain's position
in the eastern Mediterranean and his refutation of the Prime Minister's views exhibits important divergencies of perspective between the

two men. For Bevin, retreat from the Middle East would leave a vacuum which would be filled by the Russians. It would be a signal of
British weakness to the world and not least to the Soviet Union which
would assume, like Hitler's Germany, that it could achieve its objectives bloodlessly through intimidation. But the difference between
the Prime Minister and his Foreign Secretary was less sharply defined
than is sometimes suggested.[89] During the debate with Attlee, Bevin
had already demonstrated a readiness to go some way towards the
Attlee line by pulling Britain's principal centre of communications
for the Commonwealth out of Egypt and place it in Kenya. In fact,
this was more of a redeployment of British forces than the tactical
withdrawal that Attlee had in mind and Bevin intended that the British presence in the Mediterranean should remain. But the real
similarity with Attlee was that Bevin 'had not, in the way of his officials, formed a clear view of the unequivocal hostility of the Soviet
Union to Britain and the British way of life' and it continued to nag
him that among the compound of motives which governed Soviet
actions was fear and that if only this could be dispelled their behaviour might be changed.[90]

There is reason to believe, in other words, that if the substance of
Attlee's proposal was unacceptable to Bevin the underlying principle
of avoiding the assumption of inevitable, all-out confrontation was
not and that the long-term objectives of the two were not far apart.
We do not know why Attlee finally bowed to the views of his Foreign
Secretary. One version has it that the CoS threatened to resign *en
masse* unless Attlee kept his views to himself. This, however, rests sole-
ly on the testimony of Field Marshal Montgomery – not always the
most reliable of witnesses. Perhaps it is no less fanciful to assume that
it was the final paragraph of Bevin's rejoinder to Attlee with, as in his
recent comment to Nicolson, its optimism, its emphasis on patience
and its measured tone of eventual progress through negotiation –
perhaps even through the United Nations – which convinced the Prime
Minister. Bevin argued:

> Our economic and military position, is now as bad as it will ever be.
> When we have consolidated our economy, when the economic re-
> vival of Europe has made progress, when it has become finally clear
> to the Russians that they cannot drive a wedge between the Ameri-
> cans and ourselves, we shall be in a position to negotiate from
> strength. There is no hurry. Everything suggests that the Russians

are now drawing in their horns and have no immediate aggressive intentions. Let us wait until our strength is restored and let us meanwhile, with US help as necessary, hold on to essential positions and concentrate on building up UNO.[91]

Bevin had another important iron in the fire which he hoped would help restore British authority. This was his objective of moulding a system of collaboration between Britain and her neighbours in Western Europe aimed at fostering a Western group which would co-operate in economic, social, defensive and, eventually, political affairs and provide a power base that would allow Britain to stand independently from and on equal terms with its two wartime Allies. This stimulated his interest in the French proposal for international control of the Ruhr which, in his own scheme, would kick-start the post-war economies of the participating Powers and bind them together as an effective working unit.[92] The prospect of pooling the resources of the Western European states – including their colonial assets – in order to match the power of the United States was one which had fascinated him since the 1920s and energised by his first 18 months' experience as Foreign Secretary.

This was not just related to difficulties with the Russians. The co-operativeness which had tended to characterise Anglo-American relations during the war had also largely evaporated. Neither Truman nor Byrnes thought much of the 'graceless and rough' Bevin.[93] Nor did the British have a high opinion of the American leadership – particularly of Byrnes whose main objective appeared to be to reach a European settlement which would involve the minimum liability to the United States. This personal coolness tended to confirm more general misgivings. The feeling beginning to be expressed in London was that either isolationism continued to be a strong factor or that the Americans were 'just as bad as the Russians' in trying to carve out their own sphere of interest without reference to the British.[94] In Washington, already lively suspicions that the British were cannily trying to use American power to preserve British influence in the world were now joined by concerns over the direction of a socialist government. For their part, the British held a list of grievances against the Americans which did nothing to add warmth to Anglo-American relations; the sharp severance of Lend-Lease at the end of the European war which was likely to make Britain's economic readjustment to peacetime (regarded by the British as a temporary procedure) more difficult;

disappointed expectations of a grant from the United States to aid
this postwar reconstruction, which hard-nosed American attitudes had
forced them at the end of 1945 to transform into a cap-in-hand request for a £3.75 billion loan, plus increasing indications that the
Americans intended to renege on joint co-operation in atomic research. Though Bevin sought American support for British actions
over particular issues – resistance to Soviet demands to be given an
ex-Italian colony, over Iran and in Germany – his larger aim was to
devise a system which would, in the long run, permit Britain to do
without this sort of assistance.

There was a good deal of talk in the fluid international climate
following the great upheaval of 1939–45 of the emergence of various
Monroe regions, replicating the area of special interest in the Amer-
icas which the United States had delineated, via the Monroe Doctrine,
in the early part of the nineteenth century. Bevin made his own contribution to this trend at the end of 1945, when he forecast the rise of
'three Monroes' in the world. The third of these was clearly a reference to a British sphere made up of the Commonwealth and those
parts of Europe and the Middle East not embraced by the Soviet 'Monroe'. This would be, to use the jargon of the times, a Third Force to
counterpoise the influence of the USA and the USSR. One reason
why Attlee's suggestion, in the spring of 1946, that Britain should
pull out of the eastern Mediterranean and the Middle East was objec-
tionable to Bevin was that it would ruin the chances of establishing
such a Third Force. Britain, he reminded Attlee, was the 'last bastion
of social democracy' as against 'the red tooth and claw of American
capitalism and the Communist dictatorship of Soviet Russia … We
talk a lot of a "Western group" but shall we be able to bring it into
existence or maintain it once we abandon our position as a Mediterranean power? I doubt it.'[95]

The 'Western group' as we shall see, was to prove impossible to
achieve. Misgivings that both the Americans and the Russians would
interpret the proposed group negatively, with the Russians seeing it
as an offensive bloc aimed against themselves, meant that the scheme
moved forward so slowly that, at times, it seemed that its momentum
had almost vanished. Sometimes, aspects of the project had to be
jettisoned in the face of more pressing demands. Discord in Germany, for instance, meant the collapse of Bevin's support for the
international control of the Ruhr. This he ruefully admitted, would
'inevitably postpone for some years any hope of fulfilling one of my

principal ideas which is that the Ruhr should be turned into a positive element of European reconstruction.'[96] Bevin's enthusiasm for a 'Western group', however, remained undiminished in the face of such obstacles. On the contrary, the less he achieved, the more his vision seemed to expand. What had essentially began as ideas of collaboration between the states on the 'Mediterranean and Atlantic fringes of Europe' grew to encompass the still-substantial European colonial empires. In May 1946 Bevin 'reminded [the French Foreign Minister] that if our two Empires were co-ordinated we had together the greatest mass of manpower in the world.' Over a year later he was urging the French Prime Minister that this manpower and the riches of the two nations' colonial territories meant that they 'could, if they acted together, be as powerful as the Soviet Union or the United States.'[97] This, and not an urge to spoil for a fight with the Soviet Union or to forge a partnership with an unreliable United States in a contest against Communism, was what had animated Bevin since the summer of 1945. It was not a realistic aim nor were aspects of it, in the full glare of the anti-imperialist hindsight of the late twentieth century, particularly noble. It was, however, to continue to be Bevin's preferred goal over the next two years.

# 2

## CAUGHT UP IN COLD WAR,' 1947–49

According to one authority 'most historians asked to name the most plausible date for the beginning of the cold war, would suggest 2 July 1947' the day Molotov withdrew the Soviet deputation from the Paris discussions of the Marshall Plan.[1] This may be so, and even a search for origins which arrives at a less assuredly precise conclusion will find plenty to support 1947 as having been decisive. It was, after all, the year in which the term Cold War achieved common currency in its modern sense, coined either by the American Democrat Bernard Baruch or the journalist Walter Lippmann. It was certainly being used by this time in British official circles. On the opposite side of the emerging divide, the Soviet leadership aware that, whilst the Americans were not able to contemplate open warfare, none the less saw Washington 'conducting a cold war, a war of nerves.'[2] 1947 was also the year in which the influential American official, George Kennan, writing anonymously as 'Mr. X' in the journal *Foreign Affairs*, publicly etched the outlines of the United States' policy of containing the Soviet Union. On the institutional level, 1947 witnessed the inauguration of the Anglo-American Bizone in Germany, the creation of an American National Security Council (NSC) and a Central Intelligence Agency (CIA) – conveniently furnished with intelligence material by the British MI6 - to effect the struggle against Communism. Reciprocally, the Soviets set up the Cominform. It was, even more notably, the year of the Truman Doctrine and the Marshall Plan. In short, 1947 provides a spacious arena for a favourite sport of contemporary historians, that of trying to identify the start of the Cold War.

Inevitably, the picture is more complex. The efforts of counter-orthodox historians over three decades have hardly dented a popular perception of the Truman Doctrine and Marshall Plan as twin American responses to an overt Soviet attempt to spread their authority across

Europe, welcomed with unalloyed gratitude by the Western leaders of the beleaguered continent. In particular, analysis of British policy at this stage has often been over-simplified. Guided by Bevin, the traditional version goes, Britain had long been working to forge a Western European security group to thwart Soviet ambitions. The intention was to demonstrate the determination of the Western Europeans in order to draw the Americans into supporting it - the 'sprat to catch the mackerel' - as Bevin later allegedly described his approach. The apotheosis of this supposed far-sighted and patiently pursued strategy arrived in 1949 with the North Atlantic Treaty. This picture of a United States responding, with British prompting, to an aggressive Stalinist monolith requires considerable modification however.

So far as the USSR is concerned, material made available from the Soviet archives suggests, as mentioned in the preceding chapter, that at the start of 1947 Stalin was still committed to continued co-operation with the West. This was founded upon his assessment of Russia's weakened position after the war leavened, perhaps, by a psychological desire to maintain the relative camaraderie of the Big Three which had already allowed many of his territorial ambitions to be met. Though the incompleteness of this new evidence and its still undigested state demands a degree of caution, it does appear to provide quite compelling evidence that Stalin's pressure on Turkey and Iran and policy in the Soviet Zone of Germany were unsystematic developments springing less from ideological considerations than from a heavy-handed determination to press perceived legitimate security needs to the point where these met external resistance. This gives some support for the 'revisionist' interpretation of Cold War origins. But orthodoxy is partly validated too in that Stalin's underlying Marxist-Leninist imperatives coupled with his pathological suspicions meant that East-West collaboration was unlikely to be permanent. Changes in the personnel of the Big Three at the end of the war plus the American monopoly of the atomic bomb had already begun to bring Stalin's mistrust to the surface. The outcome was that, although he 'still did not want confrontation with his former allies ... he did not know how to avoid it'.[3] Even so, this inclination towards co-operation probably survived into 1947 and it has been persuasively argued that, despite a growing sense of betrayal by his wartime partners, Stalin 'was not prepared to wage the Cold War (that is, open confrontation without much diplomatic coverage) until 1948' with the Communist coup in Czechoslovakia and the blockade of Western land routes into Berlin.[4]

Similarly, the United States did not initially seek international friction. In the early months after the end of the war Washington groped towards what Leffler calls a strategy of preponderance in relation to the Soviet Union.[5] This embryonic version of what was soon to be transmuted into a more formalised policy of containment implied co-operation with Moscow, so long as this coincided with what were regarded as essential American interests and as long as the Soviets were confined within an acceptable sphere. The vestiges of isolationism meant that this preponderant power was first played out by proxy with others, the British and the French for instance, taking the strategic, military and economic strains which the United States preferred, as yet, not to exert. Only when apprehensions surfaced over what was seen as an insidious growth in Russian political and economic influence alongside a recognition that the strength of the Europeans had been exaggerated was Washington impelled towards a more confrontational approach. Though there are signs that this change had already begun in the early part of 1946, it did not solidify into policy initiatives until the spring of 1947. In other words, there is sufficient evidence to suggest that it was the Americans who were to be the authors of a decisive change in international events and that this came in 1947. In mitigation of American impetuousness it might be argued that haphazard and opportunistic Soviet activity could seem more purposeful when viewed from across the Atlantic. In the longer perspective, if Washington can be accused of misperceiving the defensiveness which seems to have characterised Soviet policy at this juncture, indications also suggest that Marxian logic implied that once Soviet invigoration had been achieved co-existence was likely to be replaced by confrontation. What seems certain in the short term is that in Moscow, as in Washington, a determination to defend what were seen to be vital interests produced a helix of misunderstanding. As Leffler suggests, 'neither the Americans nor the Soviets sought to harm the other in 1945. But each side, in pursuit of its security interests, took steps that aroused the other's apprehensions.'[6]

The British fit this scenario too. A hard-headedness in Germany and alarm over events in Greece, Turkey and Iran, which Whitehall took as part of a Soviet determination to reduce British influence in the eastern Mediterranean and the Middle East, are indicative of a foreign policy that, rather than seeking a showdown, 'was revolving around essentially primitive attempts at "squaring up" in the hope that the other side would back down first and thereby prevent any loss of status, prestige or imperial influence'.[7] Bevin's tactics were, in other words, a counterpart to Molotov's hard bargaining style which spurned major concessions in expectation of inducing a return to co-operation on a basis of mutual compromise founded on a recognition of each other's essential interests. Whenever possible, as over Iran and Turkey, the British brought in the United States to underpin this process. This approach was not without its dangers and at times of particular tension generated the austere view that the Soviets were not amenable to negotiation. But to see these periods of pessimism as the norm or to view temporary associations with the United States at specific moments of crisis as the mark of desire for a more perma-nent and intimate Anglo-American relationship is to distort the direction in which Bevin wished British policy to move.

Bevin continued to gnaw on the possibility of developing what, from the beginning of his time as Foreign Secretary, he called a 'Western Union'. His aim was the promotion of a consolidated British power-base and the economic renewal of a British-led Western Europe which would unshackle the United Kingdom from economic dependency on an overmighty and unreliable USA. The perception in the early months of 1946 of the existence of a range of direct and indirect Soviet pressure reaching from Teheran through Turkey, Greece, Italy and France to the British Zone in Germany accentuated the political appeal of a 'Western Union', which began to be cast in the shape of a possible European Third Force existing autonomously between the extremes of American capitalism and Soviet Communism. It was around this time that Bevin spoke of a world drifting towards three Monroes.

The Truman Doctrine of 12 March 1947, in which the American President proclaimed his nation's readiness to resist the aggressive or insidious advance of Communism throughout the globe, was the first definitive indication of the United States' readiness to play a more vigorous role on the postwar international stage. Though precipitat-ed by the British with their warning that, because of their continuing economic difficulties, they were unable to sustain the cost of their part in the prevention of a Communist take-over in Greece, Truman's declaration was, in fact, seen as an unwelcome intrusion into the way in which the Attlee Government thought the diplomatic game with the Kremlin ought to be played. Aside from its provocative universal assertions, Truman's statement was made just as another CFM gath-ered in Moscow making the path towards any general *modus vivendi* more intractable. Bevin wrote despondently to Attlee from the Soviet capital that 'we are getting perilously near a position in which a line up is taking place' and blamed the two 'big boys' for this developing polarisation.[8] Even in the more Russophobe Foreign Office, the Truman Doctrine came as a 'bombshell'. Concern from that direction, though expressed in homely terms, did not disguise misgivings over the arrogance of American power. 'We shall,' it was predicted, 'shortly be faced by a "Greek" situation here, in which [on the expiry of the present American loan to Britain] the grant of another will be made dependent on our accepting "US Administrators", one of whom will sit in the little room next to Uncle Ernie's where we sometimes have tea.'[9]

This had all stemmed from 21 February, the date when the Americans had been informed that British financial aid to Greece and Turkey was to be stopped. The decision had not been taken suddenly. It had been urged for some time by the Chancellor of the Exchequer, Hugh Dalton, as one way for an over-extended Power with a besieged economy to reduce its commitments. Nor was it a turn of events which was entirely unanticipated in Washington. But, like snow in a British winter, when it came, the expected somehow provoked surprise. Truman also had his own domestic agenda which a show of alarm would serve well. The emergent decision was precipitated by the impact of truly extraordinarily bitter weather. Ice and snow brought Britain's war-battered economy near to collapse and induced an air of dejection about the ability of the system itself to withstand it. Three days after the British communication to Washington, Bevin's Private Secretary complained to his diary of 'the coldest night I remember in England ... Everybody hates it, as we are cold both indoors and out having neither the right clothes nor houses rightly built for severe cold. The frosts and fogs have meant another setback for the fuel stocks.' 'Yet it is impossible to believe', he went on, 'that the country will really crash, as seems inevitable.' The Russians, it was contended 'are beginning to think that a Communist regime here is a practical proposition'.[10]

It must, indeed, from the perspective of a respectable member of the English upper middle class, have seemed that the world was about to stop spinning on its axis. Deep economic gloom was coupled with a recent Cabinet decision on the steps which would bring to an end British rule in India and to their responsibilities in Palestine. The decision over Greece was a piece in this much larger process of shedding responsibilities. In fact, despite a renewed attempt at Communist insurgency in the middle of 1946, the CoS were not alarmed by the possibility of a Communist take-over in Greece and believed that the position could be stabilised by a strengthening of the Greek armed forces. Presumably Bevin, who had up to now stiffly resisted Dalton's demands for the end of aid to the Greece, accepted the Chiefs' analysis and there seems to have been a general expectation in Whitehall that the Americans would pick up the additional financial help that the Greeks would require. In the end, what divided Dalton and Bevin was the latter's view that a modicum of British aid should continue alongside the support expected from Washington and the Chancellor's insistence that aid from London should be drastically choked off. Dalton won the contest, but both men counted upon the stepping up of existing American financial aid to Greece and not a Presidential declaration to resist the spread of Communism on all fronts.

Of the two 'big boys', as Bevin called them, it was the United States which now resolved to up the stakes of confrontation. The restructuring of British policy in the eastern Mediterranean had touched sensitive nerves in Washington where, in contrast to London, there were real worries of a Communist take-over in Greece. If this occurred, it was believed, there would be a roll-on effect with Communist successes in Italy, France and beyond. The most evident steamroller in operation, however, was not Russian, but American. Having used the British retreat from Greece to scare funds out of Congress on the basis of a developing Red menace, the Truman Administration now looked with deep apprehension upon the economic dilapidation of Western Europe. This seemed to pose a double threat to the United States. Though it was recognised that the Soviet Union was in no position to wage war, European economic dislocation which had been exaggerated by the appalling winter could play into the hands of the Western European Communist parties and add to the list of Russian satellites by default. At the same time, European economic ill-health and a tendency on the part of the Western Europeans to seek autarkic solutions were seen as detrimental to American economic well-being and, in the long run, hazardous to the principal of free-enterprise on which all other American freedoms were judged to be founded.

George Marshall, Truman's Secretary of State since January 1947, saw something of what was happening in Western Europe with his own eyes whilst on his way to the Moscow CFM in March. His experience at the Council reinforced his sense of apprehension. Germany was the key issue. With industrial production in the Western Zones lagging behind prewar levels and with civil disturbances inspired by food shortages, Germany, the political and economic heart of the Continent, seemed a particularly ripe target for Communist influence. In these circumstances, the continued insistence of the Soviets at the Moscow Conference on increased reparation and participation in the international control of the Ruhr appeared to the Americans as especially ominous. Reviving German productivity was now seen as an essential trigger for the restoration of healthy economic circumstances throughout Western Europe. Failure to promote this could result in the fearful prospect of Germany slipping into the orbit of the Soviet Union – a nightmare which, of course, had troubled some in Whitehall since 1944. To counter this, it was now believed, the level of industry permitted the Germans before reparation was allocated had to be marked upwards and the Russians excluded from participation in any international control over the Ruhr. Marshall returned home having given up on the Russians and latched on to ideas already circulating in the State Department, War Department and other Government agencies of replacing the piecemeal support which America had engaged in since the end of the war with a comprehensive aid package to the Europeans.

The public manifestation of this was a rather hazy initiative expressed in a speech at Harvard University on 5 June. A more fully developed image of what was to become known as the Marshall Plan emerged gradually over the ensuing weeks and had several interlocking objectives. First was the overriding need to strengthen Western Europe as a barrier to the spread of Soviet influence. This, it came to be believed in Washington, could best be achieved by sweeping away existing self-sufficient national economies and constructing an integrated Western European economy based on the principles of free trade. Linked to this the expectation that the habits formed in the process of economic collaboration would brush off on the Europeans in the shape of political co-operation and that they could be coaxed towards some form of federalism. A federal Western Europe based on the same 'progressive' ideals as the United States would not only be a more effective obstacle to Soviet Communism, but also, by happy coincidence, a desirable trading partner in the goal of providing a healthy American economy. As Hogan states, the Americans wanted 'to refashion Western Europe in the image of the United States'.[11] Central to attaining these aims, the debilitating exclusion of Germany from the economy of the West had to be brought to an end.

American thinking on Germany was simply catching up with apprehensions which the British had held for some time. Twelve months earlier the United States had resisted Bevin's calls for an increased level of industry in Germany and had shown some animosity towards the British approach to the future organisation of the Ruhr. By the end of 1946 the German policies of the two Powers had coincided to the significant extent that they had agreed to merge their two zones of occupation into one Bizone which had begun to operate in January 1947. Though this proved to be a turning point which was eventually to lead to the creation of two German states, this was not the clear purpose at the time. The then Secretary of State, James Byrnes, probably viewed Bizonia as a way of jump-starting the languishing Potsdam decision to treat Germany as an economic whole by by-passing the wrangles over reparation, central administrations and territorial amputation and pushing the occupying Powers – especially the Soviets and the French – towards co-operating. Despite his own deep concerns over what seemed to be at stake in Germany, Bevin was not at first convinced that Anglo-American zonal fusion held the answers. When, in the midst of the Paris CFM in July 1946, Byrnes had privately approached Bevin with a proposal for zonal merger the Foreign Secretary doubted that this would provide a solution to economic difficulties in the British Zone, and was more worried that the Americans might either put pressure on him to abandon the development of socialised industry in the Ruhr or change their minds about fusion and 'leave him in the lurch'.[12]

That he might be let down by the Americans remained a nagging fear for Bevin even after his advisers had persuaded him to pick up Byrnes's offer. A more tangible source of disappointment was the realisation during fusion negotiations that the Americans had no intention of taking a preponderant share of the financial burdens of the British Zone and doubts were raised in Cabinet whether agreement to proceed on zonal merger had been wise.[13] A typical consideration behind Bevin's irresolution was a worry that fusion might be too precipitate and provoke too clear a breach with Moscow. He 'thought that it would be a mistake at this stage to commit ourselves irrevocably to a measure which implied a clear division between Eastern and Western Germany' and should only be considered 'if ... it was clear that we must abandon hope of Russian co-operation'.[14] This was a conclusion, as his hesitation demonstrates, which he had not yet arrived at. Moreover, as he ruefully manouevered British policy into a more abrasive position *vis à vis* the Soviet Union, his old prejudices continued to haunt him that, after all, 'the Germans were much more dangerous than the Russians'.[15]

Bevin's enthusiastic reception of Marshall's purposely vague formula had the effect of breathing life into the Marshall Plan, though the Foreign Secretary's eagerness was also propelled by a desire to head off à French attempt to grasp leadership of the venture.[16] But the fundamental thrust behind his zeal was Britain's desperate need for financial assistance. The Harvard speech coincided with another period of acute economic difficulty for the British. Almost a third of the $3.75 billion loan which had been negotiated with the USA in December 1945 had been spent even before Marshall spoke. Another time-bomb was also ticking away. One condition of the loan had been that sterling should become freely convertible with the dollar a year after the agreement had been ratified. This was to come into effect on 15 July 1947. The run on the pound which was to ensue proved so potentially calamitous to Britain's dollar reserves that convertibility had to be suspended just over a month after being introduced. Apprehension over the state of sterling therefore provided part of the backdrop to Bevin's response to Marshall's offer. Yet, as the two Western European Powers were well aware, Marshall's offer was also a political initiative. On the surface at least, it did not rule out Soviet participation. Bidault, the French Foreign Minister, was especially anxious to avoid excluding them for fear of antagonising the French Communists. Bevin was not averse to going along with the French so long as the Soviets did not attempt to wreck or delay the proceedings and an Anglo-French invitation to attend a three nation conference on 27 June to discuss the Marshall proposals was duly dispatched to Moscow.

The Paris Conference went about as badly as it could. Molotov insisted on obtaining clarification of American intentions and also on a series of individual requests for aid. Both were contrary to Marshall's most emphatic prescription that the form in which aid was given should stem from the deliberations of the Europeans and would be dependent on them devising a common integrated programme. Molotov's attitude seemed to justify Bevin's worst fears over Russian obstruction. Looking back on the meetings some days later, his Private Secretary thought it had been all too predictable:

It was obvious from the beginning that the Russians could not come into any honest plan for European recovery, they didn't want it. They want to keep Europe, and GB, in a state of economic disorder for the next few years with the double object of disrupting the British Empire, communising Europe and getting their own economy on Communist methods into shape - the final objective being a Europe run politically and economically on Communist methods. The effect of an all-European programme based on American help would be, not only to put Europe on its feet which the Soviets do not want, but also to introduce Western methods and ideas into the Eastern European systems and thus undermine Soviet influence. It might even undermine the Soviet regime itself. The whole idea, furthermore, is shocking to Soviet theories. To them it is an attempt by the USA to make something happen (i.e. the recovery of Europe) which otherwise would not happen. It is thus power politics under the umbrella of benevolence. Since capitalism contains the seeds of disintegration, it would in fact lead to the disintegration and not the recovery of Europe. Above all, the rulers of the Kremlin fear for their own position and regime if Europe, under American watering-cans handled by British gardeners, blossoms into a happy Western Garden of Eden.[17]

Though not lacking in perceptiveness, this was rather too charitable an analysis of American motives which held no intention of permitting the British any special role in cultivating the new Shangri-La. It also misjudged the Soviet position somewhat.

At the time of Marshall's offer, Moscow was still leaning towards co-operation with the West. The shrillness of the Truman Doctrine had not significantly shifted this position. Stalin's assessment of the sparring over Germany which had characterised the recent CFM in Moscow was that it was 'something like combat reconnaissance. When the partners have exhausted one another, the moment for a possible compromise arrives. The result may be attained at the next session rather than the current one, but on all important issues, such as democratisation, political organisation, economic unity and reparations, compromise is within reach.'[18] This was not far removed from Bevin's own approach to East-West diplomacy. Molotov's objectives were also within this general spirit of finding a middle position. According to the Soviet Foreign Minister's advisers, Marshall's initiative had been provoked by American self-interested fears of a crisis of capitalism which required the reconstruction of overseas markets if economic chaos was to be prevented. This, it was judged, made the United States vulnerable and open to negotiation over credits to Eastern Europe and the Soviet Union. In this sense, his decision to go to Paris sprang from a genuine quest for elucidation and, if it then seemed appropriate, participation via a process of horse-trading in a way which would make the programme fit the needs of the Soviet Union and its satellites. As Molotov made his preparations for the Paris conference, Nikolai Novikov, the Soviet Ambassador in Washington offered the more wary advice that the Marshall Plan was merely an effort to replace the failed Truman Doctrine as a means of building an anti-Soviet grouping around the United States. It was when Molotov - and Stalin - became convinced during the conference that Novikov was right and that the United States along with Britain, their economic puppet, could not be suborned from such a plan to create what in effect would be a Western bloc, and likely also to include Western Germany, that he left the Conference on 2 July. The Soviet inclination towards at least a tactical form of co-existence, which Molotov represented, now evaporated as a direct result of the Marshall Plan and the ensuing discussions.

Molotov came away from Paris with the impression that the Marshall Plan was not merely intended to construct a barrier to Communism but was also intended to break open the Soviet sphere in Eastern Europe. This does, indeed appear to have been a principal motive in Washington.[19] Bevin was certainly inclined to see Marshall's initiative as a way of sucking Moscow's satellites into the Western camp. One aspect of zonal fusion in Germany which had appealed to him was that the industrial strength of a revived Ruhr might be used to attract those states behind what was now being called the 'iron curtain' into the orbit of the West and that Britain and the United States might use the economic strength of the West to 'further our common aim of arresting or reducing Soviet influence in the countries of Eastern and Southern Europe'.[20] On the other hand, Molotov overestimated the strength of his bargaining position. His stance was that American aid to Russia should be conditional on agreement over reparation from Germany and Soviet participation in the control of the Ruhr.[21] As these had provided major bones of contention since the Potsdam Conference and had stymied the recent CFM in Moscow, it either required optimism of the highest order to expect resolution over them now or else supreme confidence in the impact of the economic crisis which the Soviet government divined to be hovering over the United States. In any case, the outcome was that those forces in the Kremlin which were already warning of the need for the strengthening of a consolidated Soviet bloc to match the American-backed 'Western bloc' as a preparation for the inevitable conflict between the two were now in the ascendant. In September, Andrei Zhdanov, Secretary of the Central Committee of the Soviet Communist Party and the principal hard-liner in the Kremlin, set up the Cominform as part of Moscow's tightening of control over the Soviet Union's Eastern European satellites, a process which was now accelerated. Zhdanov, doubtless with Stalin's authority, spoke publicly of a Europe divided into 'two camps' of socialism and imperialism with the Americans intent upon using their sphere as 'a jumping-off place for attacking Soviet Russia'.[22]

Having confirmed for himself at Paris that the West were in the process of devising a Western bloc, Molotov's best ploy would have been to keep Russia and its Eastern partners in the system and disrupt it from within. This was an enticing prospect and there remained the possibility, canvassed by Molotov, that the Eastern European states should participate in further Marshall Plan deliberations scheduled to start on 12 July. But this was rejected out of fear that, not yet fully under Stalinist control, the Eastern Europeans would be lured by Western largesse and lost to Soviet influence. On the Western side, the lingering possibility of Soviet disruption of the Plan was a source of anxiety. Bevin was not immune to the dark apprehensions of his Private Secretary noted above. After Molotov's walk-out, he told the US Ambassador in Paris that he had 'anticipated and even wished for' the collapse of the Conference 'given my certainty that Molotov had come to Paris to sabotage our efforts'.[23] There was an element of *ex post facto* rationalisation in this and evidence from associates of the Foreign Secretary hints that he may well have entertained genuine hopes that the Russians would be co-operative.[24] The fact was that only 18 months earlier, British attempts to ring-fence a Soviet sphere as the prelude to a negotiated *modus vivendi* from a firm position had been ahead of US thinking. Now a bleak American policy of containing an incompatible adversary was in the ascendant and, with American money bags jingling, Bevin was bound to Washington's golden chariot.

He was fully aware of the American attitude. Before the Conference had opened, Bevin had been informed by the American Under Secretary of State, William L. Clayton, that Russia's access to raw materials made it unlikely that she would qualify for aid and that, in any case, Congress was likely to balk at assenting to it. Thus the two Western Powers had already made their play before the conference opened and Molotov learned of the 'behind-the-scenes collusion of the USA and Great Britain' via Soviet intelligence as events in Paris proceeded.[25] The American decision to use the European situation to halt and even push back Communist gains and to reduce the dangers of economic overproduction in the United States forced Bevin to make one of two choices. He could set his face against political polarisation in Europe only at the cost of throwing away the opportunity of American financial aid. There is no indication that he considered the latter. Bevin therefore must take some responsibility for creating the fissure which cut Europe in two as the Soviet Foreign Minister swept out of the French capital. In fairness, had Bevin genuinely wanted Soviet participation, he had been given little room for manoeuvre. Aside from Clayton's scepticism, Marshall's insistence that any scheme for recovery which America would fund had to be a common plan drawn up by all participants and must emerge from their own joint deliberations met square on with Molotov's half-expectation to swing a separate deal for the Soviet Union. The reality was, as Bidault pointed out at the Paris conference in the face of Molotov's demand that aid be on a state-by-state basis, 'the borrower cannot impose conditions on the lender' and any attempt to do so ran the risk of killing the offer.[26]

Before long, the Marshall Plan was being sold to American Senators as the means of restoring balance to a bi-polar world in which the USSR had stolen the advantage.[27] This corresponded to advice from hard-liners within the Foreign Office, eerily pre-empting Zhdanov's theory, that 'we must accept the existence of "two worlds" and concentrate upon putting our own world in order, and not upon fruitless attempts to appease or get on with the Russians.'[28] But Bevin remained determined to avoid this defeatist conclusion. His instinct was to use the integrationist impulses of the Marshall programme to complement his own version of a Third Force via European co-operation. One way of doing this was by attempting to persuade Clayton to enhance British standing among the Europeans by assuring that Britain should not be 'lumped' together with the other Europeans seeking American munificence but should rather be the conduit through which this aid would be distributed – the 'American watering-cans handled by British gardeners' as Dixon put it. This was not dissimilar to Molotov's appeal for individual responses to the Marshall initiative rather than the common European approach which the Americans sought and, unsurprisingly, was received in Washington with equal frigidity. Far from being granted the accolade of first among equals by the Americans, the British were soon to feel that in return for receipts from the European Recovery Programme (ERP) they were being forced to endure the indignities of pinprick attacks upon their own domestic nationalisation policy, over their reluctance to participate in an American-inspired European customs union as well as over their supposed general ingratitude towards Congressional generosity.[29] Little wonder then that the experience of Marshall Aid fuelled Bevin's determination to continue to press Cabinet colleagues for agreement on a British-led scheme for Western European economic co-operation. 'The Marshall Plan', he believed, 'offered an opportunity of making the first step in this direction by endeavouring to form a customs union. France and Italy were already considering such a union and he was anxious to explore the possibility of an Anglo-French economic association as soon as possible.'[30]

This was a familiar tune. But it was now to be played *con brio* and developed a more persistent refrain of associating European colonial possessions with the proposed economic co-operation which Bevin increasingly saw as vital if Western Europe 'was to maintain its independence as against Russia and the United States'.[31] Colonial collaboration was, in part, a recognition of the limits to economic revival if attempted by a concert of Western European states alone. Africa, in particular, provided a tempting vision of a huge market for European goods and a way of obtaining raw materials without drawing on scarce dollar reserves. It was also an important source of strategic materials, including uranium. As he was to point out to a somewhat sceptical Chancellor of the Exchequer over a year later, the 'US is very barren of essential minerals and in Africa we have them all.'[32] Political considerations inevitably impinged. Molotov's claim, first made at the London CFM at the back end of 1945, for a Soviet trusteeship within former Italian Tripolitania had aroused fears of Russian attempts to penetrate Africa. It also happened to cut across a British desire to obtain what had been Italian Cyrenaica for themselves as a means of bolstering their strategic position in the Mediterranean and as a replacement for Egypt, where pressure to remove British forces was already evident. The proposed withdrawal from India and the possibility of retreat from Suez, the two traditional foundations of British imperialism, added emphasis to Africa as a buttress to Britain's position in the Middle East and as a source of military manpower. All this played its part in the extension of Bevin's European vision to organising what he called 'the middle of the planet', ranging from the Norwegian Nordkapp to the Cape of Good Hope and embracing all the African possessions of the Western European states. This potentially massive Third Force was seen as a way of containing Soviet expansion, escaping from the servitude of American economic domination, and restoring Britain's position as a full member of the Big Three as a prelude to the return to inter-Allied co-operation .

On at least two occasions in 1947, in April and in September, Bevin revealed his enthusiasm about joint developments in Africa to leading French politicians. But independence from the United States could not be a publicly declared objective whilst Britain still remained reliant upon American economic and diplomatic support. Significantly too, Bevin remained wary of advertising a policy which was bound to be provocative to the Russians who, it was well known, were deeply apprehensive over the possible development of a 'Western bloc' against them. For these reasons, the Third Force notion was promoted throughout 1947 with persistence, but with some circumspection. Feasibility studies and working parties on European colonial co-operation sprouted in Whitehall with Cabinet support and objections from officials outside the Foreign Office (where there was a belief that the political gains would be well worth short-term economic disruption) that a satisfactory economic infrastructure did not exist in the African colonies, that there was a shortage of the necessary equipment to begin to construct it, and that the similarity in the raw materials produced in the British and French colonies made their integration superfluous were, for the time being, brushed aside.

Deteriorating East-West relations at the end of 1947 pushed Bevin's Third Force plans into top gear. As so often, Germany was the accelerator. Implicit in the ERP, as all the Powers recognised, was the economic revival of the Western Zones of Germany funded by credits from the USA. The dispute over this came to a head in December when the CFM system of preparing the way for peace finally collapsed following a sterile meeting in London which left disagreements over Germany unreconciled. In effect, East and West were no longer talking to each other. Immediately after the disintegration of the Council, in what was to mark a pivotal development, Bevin separately approached both Marshall and Bidault with a rather nebulous proposal for some kind of Western federation.[33] Following this, on 22 January, in a famous Commons statement, Bevin spoke publicly of his desire for what he termed a 'Western Union'.[34] As a consequence, within a matter of weeks negotiations had been opened between Britain, France and the Benelux countries which were to produce the Brussels Treaty in March.

The Brussels Treaty was not, as is so often claimed, a determined first step towards an American alliance. Bevin's intention remained to avoid that route and he had arrived at this position from a quite different direction. As we have seen, since 1945 he had been fascinated by the possibility of building a 'Western Union' of states on what he called 'the crust' of Europe under British auspices. He envisaged the political core of this to be an Anglo-French alliance and much effort had been put into achieving this during his first months in office. Although Bevin may with a certain justice be accused of over-caution in his approach to an alliance with the French, the obstacles in the way of a Franco-British accord had been real enough to be more than just an excuse for the British to evade the issue.[35] Yet by the time an agreement had been cemented in March 1947 by the Treaty of Dunkirk, tensions had already begun to transform the international pattern which had existed when Bevin had first entered the Foreign Office and temporarily deflected him from his primary purpose. Because of this, Dunkirk was motivated more by the need to provide some psychological boost for the non-Communist forces in France than in laying the foundations for Western European co-operation. It certainly had nothing to do with preparing the ground for a military pact against the Soviet Union.[36] At the end of the year, however, the Treaty of Dunkirk did seem briefly to provide a suitable foundation for a Western association. Still unclear how precisely this edifice might be constructed or even defined, there remained wide support among Foreign Office officials that, nevertheless, Britain should build it. Failure to do so, it was asserted, would result in being 'outclassed' by Russia, dependent on the United States and with Britain and Western Europe reduced to 'pigmies between two giants'.[37]

It was the weeks immediately following the tense international atmosphere surrounding the failure of the London CFM in December which were to see the high-watermark of Bevin's hopes for Western European collaboration. The breakdown of the CFM and the progress of the ERP had banished his long-standing caution over appearing to build a bloc against the Russians and 'had opened the way for an attempt to secure a greater measure of co-operation among the countries of Western Europe.' At a Cabinet meeting on 8 January 1948 he laid out his views in a clutch of important papers.[38] The most important of these, 'The First Aim of British Foreign Policy', developed the notion he had already tentatively put to Marshall and Bidault that physical barriers and economic progress were not sufficient to 'stem the further encroachment of the Soviet tide' and that 'spiritual forces' must be mobilised to defend the West. 'Spiritual' was used on five occasions in the paper, prompting his colleagues to suggest the need for more precision and a 'positive point of focus'. Bevin himself admitted that his proposal might seem 'a somewhat fanciful conception'. Yet, if these papers and the surrounding discussion lacked illumination as to how his goal might be realised - he was, for instance, unsure whether formal alliances would be appropriate – his general thrust was clear. The core of this moral alliance would be those Western states which held common ideals on civil liberties and human rights. More specifically:

> it would be necessary to mobilise the resources of Africa in support of any Western European union; and if some such union could be created, including not only the countries of Western Europe but also their Colonial possessions in Africa and the East, this would form a *bloc* which, both in population and productive capacity, could stand on an equality with the western hemisphere and the Soviet *blocs*.

The aim was to win 'material aid' and 'backing' from the United States but the Western Europeans who 'despise the spiritual values of America' would look to the UK and not the USA for leadership. 'It is', Bevin asserted, 'for us as Europeans and as a Social Democratic Government, and not the Americans to give the lead in the spiritual, moral and political sphere to all the democratic elements in Western Europe which are anti-Communist and are, at the same time, genuinely progressive and reformist, believing in freedom, planning and social justice – what one might call "The Third Force".' In response, the Cabinet gave its approval to a policy of the consolidation of 'the forces of the Western European countries and their Colonial possessions' which was to lay behind Bevin's 'Western Union' speech on 22 January.

For a fleeting period the idea of a 'spiritual federation' of the West became the focus of an official propaganda offensive against a general encroachment of Communism in an attempt to expose the dark side of Stalinism whilst presenting British Social Democracy as a superior exemplar to unrestrained capitalism. Indeed, Bevin was doing more than rehearsing to the Cabinet the terms of the political initiative he was about to make. He was also reclaiming the ideological middle ground for those with faith in the Labour Party's brand of Social Democracy as a distinctive alternative to Communism or capitalism and implying that a vision of a 'socialist foreign policy' was not the prerogative of the Labour Left alone. So far, Bevin had been generally resistant to efforts by members of the Foreign Office's Russia Committee to use the BBC and MI6 to undermine Soviet influence through a propaganda campaign to expose the deficiencies and ruthlessness of Communist rule. This reluctance is perhaps to be explained, in part by a natural unwillingness to increase his domestic difficulties with left wing back-bench Labour MPs who were critical of his apparent hostility to the Kremlin. Significantly, even over Iran, where Bevin did judge the situation to be sufficiently menacing to permit a political warfare campaign against Moscow, he complained to his zealous officials of 'too much emphasis on anti-Communist propaganda' as opposed to 'the positive features of British theory and practice' warning that 'it was a mistake to rouse Communist enthusiasm by excessive attacks on Communism.'[39] At the beginning of 1948, the world seemed dangerous and divided enough for Bevin to accept some change of direction. There was also a developing thrust from permanent officials and from the military that government should take the offensive in what the latter called the 'political war' – that is, counter-subversion and propaganda. It was their assertion that if this 'political war' was not won 'a war of physical violence was almost inevitable.'[40] Therefore, at the same time as the Cabinet agreed to Bevin's attempt to consolidate Western Europe, it also approved the creation of what was called an Information Research Department (IRD) a secret section lodged within the Foreign Office which from unimposing headquarters in Carlton House Terrace would collate intelligence and disseminate anti-Soviet material to counter the temptations of Soviet ideology and 'seek to make London the Mecca for Social Democrats in Europe'.[41]

Ministers, journalists and trade union leaders began to be supplied by a team of IRD writers with anti-Soviet material as ammunition for the ideological struggle in which the British were now joined and which would be channelled in the form of speeches and articles via news agencies, the BBC or planted press stories into Europe and the Middle and Far East. Around the same time, a Foreign Office 'Working Party on the Spiritual Aspects of Western Union' argued for an institute of young 'rising men' which would educate its audience in 'the British contribution to Western Civilisation'. In August, these efforts were supplemented by the creation of a Colonial Information Policy Committee to oversee the broadcasting of pro-British, anti-Communist publicity within the colonies.[42] This was, however, not quite, 'Britain's declaration of the Cold War'.[43] Bevin remained impervious to pressure from within the Foreign Office for more 'unscrupulous methods' such as instigating a purge of the Communist leadership of the Italian Trade Unions.[44] Although he now accepted that 'Soviet policy is actively hostile to British interests everywhere', he also considered that they were not planning war and underlying the shift in policy was a surviving, though less sanguine, belief that if faced with a demonstration of the virility of the West, 'the Soviet Government might radically change its policy'.[45]

A Third Force thus remained a highly seductive model not only to Bevin, but also to significant elements in the Foreign Office and to his Cabinet colleagues. Nevertheless, it was a notion which charmed to deceive. The persistence of Britain's economic difficulties and the dawning realisation that, whatever potential they might hold, the African colonies could not provide the quick fix that the Western European economies needed supported the persistent resistance of both the Treasury and the Board of Trade to Bevin's ideas. The Colonial Office was also reluctant to support projects which smacked of European exploitation of indigenous peoples. In the longer term, as we shall see, these impediments were to play their part in destroying the Third Force idea. To these were added the weight of the Chiefs of Staff.

If Western Europe was to become a platform for British power, it had to be a base that was secure from external threat. No less importantly, if the Western Europeans were to be persuaded to come together, they must feel assured that Britain, the most powerful among them, was prepared to defend them against the most pressing potential threat of the day – Soviet Communism. The attempt to cover both these requisites was to have the effect of skewing emphasis towards the security aspects of 'Western Union'. The Foreign Secretary who had earlier supported the insistence of the CoS – in the face of firm opposition from Attlee – that it was the Middle East and not Western Europe which was the key to Britain's defence, should not have been surprised to discover that the Chiefs were not his allies as he switched his attention to Europe. Their position remained unaltered. Moreover, they were also convinced that if war should come, American support would be vital – though they had no more reason than had Bevin to expect that this would be likely.[46] The Western European states, including France, they felt, had little to offer. On these grounds, and also on the basis that Communist influence in France made French military and political security a dubious commodity, the Chiefs were opposed to staff talks with the French even after France was offered full British support against an attack by Germany in the 1947 Franco-British Treaty. Britain's own military weakness – military manpower had been reduced by over four million since the end of hostilities and further economies meant that this was not yet the end of the decline – and the even worse state of the French armed forces, set the Chiefs further against the idea of any future expeditionary force for the Continent and provided another argument for not exposing British defence thinking to the French in military talks. There was one more potential embarrassment. Tentative British planning with the United States envisioned that, should war break out, existing Allied forces in Europe would undergo a Dunkirk-style evacuation of the Continent ('Dunkirk' was, in fact, the rather insensitive code-name for Anglo-American thinking on such an operation) followed, in the distant term, by an eventual rerun of D-Day.

Bevin, however, increasingly saw his Third Force ambitions as dependent on Anglo-French staff talks which would provide an avenue for persuading France to embark upon more general co-operation. Bidault's apparent anxiety after the failure of the London CFM that the Western Powers' attempts to integrate their German zones of occupation into the economy of the West might provoke the Soviet Union into a military strike in Europe gave added impetus to this. Bevin's dilemma was how sufficiently to reassure France and the other Western European states over their security that coming together in a 'Western Union' was a practical proposition when the British Chiefs were against a military commitment to the Continent. The solution appeared in the second week of 1948. Grasping at a possibility which Bevin also seems to have alighted upon, one Foreign Office adviser noted that:

in this predicament it seems to me that our only method of satisfy-
ing the need for security is to involve America as far as possible in
the defence of Western Europe. It is quite likely that the Americans
too will refuse specifically to commit their forces to the Continent
of Europe; but if they would enter with ourselves into some general
commitment to go to war with an aggressor it is probable that the
potential victims might feel reassured as to eventual victory and
hence refuse to embark on a fatal policy of appeasement.[47]

Bevin had already made certain overtures along these lines to Marshall when he had spoken to him after the failed London CFM in
December. But first he had spoken to Bidault of the need for 'some
sort of federation in Western Europe'. Only then did he go on to test
the Secretary of State on possible Anglo-American military collaboration – though he purposely exempted the French from these. Bevin's
motive at this point has often been interpreted as one of angling principally for American support, whilst simultaneously constructing a
Western European group capable of defending itself and therefore
deemed worthy of US backing in Washington. There is, indeed, evidence which might suggest that it was this, and not a 'Western Union',
that he was working towards. Though he mentioned to Marshall certain limited staff conversations between London and Paris, which by
now he had persuaded the CoS to agree to, he also cast some doubt
upon the value of these as compared to military talks between Britain
and the United States which would be 'like those between members
of one country'.[48] The two now agreed to pick up the suggestion of
tripartite security talks with the Canadians, which the latter had put
forward two months earlier, and that the French should not be asked
to join. It may be, that on occasions the mind-searing intricacy of
constructing a 'Western Union' and a sensation that the existing international situation presented such an immediate danger that it would
not allow too much prevarication caused his optimism to falter and
that his preference sometimes *did* swing towards reliance on the Americans. Certainly the prerequisites for the alternative construction of a
Western European base were exasperatingly difficult to mesh. Before
the Europeans, especially the French, would themselves countenance
Bevin's 'spiritual union', they made it apparent that they wanted assurances of military support. This the British CoS were reluctant to
give without American backing. As for the Americans, they could not
be persuaded to become involved without indications that the Euro-

peans were already working together. Added to this, whilst the French made it clear that they favoured a series of bilateral treaties based on the Treaty of Dunkirk example and which would provide territorial guarantees, the Dutch and the Belgians wanted a single multilateral pact which committed the participants to detailed military discussions. The latter were, as we have seen, quite uncongenial to the British CoS. It may be that Bevin was playing a double game, not precisely sure which of the two paths he straddled was the best finally to adopt. It was certainly a complex one.

A significant burden of evidence suggests, however, that in the first half of 1948 Bevin's more consistent endeavours still lay in the European and not the Atlantic direction. In his talk with Bidault in December, Bevin had pointed out that the Americans would have to be kept informed of moves towards a European federation but mainly to the extent that this would allow them to 'think it was they who were acting'.[49] When, early in January, the Americans were told of the Cabinet's ambition to build, with their assistance, a Western European system the information that this organisation was intended to eradicate Western European subservience to the USA and the USSR was excised in communications to Washington.[50] In other words, American support was vital and they had to be lured into giving it, but Bevin's intention was to use the military, as well as the economic, might of the USA to underpin a temporarily weakened half-Continent, thus out-flanking the CoS and reassuring the Western Europeans. In this way, the Americans were to be the 'sprat' to catch the Western Europeans – not the other way around. No doubt, as Leffler suggests, by this time, the American 'goal was to expedite Western Europe's recovery, undermine the appeal of Communism, co-opt Western Germany, and thwart the Kremlin.' But the aims being pursued by the US and the British were 'complementary' rather than identical.[51] In the first place, Bevin shared all Washington's objectives, but was determined *in addition* upon an independent power base for Britain. American assistance would then be discarded like so much superfluous ballast. In March, the Cabinet was urged that 'we should use US aid to gain time, but our ultimate aim should be to attain a position in which the countries of Western Europe would be independent both of the US and the Soviet Union.' If Britain 'only pushed on and developed Africa', Bevin asserted in October, 'we could have the US dependent on us and eating out of our hand in four or five years.'[52] By the same token, the Truman Administration wanted to contain

Communism where it encroached upon their own interests and these did not necessarily coincide with the interests of Whitehall.[53] But the British had less taste for an all-out crusade against Communism than was burgeoning in Washington. It remained an important consideration for Bevin not to be judged to be constructing a system aimed at the Soviet Union and he remained anxious to 'leave the door open to a Russian conciliation with the West'.[54]

The direct outcome of Bevin's 'Western Union' speech of 22 January – and of his concurrent manoeuvring – was the Brussels Treaty which was signed by Britain, France and the Benelux states on 17 March 1948. The Brussels Pact was something of a hybrid arrangement suggesting its status as an intended staging post to wider European co-operation. Alarm over the Communist take-over in Czechoslovakia in February had helped put aside divisions between the participants over the form the Treaty should take. Events in Prague were taken as a possible overture to the extension of Soviet influence in Finland and Norway. There was also fear that pressure would be put on Italy where elections were due in April and therefore, as had been the case in France a year before, ways were sought to give public support for the anti-Communist Socialists. Each of the contracting parties now agreed to come to the aid of the others if they were the object of an armed attack in Europe. Nevertheless, the Soviet Union was not specified as a likely aggressor. Germany, however, at the insistence of the French who were deeply anxious at German rehabilitation through the ERP, was named as a potential trouble-maker. On the other hand, the Brussels Treaty did not conspicuously advance Bevin's hopes for reassuring the Europeans as a preliminary to deeper co-operation. Despite the anxieties of the Western Europeans on this point, only the existing occupation forces were considered appropriate to cope with the named potential assailant and no additional military provision at all was made to face the implied enemy. American underwriting of the new association was informal and imprecise, partly because of surviving isolationist opinion and partly because even those in Washington who felt that the Western Europeans should be supported did not believe that a military alliance was necessarily the way to do it. Truman did endorse the announcement of the Brussels Treaty in Congress but, as yet, this amounted to little more than a Presidential promise to be a good neighbour.

On the British side, the CoS were hardly budged from their determination to view the interests of Britain lying principally in the defence of the Middle East with as much American support as could be obtained. Pleas from Bevin at a meeting of the Defence Committee of the Cabinet on 8 January that 'he would be embarrassed in his dealings with Britain's potential European allies if planning were based on the assumption that an army was not to be sent' to the Continent met only limited success. Despite support for the Foreign Secretary from the new Chief of the Imperial General Staff, Bernard Montgomery, and notwithstanding a directive from the Cabinet that they should realign their defensive thinking to Bevin's foreign policy objectives in Europe, the Chiefs as a whole could only be leaned on so far as to accept that if hostilities broke out, the existing occupation forces would not be withdrawn. They were even prepared to renege on this. A month after the Treaty was signed, the CoS agreed with the Americans, in a plan the British code-named 'Doublequick', to arrange for the withdrawal of all their forces from the Continent in a European emergency, though this was revised in May, for fear that the Brussels Treaty Powers would hear of it.[55] Planning for the defence of a Europe under attack reverted to the January decision to keep occupation forces in Europe without reinforcement. This muddle reflected the dissonance between Bevin's urgent political wish to provide confidence-boosting assurances to the Western Europeans as a means of getting 'Western Union' to work and the rather more leisurely views of the military planners who envisaged no immediate Soviet invasion of Europe and, in any case, did not believe that a European bloc alone could stop it.

These frustrations did not work entirely to Bevin's disadvantage. When the prospect of treaty negotiations had emerged at the start of the year, he had insisted to Bidault that these 'should not be subject to [American] approval.' In April, with the Brussels Treaty signed and when it looked as though the Americans were now ready to become more involved in European security arrangements, Bevin was against their participation 'from the beginning' because they would 'tell us what we should do'. As John Kent and John Young point out, 'this shows that Bevin was still determined to build up Western European co-operation under British leadership *before* US involvement: Western Europe should prepare its *own plans* while securing American *support*.'[56] 'Western Union' – the term used privately by Bevin to describe his dream in 1945 and now actually bestowed upon the five signatories – remained the crux of the pact so far as Bevin was concerned and, with the constituent core now signed up backed by

American approval, he presumably hoped that the rest of the structure would fall into place. It is interesting that of the ten Articles which made up the Treaty, only four were specifically concerned with issues of mutual defence and the first three asserted common purposes in economic, social and cultural matters. Similarly, the first four of seven preliminary resolutions of the Treaty stressed the bonds of heritage, culture and the desire for economic recovery. Given Bevin's reluctance to commit his thoughts to writing and his preference for broad rather than detailed statements, the Brussels Treaty provides us with the first fractured image in hard print of his 'spiritual union'. It was also to be the last. This emphasis was absent from the North Atlantic Treaty one year later.

The fact remained that the Western Europeans had scrambled to sign the Brussels Treaty without guarantees of additional military support not out of interest in constructing a Third Force – 'spiritual' or otherwise – but largely because the recent coup in Prague had highlighted the sensation of danger from the East. A note almost of panic in Washington also helped crystallise an American decision to provide verbal and the prospect, perhaps, of more concrete support for what the Western Europeans were doing.[57] Even before the Treaty was signed, Bevin's apprehensions were aroused that this lowering international climate would dilute the whole idea of a 'Western Union' and reduce it to no more than a mere instrument of security. This was, indeed, what was to happen. The economic declarations in the Brussels Treaty were already not much more than a remnant of what Bevin hoped the signatories might achieve. Foreign Office attempts, for instance, to have the Treaty embrace colonial co-operation were made, but this was rejected by the Benelux states as inappropriate.[58] The start of a crisis over Berlin in June ensured that security considerations crowded in even further, pushing Bevin away from his grand design towards the more prosaic path of being a partner in a Euro-Atlantic system to contain the spread of Soviet Communism.

Stalin's decision to cut off all overland routes between the Western sectors of Berlin and the occupied zones in the West on 24 June 1948 originated in his recognition that a part of the purpose of the Marshall Plan was to draw Western Germany securely into the Western orbit. The London CFM in December 1947 was a last attempt, and not an auspicious one given the West's fixation with the ERP, to settle wrangles over Germany since 1946 and have the state treated as a single economic unit. Systematic measures taken by the Western Powers after the collapse of the CFM to restructure the economic and political life in their zones were clearly intended to lead to a separate West German state and met with the Russian response on 1 April 1948 of making access to Berlin difficult for the Western occupiers. The introduction of a full land blockade in June, and the consequent decision by the West to relieve the siege by air, marked such a new level of confrontation in the Cold War that it may well be argued that the contest itself did not truly begin until this moment. Until now the prospective combatants had engaged largely in shadow-boxing using bluff, subversion or economic weaponry, but backing off – as over Iran and Turkey in 1946 – from escalation towards a final showdown. By definition, all of the Powers were to balk from this final encounter in the Cold War. But it takes more than one side to fight even a Cold War and, thus far, it might be said, a set of fully committed combatants had failed to muster. Bluff, it goes without saying, was exerted over Berlin too. Yet the crisis which now developed, and its extension over 11 months, reflected not only the exhaustion of patience in the West over what they considered to be two years or more of Soviet obstruction over Germany, but also the crucial significance which the future orientation of Germany had to both blocs throughout the period. This time, though neither side wanted war over Berlin, each was prepared to contemplate action which skirted the risk of open conflict.

Stalin had to face the possibility of an armed thrust by the West to Berlin or, during the airlift, an incident which would lead to conflagration. In the West there were those who favoured dispatching armoured convoys along the autobahns to relieve the city. Though the British Government was not prepared to go so far as Churchill who advocated threatening the annihilation of Soviet cities by atomic bombs unless the siege was raised, American B-29 bombers were deployed in the eastern counties of England. Agreement that British bases should be developed to take these had been arrived at in the summer of 1946, at the time when there were fears that Russian pressure on Turkey might result in the outbreak of war.[59] In fact, in 1948 the B-29s came without atom bombs or the necessary modification to deliver them, although the implication at the time was that these were 'atomic-capable'. Anxieties were multiplied because of the fear in most minds that though war would not be deliberately provoked, it might occur by crisis mismanagement. Moreover, if war did come, Britain's lack of military preparedness was such that, according to the CoS, there would 'be complete disorganisation, leading to disaster … '.[60]

In contrast to the pervading hesitancy in Washington and pessimism over whether West Berlin could be held once the full crisis broke in the summer, Bevin had already decided the previous February that 'we must stay'.[61] 'The Russians', Bevin argued, 'think our Government is weak, but this time we're sticking. No-one has stood up since the war to Russia: we are going to stand up now.'[62] The Cabinet endorsed this stance and quickly settled on an attempt to support the West Berliners by airlift. It seems a fair judgement that, as the crisis escalated, 'London moved with greater speed and decisiveness [than Washington] in making its basic strategic choice to stay in Berlin, in announcing this decision and in prompting the American government to follow suit' and 'much of the inspiration and initiative for the airlift came in fact from the British side.'[63] As the crisis unfolded, Bevin was irritated by American efforts to deal directly with Stalin, viewing them as appeasement and an unhealthy sign of their impatience. To him it was 'an issue of will' which would lead the Russians to come to terms if the West stood firm.[64] This was his characteristic approach to the Russians: 'We have to be firm and we have to be patient, and then we shall see.'[65] The symbolic significance of making a stand over the former centre of German power was important. More so, however, was his determination to avoid any settlement over the future of the city which involved concessions to Moscow over Western Germany and the Ruhr. Even so, if at the conclusion of the crisis almost a year later it was Stalin who was the worse off through having to acknowledge the consolidating Western bulkhead in Germany – the Federal Republic of Germany (FRG) was proclaimed four months after the end of the Berlin siege – and recognise the status of West Berlin, then Bevin was to lose a good deal too.

The struggle over Berlin accentuated the shift towards a military emphasis in 'Western Union' still further. Obviously the immediate danger was in Europe and, more than ever, it was now necessary to convince the Western Europeans that in the event of a Soviet attack, collaboration would mean that they would not be left to fend for themselves. As the CoS had made apparent, the crisis also pointed up British military weakness which, as Bevin admitted at the time, made nonsense of any effective resistance to a Soviet thrust without backing from the United States.[66] American support did now seem more likely with the United States displaying a greater readiness to consider their response to an attack on Western Europe, which was encouraging to those who sought an Atlantic alliance, though requiring careful handling if a British-led 'Western Union' was the primary objective. In other words, the centre of gravity of any proposal for a security arrangement was drifting away from Western Europe and 'the middle of the planet' towards Atlantic, and therefore American, predominance. An Atlantic defensive system was, in fact, the only kind of association that Washington was prepared to consider as appropriate to their own strategic requirements, though their preference remained to provide moral support and they came up with no offer to send military forces to a future beleaguered Europe. Instead, American military planning continued to be based on withdrawal from a Europe under attack and the pursuit of war by air strikes from bases on the periphery.

For a time, Bevin seems to have held onto the hope that an Atlantic Pact could be complementary to the Brussels Treaty without absorbing it, allowing the participants of that group to retain their discrete entity and independence, whilst buttressed at a distance by the American military in much the same way as Europe was being supported financially under the Marshall Plan. One authority suggests that it was this possibility which encouraged the British to take the road which was to lead to an American alliance in the shape of the North Atlantic Pact in April, 1949. In this view, the North Atlantic Treaty Organisation (NATO) emerged from an expectation that if the Western Europeans joined the kind of Atlantic structure which the Americans wanted, Washington could then be persuaded to guarantee the Brussels Treaty states which would provide the cohesion necessary for them eventually to go forward towards the kind of 'Western Union' which Bevin had always envisaged.[67]

In fact, Bevin's intended Third Force was already drowning under a torrent of other difficulties making its viability increasingly unlikely. Although, in January, 1948, the Cabinet had given its support to the general notion of constructing a 'Western Union', it then failed to back the measures which Bevin judged necessary to achieve this. Central to his vision was the provision of an economic system which would eventually give the Western Europeans – and Britain – economic independence from the USA. But as ERP funding began to flow, the Western Europeans became increasingly engaged in disruptively competitive economic policies as each state vied to boost its own exports in the hope of economic take off and to reduce dollar expenditure before Marshall Aid came to an end in 1952. An appealing way to counter these centrifugal tendencies for Bevin and his advisers was to supplement the Brussels Treaty with some form of customs union, including the setting up of a supranational Western Union economic bank. Both were rejected by the Chancellor of the Exchequer, Sir Stafford Cripps, and his Treasury experts as too 'grandiose'. In their view, the fragility of Britain's economic recovery would be best protected within the shelter of the sterling bloc rather than risking the free-for-all of a customs union. Though not opposed to integration, their preference was for a gradual series of separate joint projects aimed at improving trade relations and economic efficiency without endangering British freedom of action or cutting across the Labour Government's preference for economic planning. This strategy was endorsed by the Cabinet in March. Bevin seems to have gone along with this, though he continued to tell the French that he favoured 'a Western Union bank and currency' to make the group 'more independent of the United States.'[68] The reality was that the Cabinet decision was bound to restrict his room for manoeuvre with the Europeans, more especially with the French who, to Bevin's discomfort, were notably beginning to embrace federalist views on European cooperation and, ironically, favoured something along the lines of Bevin's more radical approach which had been blocked by the Treasury.[69]

Within a year of the onset of the Berlin Crisis, the British were to experience such a depletion of their dollar reserves that the value of the pound and the viability of the sterling bloc itself was threatened. This coincided with the negotiations which led to the signing of the North Atlantic Treaty in April, 1949. In other words, Britain's inescapable reliance on the USA for defence coincided with the need for further American financial support. By the summer, the situation had significantly deteriorated and Cripps, searching for a way to stop the haemorrhage of British dollar reserves, specifically rejected developing a bloc made up of the Western Europeans and their colonial dependencies in favour of some kind of arrangement with the United States.[70] When the decision was finally made in September, 1949 that sterling would have to be devalued by over 30 per cent, it was taken in close consultation with the Americans and surrounded with agreements by Washington to increase trade with the sterling bloc and the Empire, stimulate investment there and reduce restrictions to British trade with the United States. It was the clearest of signals to the Western Europeans, who had not been informed of the forthcoming British devaluation or invited to the Anglo-American talks which prefaced it, of a British determination to lean on the United States in order to preserve their own commercial bloc.

On top of this, as mentioned above, colonial co-operation had not found its way into the Brussels Treaty. Discussions leading to the Treaty had included collaboration between the overseas territories of the signatory Powers and a statement of intent inserted into the initial draft of the first Article of the pact. It was omitted from the final Treaty, however, because the Benelux states, the Dutch in particular, deemed it irrelevant to the kind of organisation they wanted. This was a source of disappointment in the Foreign Office, but experts in the Colonial Office had always judged Bevin's collaborative ideas to be fundamentally exploitative of the colonies. Their point of view was strengthened as the shortage of capital investment and the scarcity of dollars encouraged the extension of import restrictions on the colonies, whilst colonial exports were used to promote Britain's economic recovery and add to the British dollar pool – a topsy-turvy way of promoting colonial development. By 1949, the collapse of the dollar earning power of the colonies eroded the value of even this short-termism. Around the same time, the Dominions Office was warning that if Britain chose to associate itself with an economically weak and imperfectly defended Third Force, the result would be to push the Commonwealth states of Canada, Australia, New Zealand and South Africa towards reliance on the more potent attractions of the United States.

Exactly when Bevin finally abandoned the idea of an independent British Third Force remains unclear. The traditional view that Bevin, driven by an anti-Communism learned during his time as a trade union leader, worked consistently since 1945 to draw the United States into a defensive arrangement with Western Europe no longer holds water and may safely be discounted. A modified version of this suggests that since coming to the Foreign Office 'Bevin had a number of broad objectives which he sought to pursue. There was no blueprint but a series of alternative visions which he pursued simultaneously in his search for a stable international order and the re-establishment of British power and independence.' It may be the case that Bevin's decision to follow the Atlantic path and to abandon other 'alternative visions' came in between the failure of the London CFM in December, 1947 and the signing of the Brussels Treaty the following March. Signs of Soviet pressure on Norway early in 1948 may well have convinced him that resistance to the USSR was required on such a disconcertingly wide European front that Western European weakness could only be counterbalanced by a larger instrument than the Brussels Pact and which should include the United States.[71] This is a perfectly plausible scenario and offers an explanation for what otherwise may appear elaborately intricate, and apparently conflicting, manoeuvres. Particularly, it fits in with the fact that the Anglo-American-Canadian discussions of a possible Atlantic arrangement began within a week of the signing of the Brussels Treaty. These so-called Pentagon Talks fed into wider security talks in Washington which were, in their turn, to produce the North Atlantic Treaty (consisting of the Brussels Treaty signatories plus Canada, Denmark, Iceland, Italy, Norway, Portugal and the United States) in 1949.

This version of events, however, leaves us with the problem of the persistence of Bevin's Third Force ideas and the auxiliary status which he had always given to the idea of intimate Anglo-American collaboration. These were not, in Bevin's mind, two equal 'alternative visions' and the quest for a self-reliant base for British power, though moderated after the Brussels Treaty and stated in fainter and palpably more desperate tones than earlier, remains perceptible. It is quite feasible therefore to view the Pentagon Talks and the subsequent Washington security conversations as leading to a North Atlantic treaty by default and intending rather to provide trans-Atlantic support for, and not an alternative to, a free-standing Western European grouping. Whether, however, Bevin continued to cling on to a serious expectation, right into the negotiations for a North Atlantic Pact, that such an arrangement would shelter, rather than assimilate, the essential germ of the 'Western Union' appears doubtful. After all, by early 1949 two essential components of Bevin's ideal, a European customs union and colonial co-operation had either been abandoned or resulted in nothing of substance. It seems more likely that intermittent references to 'Western Union' were by this time little more than vestiges of a once doggedly pursued policy which logic now suggested was no longer attainable; 'wishful thinking', as the principal protagonist of this interpretation admits.[72]

Rather it was the Berlin crisis which dealt the *coup de grâce* to the Third Force idea. With the economic and colonial aspects of Bevin's European policy already in serious trouble, a war in which the Europeans would be completely outclassed loomed as a serious possibility. The security talks in the Pentagon, which commenced in the March before the crisis broke, were viewed by Bevin either as a probe to discover the extent to which the United States might underwrite his 'spiritual union' or perhaps as possible insurance if Bevin's European policy came to nothing. Either way, progress was not encouraging. Little in the way of a formal commitment from the Americans emerged from these talks and Bevin was not optimistic that Washington would feel able to break with tradition and provide one. An extension of these conversations had been mooted since late April, but it was the contest over West Berlin which made this a reality. As these new negotiations were taking place during the summer between the United States, Canada and the Brussels Pact states, the American Ambassador in London summed up how the British now saw their position:

> with help from US [and] in conjunction with British Commonwealth and Empire, they will again become a power to be reckoned with, which associated with the US, can maintain the balance of power in the world. For geo-political and historic reasons, they feel we need them almost as much as they need us; that US can never again retreat into isolationism; and that in all the world there is no more stable, predictable, or reliable ally than British Commonwealth and Empire led by UK.[73]

Independence slouched towards interdependence; pretensions of equal authority began to be eclipsed by the role of loyal subordinate to the trans-Atlantic Superpower. Instead of organising the 'middle of the planet', Britain, in Hogan's words:

> might at least become the pivot in a Western system of overlapping blocs, the sovereign of a middle kingdom that included the sterling area and the Commonwealth, the leader of Western Europe through the Brussels Pact and the Organisation for European Economic Co-operation, and the ally of both Western Europe and the United States through the ERP and the North Atlantic Treaty then being negotiated in Washington.[74]

The enormous ramifications of all this for British power were set out during the spring of 1949 in an important paper by a newly formed Foreign Office body, the Permanent Under-Secretary's Committee (PUSC). The paper's conclusions were founded on two assumptions which, until now, the Foreign Secretary had been loath fully and finally to admit – the 'implacable' hostility of the Soviet Union and

Britain's 'economic dependence on the United States'. The argument now was that 'economic integration with Western Europe involves great risks which would only be worth taking if we could be confident that economic integration would create a unit economically and militarily strong enough to be capable of resisting aggression. For the moment there seems little prospect of such a development and we might, if we went too far along this road, find Europe overrun and our own segment of the economy unable to function on its own.' Britain's future, it was posited, lay in the consolidation of the West in which the United States would obviously be the most powerful force, but with the hope that 'as time goes by, the elements of [British] dependence [on the USA] ought to diminish and those of inter-dependence to increase.' The 'concept of Western Europe as a Third World Power' acting independently of the United States was rejected as 'inconsistent with the consolidation of a Western system'.[75] Bevin read the paper on 27 March and expressed his agreement with the Committee's analysis.

The PUSC was in itself an indication of a new direction in British policy. During the Berlin crisis the Russia Committee, up to now the jealously guarded preserve of the Foreign Office, was opened to a representative of the CoS. This was the result of considerable pressure from the military, who were critical of Bevin's low level of enthusiasm for clandestine operations and anxious that the Cold War was being lost through inadequate funding and the lack of integrated planning to fight it. A sustained attack from the military planners throughout 1948 urged that a co-ordinating body to oversee special operations and psychological warfare and with a wider brief than the burgeoning IRD was immediately necessary 'to wage the cold war'.[76] Attending the Committee for the first time on 25 November 1948, Air Chief Marshal Sir Arthur Tedder, The Chief of the Air Staff, asserted, to some scepticism from Foreign Office members, that the British should 'aim at winning the "cold war"'. By this he meant overthrowing the Soviet regime in five years. He proposed the need for a permanent team to plan and execute this via subversion and psychological warfare. Bur Bevin's disquiet over creating a group which might undermine his own authority over the running of foreign policy meant that Tedder's planning team never materialised, though the germ of failed attempts to foment civil war in Albania which began the following year emerged from this meeting of the Committee. The PUSC when it was created in February 1949 was something of a compromise in that its task was for long-term planning of foreign policy, though the authority to oversee the operation of its recommendations was absent. The Russia Committee began to meet less regularly until it finally faded away in the early 1950s. The PUSC, on the other hand, backed by a Permanent Under-Secretary's Department (PUSD), joined the JIC as key co-ordinating organs for intelligence gathering to resist Soviet overt and covert activities and to take the Cold War, by clandestine or psychological means, into what was now regarded as enemy territory. These propagandistic and subversive attacks on the Soviet system, which by the end of the year were in full swing, were conducted through semi-official or non-governmental bodies and via influential individuals judged best able to disseminate information about Communist methods and tactics fed to them by the expanding resources of the flourishing IRD.[77]

By the end of the 1950s the IRD had a staff of around 400 personnel guided by seniors who had honed their skills in the war of deception and subversion against the Axis Powers. The IRD's preferred medium was 'grey' propaganda – 'the truth imparted with a certain "spin"' – as opposed to 'white' (uncomfortable truths) or 'black' (false) propaganda and was diffused (sometimes in association with less-secretive Foreign Office information machinery) by radio, briefing notes for MPs, the press and sympathetic publishing houses to the eyes and ears of individuals in Western Europe and the Middle and Far East to demonstrate the superiority of Western over Communist systems. These were judged to be the areas most open to Soviet penetration, though the disappointing results of a campaign in the late 1940s and early 1950s to stimulate defection among Red Army units serving in the Soviet European satellites seems to have encouraged the IRD from then on to concentrate its efforts in the Third World.[78]

To return to 1948, the inclusion of the CoS in the Russia Committee was a recognition of the conjunction of British foreign and defence policy objectives and symbolised an end to the disharmony which had existed between the two for four years – though some disagreement over how the Cold War was to be fought remained. It was, of course, a victory for the military point of view and British foreign policy was now geared to matching a Soviet menace which the CoS had long forecast. The North Atlantic Treaty, casting aside the non-committal traditions of both Britain and the United States, was to have the highest profile in this contest. It proved to be an enduring accomplishment surviving until and

beyond the source of the external threat had succumbed. But to suggest that 'without question the North Atlantic Treaty was the crowning
achievement of [Bevin's] foreign secretaryship' is too assertive.[79]
Wherever one might choose to identify the mutation from a European to an Atlantic policy, it remains the case that the latter became
Bevin's goal at quite a late stage and was the by-product of failed
attempts to attain his objective of constructing an independent Third
Force dominated by Britain. Triumph though it turned out to be, the
North Atlantic pact was also a kind of consolation prize earned after
reluctant acceptance that the economic and military weakness of Britain and her proposed European partners in the face of the looming
power of the Soviet Union ruled out any such creation in the short
term and made it too dangerous to hang on for in the longer term.

It is easy to criticise Bevin's 'Western Union' intentions as vague, im-
practical, over-ambitious or 'half-baked pie in the sky'.[80] But they were,
at least, an imaginative attempt to come to terms with profoundly altered international circumstances. The more 'realistic' advice of Bevin's
opponents in the economic departments, and which he eventually fell in
with, that the best way forward was to consolidate Atlantic and Commonwealth connections, turned out to be a lengthy journey down a
dead-end. There is, as one French Minister put it to Bevin, 'the need for
some illusions and dreams' to inspire the people of Europe.[81] Ironically,
this was a reference to a French proposal in the summer of 1948 for a
European Assembly which Bevin judged a premature diversion. Provoked,
in part, by the limited defensive arrangements of the Brussels Treaty
and the laborious progress towards economic co-operation, the Belgians
and the French had begun to take the initiative in promoting closer co-
operation on federalist and supranational lines. This was a double blow
to Bevin. In the first place, events had forced him to recant his brief,
untypical dalliance with supranationalism in favour of gradual, pragmatic developments. More importantly, the point of his European design
was that it held the key to enhancing British power. The initiative was
slipping from his hands and the 'illusions and dreams' for the future of
Europe were being appropriated by the European federalists. Objective-
ly, their vision was no more 'practical' than his own and, as Bevin was
keen to point out, its success was based on long odds. But they were able
to persist and Bevin could not. Instead, in a postwar turning point quite
the match of British rejection of moves towards integration in the 1950s,
he abdicated the leadership of Europe and nudged Britain towards an
American-dominated Atlantic system.

# 3

---

# EMPIRE WITHOUT CLOTHES, 1945–51

Bevin's dream of using the resources of Africa to boost British authority and escape from the economic thraldom of the United States reminds us that in the late 1940s, Britain was, and intended to remain, a global power. The fact that there was no quarter of the globe in which Britain was without influence underpinned a status not matched by economic or military strength. If the British were to retain this position of political eminence or hope to improve their economic performance, this world role would have to continue. The Middle East merited particular attention. A tangible British presence was provided by troops stationed in bases in Egypt, Iraq and Aden. The Jordanian Arab Legion had a British Commander-in-Chief and British protectorates were strung along the Persian Gulf. The potential of the Middle East as a market for British manufactures and its resources – especially oil from the Abadan fields in Iran, deemed 'vital to the economic stability of the British Commonwealth as a whole', and available without dollar expenditure – ensured that the British stake in the region was of the highest order.[1] Bevin's thinking shortly after becoming Foreign Secretary mingled regard for such material factors with a nod towards socialist principles. In October 1945 he told the Cabinet that 'in his view it was essential to broaden the basis of British influence in the Middle East by developing an economic and social policy which would make for prosperity and contentment in the area as a whole. It would be the object of this policy to remedy the mal-distribution of purchasing power in the Middle East communities and raise the standard of living of the masses of the people.'[2] A Middle East Office with its headquarters in Cairo was set up to perform these tasks.

This, what might be termed, self-serving humanitarianism was coupled with a recognition that 'although the level of political

73

consciousness of the masses is low' the poverty and destitution of most of the Arabs might make them ripe for Communist propaganda and subversion.[3] Bevin himself believed that 'the most effective counter to Russian advances in the area is the economic and social betterment of the people whose lot under the existing social system makes them ready listeners to the propaganda of Communism.'[4] Increasingly, this became the predominating consideration, founded on a fear that the Russians' 'exaggerated sense of security, which is almost undistinguishable from an imperialist instinct' would cause them to fill any vacuum in the Middle East.[5] JIC Reports during 1946, whilst admitting that their speculation was based on sparse intelligence, were not prohibited by this ignorance from affirming that the Middle East was of particular interest to the Soviet Union because of the shift of gravity of her industry eastwards and the importance of the Caucasian oilfields. The Russians needed a strategic *glaçis* to protect this area and viewed Britain as a potential threat to her security in that part of the world. Without running the risk of a major war, the Russians would aim to suck into a protective belt vulnerable states such as Turkey or Iran where they sensed a less solidly united Anglo-United States front than elsewhere. Lurking behind the Committee's speculations were ancient fears of a threat from the North which would infiltrate a disaffected populace, oust Britain from the region and, having done so, press on towards Africa. In the opinion of the JIC, 'the Soviet Government have, in fact, resumed the traditional Russian policy of southern expansion, which was temporarily suspended between the fall of the Czarist regime and the war of 1939. The Soviet Union will implement this historic policy by every means short of war.'[6]

That a strategic determinant was now competing with the economic in British thinking about the region was most evidently demonstrated by the victory of the CoS, against Attlee's instincts, to preserve a presence in the Middle East. Events in Iran in early 1946 where, it was felt, the Soviet Union was 'endeavouring to extend her domination over the whole country' and where Bevin was first persuaded to initiate an all-out anti-Russian propaganda offensive nourished the arguments of Attlee's opponents.[7] The decision taken in September 1947 to quit Palestine could be taken as confirmation of their wisdom. In any case, by January 1947 (as stated earlier) the Prime Minister's arguments for withdrawal had been silenced and agreed policy, spelled out by the Chief of the Air Staff, was that the defence of the United Kingdom, the maintenance of sea communications, and the retention of Britain's position and influence in the Middle East 'were the three vital props of our defensive position: they were all interdependent and if any one were lost the whole structure would be imperiled.'[8]

The favoured solution of the CoS to the security of the Middle East was the construction of a defence group in the region. Characteristically, in early 1948 Bevin welded this proposition onto his own notion of a Third Force, envisaging a Middle East Union to match the recently founded Western Union in which, as he put it, the participants 'worked together not only for defence purposes but economically and he would like to do the same with Egypt and the Middle East Governments.' As in Europe, his intention was to keep the US at arms length and he was 'opposed to the adoption of a combined Anglo-American policy for the Middle East as this area was primarily of economic and strategic interest to the United Kingdom.'[9] This was an illusion. Like his Euro-African scheme, Bevin's policy in the Middle East ran into the buffer of Britain's unrelenting economic difficulties and overstretched commitments. A sign of this was that the Middle East Office, seriously under-resourced, soon drifted from its original purpose of promoting economic and social development among the Arabs towards a more traditional intelligence-gathering function.[10] Inevitably too, Cold War considerations had the effect of accentuating military rather than economic planning. Western Union, itself a victim of this tendency, brought additional pressures on London to commit more of its forces to the defence of Europe. In any case, despite their assertions that Britain must stay in the Middle East, the military planners were also aware that if the USSR did advance, they had not the resources to defend it. Nor had they bombers with sufficient range to strike at the Soviet Union from their Middle East bases.[11]

Early irritation that 'the Americans are commercially on the offensive in the Middle East' and Bevin's reluctance to work closely with the USA in that area were soon overtaken by recognition that Britain's predominance there could only be defended with support from the United States and the Commonwealth.[12] Ironically, the Americans regarded the Middle East principally as a British sphere and showed little interest in making a significant contribution to its defence. Once American external policy did begin to stir its focus was Europe. The Berlin Blockade and the shock of the emergence of the Soviet Union as an atomic power in 1949 amplified fears of Soviet adventurism in Europe. Strategically, the development of longer range bombers meant that the United States no longer needed to bank on the British providing them with Middle Eastern bases to outflank this threat. To Washington the threat of a Communist advance in that part of the world seemed less than urgent. On the other hand, clashes between the British and local nationalists tended to be viewed with distaste through the moral spectacles of anti-colonialism.

The more intractable and corrosive problem for the British in the Middle East was indeed nationalism. The development towards Indian independence gave rise to fears of increased Soviet influence on the sub-continent which would, in turn, imperil the British position in the Middle East. Similarly, the decision to withdraw from Palestine wound up a costly and bloody policing operation but also deprived Britain of what the CoS believed to be a vital defence screen for the strategic junction of Egypt. The truth was that a significant proportion of the population throughout the Middle East was no longer prepared to suffer Western colonialism and forces which the British deployed for a possible war with the Soviet Union increasingly found themselves actively in conflict with anti-British insurgents. Nowhere was this more problematical than in Egypt which the CoS persistently referred to as 'the key strategic area of the Middle East'. From 1946, contingency war plans had assumed the use of Egyptian airbases (the construction of alternatives in Cyprus or Saudi Arabia being rejected as too costly) to strike against the Soviet Union. Three years on, with their own capacity to inflict serious damage on a hostile Soviet Union from these garrisons in doubt, with the USA plainly opposed to providing the weaponry which could do so, and with nationalist pressure perceptibly prising the British out of their remaining toe-hold in the Suez Canal Zone, the British determination to remain in Egypt might look quixotic. It has been argued that 'the commitment to informal empire had to be maintained, not because of the requirements of Middle Eastern defence, but because of the need to preserve prestige and status.'[13] Clearly, British esteem as a world power was a crucial factor to policy-makers in Whitehall and it would be surprising to discover that they were not working towards perpetuating this. But there were other considerations which gave an urgent edge to British activity, notably over the attempt to negotiate a continued military presence at Suez. In the first place, there was a near obsession, expressed by Bevin and after him by Eden, of British retreat leaving a power vacuum which the Russians, willy nilly, would fill. This, and more particular apprehensions over Russian adventurism, could be, and sometimes was, over-drawn. But exaggerated fears are not necessarily entirely unreal ones and, with an atomically armed USSR, they could hardly be ignored. On the other side, if it was understood that Britain was no longer in a position to ward off a Soviet threat to the Middle East alone, it was not far fetched to expect that the Americans might eventually be persuaded to pick up the tab. Combined Anglo-American talks on the Middle East at the Pentagon in late 1947 (at a point when Bevin did not want formal military support from the US) and, more so, the existence of NATO (at which juncture he did) gave reasonable grounds for such optimism.

These were the assumptions which underpinned an important review of the strategic situation drawn up by the CoS in the summer of 1950.[14] The Soviet Union, it was asserted, was striving for a Communist world dominated by Moscow. Nevertheless, so long as the Western Allies maintained their resolution and built up their military strength, a 'shooting war' was considered neither inescapable nor likely. This meant that the Cold War was now world-wide and that 'it makes no sense to think in terms of British strategy or Western European strategy as something individual and independent … the cold war against Russian Communism is a global war as a hot war would inevitably be.' This involved taking '"cold war" offensive measures' to weaken the Kremlin's grip on its satellites and strengthening Allied defences 'against what would inevitably be a most insidious and mortally dangerous form of attack, namely, the Fifth Column, whose aim is to rot resistance from within, as similar methods rotted France before 1940.' Defence research should aim at developing weaponry to bring victory 'if real hostilities are forced upon the Western Allies'. Emphasis was given to a build-up of the conventional military strength of the West. But the CoS also envisaged the evolution of 'some form of supersonic unmanned bomber or other vehicle which will take atomic and other weapons to the heart of Russia in the face of the latest scientific defences'. Because European civilisation could not endure a Soviet occupation of Western Europe, because Britain itself was unlikely to survive such catastrophe and because the 'free world' itself could not withstand the submergence of the two, the preservation of the integrity of Western Europe was deemed 'absolutely vital … top priority'.

The Middle East remained a critical theatre. Allied resolve in the Cold War would be crucial here as the Russians 'do draw back when faced with determined opposition'. A thread throughout the paper was that just as Britain could not take on Russia without American help 'nor could the United States fight Russia without the help of the British Commonwealth' and that 'the United Kingdom cannot afford all the forces required for the Middle East in addition to those required to defend herself and Western Europe. Additional forces must therefore be found from other parts of the Commonwealth and from the United States' where a 'small contribution' from the United States 'would pay a disproportionately large dividend'. In its assertion that 'Allied defence policy cannot be divided into water-tight compartments of "cold" and "hot" strategy', in its merging of the measures required to win a 'real' war and a 'cold' war and in its concept of the Cold War as a conflict requiring a global strategy to combat it, the CoS were moving forward at least in tandem with influential thinking across the Atlantic and may even have been ahead of it. Circumstantial evidence hints that the British may have had a hand in shaping American strategic thinking at this point.[15] In any case, around this time, the National Security Council in Washington was pushing Truman in the same direction. In April it presented the President with a planning report known as NSC-68. Comparing the Soviet Union, as did the CoS paper, with Nazi Germany, it recommended the American resistance to Communist advance everywhere and proposed a massive increase in defence spending to support this policy.

Only four days after the CoS report was approved by the Attlee Government, the Chief's inference that 'cold' war might easily flare into 'hot' at any danger spot around the world seemed to be powerfully vindicated as the troops of the Democratic People's Republic of Korea surged across the 38th Parallel into the South, turning attention away from the Middle East to what the CoS believed to be another 'immensely important front' – the Far East. In fact, the British had already been engaged in fighting an anti-Communist 'hot' war in Malaya fully two years before the Korean crisis erupted. Their troubles in Malaya had confounded Britain's early postwar objectives in Southeast Asia which closely resembled their aspirations to organise the Middle East and Africa. Back in April 1946, Bevin had proposed to a gathering of Commonwealth Prime Ministers in London that cooperation to develop the vast untapped economic potential of Southeast Asia would be to the advantage of all, including the indigenous peoples, whilst an increase in the prosperity of the region would combat the 'rising tide of nationalism'.[16] This was a replica of his hopes for Middle Eastern development, but here too nationalism was a severe impediment to British plans. Given that both the French and the Dutch were already employed in military action to restore their prewar positions in Indochina and Indonesia respectively, proposals for co-operation between the European colonial powers had to be handled circumspectly for fear of antagonising local susceptibilities as well as those of India which, once independent, would be an important component in future co-operative ventures in Southeast Asia. An additional difficulty was that failure to support the French and the Dutch risked cutting across the consolidation of Western European co-operation. As it was, the creation of 'Western Union' in March 1948, merely enhanced suspicion amongst Asian nationalists of imperialists ganging up to bolster their own economies via a more co-ordinated system of colonial exploitation.[17]

At this juncture apprehensions in certain British quarters over the appeal of Communism noticeably began to displace the attractions of nationalism as a threat to their influence in Southeast Asia. It had long been recognised that a combination of poverty and nationalism could provide fertile ground for the growth of Communism. Such anxieties now quickened. The grant of independence to India, Pakistan, Burma and Ceylon in 1947 had, it was feared, sent signals of the apparent weakness of the colonial powers. Some detected signs that Western consolidation in Europe under the Marshall Plan was forcing the Kremlin to search for new opportunities for expansion in Southeast Asia and this seemed to be encapsulated in the manifesto of the Cominform where there was a specific reference to Southeast Asia. Added to this, there was the example of the growing success of the Chinese Communists in their long internal struggle against the Western-backed Nationalists.

This amalgam of factors probably played a part in the decision of the Malayan Communist Party in the summer of 1948 to embark upon a campaign of violence to drive out the British. That the Malayan Communists were predominantly supported by the Chinese population of Malaya out of a sense of grievance that they were being discriminated against by their colonial masters rather than as a prelude to the construction of a workers' and peasants' state added complexity to the Malayan situation, but was no less disconcerting to those British authorities who sensed an escalating influence of the Chinese Communist Party in the peninsula.[18] When developments in Malaya were set alongside mounting French difficulties in Indochina,

Communist activity in Burma and (briefly in September, 1948) in Indonesia, officials in the front line constructed an alarming figuration of an ideological juggernaut crushing all before it. Firm evidence of a concerted Soviet effort in Southeast Asia was, admittedly, sparse – but the Foreign Office and the JIC decided to see it in the worst light. Though the Colonial Office remained unconvinced. The man on the spot, Malcolm MacDonald, British Commissioner for South-East Asia who declared the State of Emergency in June 1948 which inaugurated an attenuated and often brutal military clamp-down on the rebels, devised a prototype domino theory in his expression of his fear that:

> when the Chinese Communists had conquered the whole of China, they would probably try immediately to crumble the anti-Communist front in Southeast Asia, while the going was good. They could probably seize a large part of Indochina in the next six months: Siam would be unable to resist them ... The possibilities of Communist domination in Burma were well known. If these three countries were to fall, Malaya and India would be exposed to a direct Communist threat.[19]

This proved a persuasive justification for standing firm in Malaya. A tactical retreat in the face of rioting Zionists or disorderly Indian and, maybe, Egyptian nationalists was one thing. To contemplate handing over power to Communist insurgents was quite another. After all, Malaya, with Singapore, was regarded as a focal point of British defence communications in Southeast Asia providing depth to the defence of Australia and New Zealand. There was another equally compelling motive. The Emergency, as the British were to continue to call it, came upon them mid-way between two periods of severe economic stress; the convertibility crisis of the summer of 1947 and the persisting dollar shortage which was to lead to the devaluation of sterling in the summer of 1949. This reinforced the necessity of holding on to Malaya which, with its wealth of rubber and tin, was the chief dollar earner in the sterling bloc. At the back end of 1948, Bevin was inclined to promote a version of the ERP for Southeast Asia. But cold water was thrown on this by Foreign Office experts on the ground that it would require aid packages that Britain could not afford. Those who could afford them, that is, the United States, would carve out their own economic bloc which would inevitably weaken the sterling area.[20] The CoS's strategic assessment of June 1950 drew together the political and the economic significance of the colony in their assessment that 'there is no alternative to the existing régimes in Indochina, Malaya, Siam and Burma except to become Chinese Communist colonies – which would mean the rice-bowl of Asia in Communist hands and a terrific blow to the Allied economy – particularly to the British Commonwealth.' Even so, the Chiefs did not believe that Malaya had strategic pre-eminence. To them 'the front line of the cold war in Asia lies in Indochina.' If that front collapsed, it would be only a matter of time before Siam, Burma and Malaya fell under Communist sway. In this view, 'nothing is more important than to make sure that the French restore order and establish a stable and ultimately independent friendly government in Indochina.'[21] This appreciation was, as some in the Foreign Office pointed out, 'an over-simplification of the problem' and that 'as much must depend on the position in Malaya'.[22] This was also the Government's bottom line and it was determined to eradicate the Communist 'bandits' principally via a military assault against them, but also using a local outpost of the IRD, the Regional Information Office (RIO) to disseminate propaganda intended to demonstrate to all the inhabitants of the peninsula that the territory could and should be held.

To the frustration of RIO/IRD officials, government policy was to refrain from linking The Emergency with the forces of international Communism in the hope of fomenting anxiety between Moscow and Beijing and to avoid augmenting the popularity of the 'bandits' among the Malayan Chinese. This, until the injunction was reversed under the impact of the crisis in Korea, meant that the IRD was forced to follow the instincts of the Colonial Office, which did not assume a Soviet/Chinese connection with events in Malaya, and to attempt to suppress their own conjectures, which did. Simultaneously, attempts were made to persuade the United States to increase their purchase of Malayan rubber and tin as a way of easing Britain's dollar shortage and attempting to erode Communist support by developing the prosperity of Malaya. Finally, though they had little faith in the ultimate success of the French struggle against the Vietminh (regarded by the British as predominantly Communist rather than nationalist), provision of moral and, where possible, material aid to keep in place Malaya's Indochinese shield.[23]

In late 1949, Truman had also decided to furnish financial aid to Southeast Asia and especially to the military defence of the French-backed government in Indochina – a judgement which was to lead to the catastrophe of US involvement in Vietnam. How forcefully British influence weighed with the United States on this issue is open to question. Certainly the British had sought such intervention for some time, but they had come up against the same American response as they had had to contend with in the Middle East; that Southeast Asia was the province of the Western Europeans. What was more, it seemed for a time that America's attitude to Asia had been knocked askew by the Communists' success in China in 1949. In the opinion of the British, the American perspective was erroneously coloured by Mao Zedong's victory. To them, here, as elsewhere, it was Russia ('a predatory expansionist Power ... prepared to use any method to achieve its end of world domination', Bevin now professed) and not China which presented the commanding threat.[24] Though neither of the Communist giants, it was assumed, would risk military aggression and would confine themselves to policies of subversion, the widespread unpopularity of Chinese settlers in Southeast Asia would blunt the propaganda of the Chinese Communists whereas, owing to its wartime performance, the prestige of the Soviet Union was quite high. It was accepted that, for the time being, American 'inexperience' and America's 'grave emotional disappointment' at having backed the inefficient and corrupt Nationalist forces in China only to see them overwhelmed by the Communists, meant that the 'spread of Russian influence in that region ... depends mainly on the United Kingdom.' But so important was it for the consolidation of Western influence to have an American stake in the region that the British set aside earlier disquiet over US economic predominance sensing 'another opportunity for the United Kingdom, with her longer experience, to guide the policy of the USA.'[25]

What the British tried to do was to show that they were able themselves to construct defensive partnerships in Asia. This was easier to wish for than to achieve. French and Dutch entanglements in the area continued to offend those who might participate in a regional initiative – particularly India, which was considered by the PUSC to be the 'key to the whole problem'.[26] Although the Attlee Government had assiduously avoided mixing up the question of Indian independence with security issues, the CoS were anxious that the new India be attached to Britain and its interests through membership of the Commonwealth, and had been dismayed to discover that partition would leave the weaker state, Pakistan, in the most sensitive geostrategical position *vis à vis* the Soviet Union. By the end of the 1940s, defence arrangements had been made with two other recently independent states, Burma and Ceylon. Delhi's position of non-alignment coupled with its ambition to be the fulcrum of South and Southeast Asia, however, made it impossible to arrive at a similar agreement with India. Pakistan, which would have liked a defensive association with Britain, was ignored for fear of offending her more powerful neighbour.[27] The 'old' members of the Commonwealth in the Pacific presented different problems. Australia and New Zealand both appreciated the threat from Communism but responded differently. Until 1949, Australia was inclined to take an isolationist stance and to concentrate on attending to its own security in the Pacific. New Zealand, alternatively, stressed its affinities with Western Europe rather than with Asia. Although a meeting of Commonwealth Prime Ministers at Colombo in January 1950 produced a resolution for the economic development in South and Southeast Asia as the most effective way of combating Communist infiltration, this had marginal practical effect. Moreover, the Indian Prime Minister rejected the idea of a defensive pact in the region.

Despite such evident lack of progress in demonstrating self-help, there were, anyway, by the end of 1949 indications of a change of direction in Washington. Increased purchases by the United States of Malayan tin and rubber helped transform a dollar deficit in the sterling area to a surplus in a matter of months.[28] More significantly, in December Dean Acheson, Truman's Secretary of State, revealed America's intention to provide financial aid to Indochina, Indonesia and, perhaps, Thailand and spoke of a 'rough geographical division of responsibilities' between Britain and the United States in Southeast Asia. This approach, enshrined in the State Department's Policy Planning Staff paper NSC 48/2, was accepted as policy by the Truman administration that same month.[29] According to Ovendale, 'it was a considerable achievement on the part of Bevin, and his Foreign Office officials, to help secure the American commitment to stop Communist expansion in Asia outlined in NSC 48/2. In effect, the United States once again was helping to pull British and French "chestnuts out of the fire".'[30] This probably exaggerates British powers of persuasion in Washington and a more judicious assessment seems to be that the British could claim no more than to have 'strongly influenced' American policy towards Southeast Asia for, like America's earlier turn towards the defence of Western Europe, other, more self-interested factors helped change Washington's Asian policy.[31]

In November 1949, the State Department's Policy Planning Staff and the British PUSC had exchanged views on SouthEast Asia and discovered an affinity of approach. But it was the jolt of the Soviet detonation of an atomic device in August and the proclamation of the People's Republic of China in October which, more than British coaxing, pushed American policy on to a new track. The Americans, like the British, were stumbling towards the global containment of Communism. A fortnight after the Communist victory in China, the CIA had begun to cultivate its own version of the domino theory, contemplating the extension of Communist influence from Beijing through Indochina to Thailand, Burma and Malaya.[32] Though recent events in China may, in British eyes, have caused Washington to focus on the wrong ball, at least the ball was still in court and by late 1949, the Americans were constructing their own motives for entering the game. Without the twin shocks provided by Stalin and Mao Zedong and the serious domestic problems which both of these provided for the Truman Administration, British pressure for partnership in containing Communism in Asia was likely to have remained as welcome as a cold-call for double glazing. The stepping up of American purchases of Malayan rubber and tin had more to do with a perceived need to bolster the British as associates in the defence of Western Europe as a desire to counter the attractions of Communism in the Malay peninsula. Even the American decision to help the French in Indochina was initially founded on the consideration that France's military exertions in Southeast Asia inevitably reduced French capacity to station divisions in the path of a possible Soviet onslaught through Germany. At the beginning of 1950, however, the British were less concerned with why the Americans had begun to act than that they were being galvanised at all for the CoS were 'firmly of the view that the battle for the defence of Southeast Asia in a war with Russia has already begun'.[33] What is clear is that a determination to defend Southeast Asia from Communism was palpable both in London and in Washington even before the summer of 1950 and the next surprise – Korea.

Both Western Powers therefore – though neither had any strategic interest in the peninsula – were psychologically predisposed to assist the South Koreans when the stunning blow fell from the North. What was more, on this occasion, the need to convince Republican opponents at home that it had some backbone in the struggle to contain Communism made the Truman Administration even more eager than the British, impelling them not only to intervene, but also, before consulting London, to deploy the Seventh Fleet between the Chinese mainland and the island of Formosa (where the Nationalist Chinese had decamped in 1949) to forestall a possible Communist Chinese invasion. Nevertheless, the British response was immediately to support the American sponsored resolution in the United Nations to give assistance to the Republic of Korea. Appeasement of Hitler in the 1930s was the analogue. In a radio message to the nation from Chequers, Attlee compared the situation with events before the Second World War; 'the fire that has started in distant Korea may burn down your house.'[34] From the start, the Foreign Office felt it 'virtually certain' that Moscow had prompted the North Korean action and that it 'marked the beginning of a Nazi technique of isolating and defeating one state after another' with Formosa, Indochina, Thailand and Malaya next on the list.[35] A more astute assessment of Stalin's motives was provided by the Ambassador in Moscow. In his view, the North Korean attack was intended to exploit a favourable local situation, not provoke a general conflict. A swift victory by the North would have been a shattering blow to Western prestige, but the unexpected military intervention by the United States put the Soviet Union in the awkward position of trying desperately to avoid becoming directly engaged with the Americans.[36] This is very close to the picture provided by material from Soviet archives which suggests that after months of resisting the pleas of the North Korean leader, Kim Il Sung, to support his ambition to unify Korea, Stalin eventually acquiesced in April 1950. True, 1949 had witnessed the creation of the NATO. But it was the success of Communism in China, the possession of the atom bomb and indications that the Americans were not actively interested in Southeast Asia which provided the blend to change Stalin's mind. Put another way, 'Stalin was now more confident of the Communist bloc's strength, less respectful of American capabilities and less interested in the reaction of Western public opinion to Communist moves.'[37]

When hot war flared up in Korea it was not, as is sometimes suggested, immediately perceived by British officials as a deliberate Soviet feint prior to an assault elsewhere. Tremors of anxiety that activity in Korea might be a cover for an engagement in Europe were perceptible in Norway and Germany. The British shared this concern to the extent that, as the Moscow Embassy suggested, there could be a spillover effect with Stalin manufacturing an incident where the Americans would be less likely to intervene such as Iran or Yugoslavia. But this would be more to get himself off the hook in Korea than part of a preconceived strategy. For the most part, the British tended to share George Kennan's assessment that events in Korea were a probe which, if successful, could create stepping stones for further Soviet expansion in Asia rather than being a distraction for an imminent offensive. This was an important reason for the swiftness of the British decision to support the South Koreans against aggression and join what was notionally an American action, but under the UN flag and, significantly, termed an 'international police operation'. Underlying this was a belief that 'the symbolic significance of the preservation of the Republic [of South Korea] was ... tremendous' and also the need for the West to construct a barrier to the advance of Soviet Communism.[38]

Of course, account had to be taken of the actions and attitudes of the United States. Bevin felt any reluctance to support the Americans might discourage the United States from helping Britain in Malaya and France in Indochina – though this ignored the recent reversal of American policy in Southeast Asia. His inclination to provide swift support for US intervention jarred with the view of some of his Cabinet colleagues that American action in stationing naval forces between Formosa and the Chinese mainland had extended the immediate issue and ran the risk of provoking Beijing. There was a sensitivity too not to push Stalin into a corner by openly accusing him of complicity with the North Koreans and the tone of the American sponsored United Nations resolution, that what was happening in Korea was the product of 'centrally directed Communist imperialism', was deplored.[39] Success in damping this down may have engendered confidence in Whitehall that it could act more generally as a moderating influence on US policy. But restraining Washington was to prove unexpectedly costly. For instance, the initial British assumption was that the 'symbolic significance' of their intervention would be brief and confined to modest naval support for the UN forces. Pressure from the Americans during the first month of the war to provide ground forces was at first resisted on the basis that there were other 'danger spots' in Asia and in Europe.[40] However, the grave military situation on the peninsula with the South Korean and UN forces in headlong flight gave pause for thought and there was some apprehension that without reinforcement, the Americans might be tempted to use atomic weapons. Political motives, however, outweighed military considerations. A feeling that consultation between the two Powers would improve if ground forces were provided, and that relations would deteriorate if they were not, persuaded Attlee, against the recommendation of the CoS, to overturn the earlier Cabinet decision and send an infantry brigade (later supplemented by another) to help the beleaguered UN forces, which had retreated to Pusan in the far south.[41] The compelling voice of Sir Oliver Franks, London's Ambassador in Washington and whom Attlee acknowledged in Cabinet as an influence, that the British example would be followed by others was born out only to a degree.[42] By the end of the war Britain's military contribution, though moderate by comparison to Washington's, was second only to that of the United States with contributions from other UN member states trailing far behind.

Nor, as Franks had argued, was the partnership between the two states perceptibly enhanced by Britain's increased military efforts. Washington's 'undertaking to act as a policeman in the world', as the Ambassador put it, was appreciated in London because the consequences of a failure so to act might have serious repercussions in trouble spots throughout Asia. But this feeling of gratitude was also encumbered by a deep concern over the American tendency provocatively to widen the issue without UN authority through increased assistance to Indochina, as well as their deployment of a naval task force to 'neutralise' Formosa, which might conceivably lead to reprisals from Communist China. The latter, which went against agreements made during the Second World War to return the island to China, could, it was feared, 'precipitate a general war in the Far East and thus a World War.' Having joined the Americans and therefore made their public statement over Korea, these anxieties now impelled the British to investigate the possibility of a settlement based on the *status quo ante bellum*, with the hope of a North Korean withdrawal being exchanged for full diplomatic recognition by the West of the Beijing Government and the eventual reunification of Formosa with mainland China. To British eyes this was merely accepting reality. Bevin's attitude was that 'the Peking Government is without any shadow of a doubt the Government of China and that the Nationalist representatives in the United Nations represent nothing but a small clique in Formosa which in itself represents nothing.'[43] British diplomatic recognition of the People's Republic of China (PRC) had already been given in January on this pragmatic ground. There was also the desire to protect Hong Kong and British commerce in China generally. On top of this was a realisation that Beijing was not the tool of Moscow and could, by a sensitive approach, be prevented from becoming such. More specifically, they believed Formosa should eventually revert to the Beijing Government and American determination to resist this seemed a 'most dangerous' approach which could turn Asian opinion against the West, and thereby 'greatly assist the communist forces in SE Asia.'

In Washington, where there was irritation at Britain's recognition of the PRC, coming to terms with the victory of Communist China was a psychological and, given current domestic anti-Communist hysteria, a political impossibility. In a reversal of the position over Berlin two years earlier, the US response to Whitehall's attempts to explore the prospect of an early peace via Moscow early in July was a blank refusal 'to appease or bargain either with the Soviet Union or China over Korea' and the obligatory implied threat to the British 'that unless we come into line with this view the consequences for Anglo-American relations will be very serious'.[44] To keep on good terms with the United States, the British now denied that they envisaged any *quid pro quo* as a means of ending the conflict. Bevin, however, obtained Cabinet approval for the return of Formosa to Beijing 'when the time was ripe' and it was made clear to the Americans that if PRC membership of the Security Council came to a vote in the UN in a way unconnected with Korea, Britain, in order not to 'seal China off from the West', would feel obliged to support its admission.[45]

Attempts to weave between offending their major ally and prevent them from provoking escalation remained a British preoccupation throughout the war. Apprehensions that China might be incited to enter the struggle mounted after the spectacular reversal of fortune in the war provided by General Douglas MacArthur, the commander of the UN forces in Korea. His amphibious landings at In'chon behind enemy lines on 15 September put the North Koreans on the run back across the 38th Parallel. Success further inflated the General's already monumental ego and suspicions grew in London that, acting under his own steam and beyond the control of either the UN or the US, he might take the war across the Yalu River into China.[46] These fears were far from groundless, though the British leadership was not devoid of responsibility for the situation which was now to give them such cause for concern. After the In'chon landing the Labour Government was tempted by the scent of victory to abandon the idea of merely restoring the *status quo* and support American wishes to press on and reunite Korea. Dismissing the cautious advice of the CoS, Attlee chose to believe that the Chinese 'would not be sorry if Russian influence was eliminated from Korea'. Bevin, arguing on similar lines to MacArthur that threats of intervention from Beijing if the 38th Parallel was crossed were simply bluff, predicted that the Chinese would not 'throw discretion to the winds, and ... embark upon hostilities against the United Nations'.[47] The, by now, ritual desire to avoid recriminations from the US also swayed Bevin's decision.[48] MacArthur's advance beyond the Parallel was approved following a British resolution in the UN on 7 October. Both Ministers were then appalled when it was reported on 28 November that in response, 200 000 Chinese regulars had crossed the Yalu into North Korea. In fairness to the Prime Minister and his Foreign Secretary, MacArthur proceeded with less caution than they seemed to have envisaged. Their misjudgment was also shared by the Russia Committee and the JIC, both of which considered Soviet or Chinese intervention unlikely.

On top of this, we now know that China's decision to join the contest was not taken lightly and it seems that only on 13 October was a reluctant Mao Zedong persuaded by Stalin and pro-Moscow members of the Chinese leadership to agree to enter the war.[49] Anyway, with China now in the conflict and with UN forces again in unrestrained retreat, the British reverted to their limited view of the war as 'important as a symbol of ... resistance to aggression', that 'Korea was not in itself of any strategic importance to the democracies and it must not be allowed to draw more of the [United Nations'] military resources away from Europe and the Middle East.'[50] Behind this were disconcerting signs that the Americans were now less interested in pursuing the war in Korea than in pulling out of the present conflict and finding a way of having a showdown with the PRC. To the irritation of the Americans, the British also raised once more the possibility of US recognition of the Beijing Government and the return of Formosa to the PRC as concessions for a cessation of hostilities on the 38th Parallel.[51] At the same time, it was also made clear in Washington that Britain would not support an American UN resolution condemning China as an aggressor.

These matters, as well as MacArthur's conduct of the war, were discussed when Attlee met Truman in Washington at the beginning of December. The main purpose of the meeting, which Attlee had instigated, was rather more urgent. In the face of new and serious military reversals, the President, at a press conference on 30 November, had indicated 'active consideration' of the atomic bomb in Korea. Its use would be 'up to the military men in the field', i.e. General MacArthur, without seeking advance approval by the other UN states. Though Truman quickly backtracked and his alarming statements were interpreted by the Washington Embassy as off-the-cuff responses to unexpected questions and attempts to indicate toughness to the Republicans, even so, this 'did not make the reply any less dangerous'.[52] Despite Truman's retraction, his remarks gave rise to sufficient anxiety that only a personal discussion between the two Western leaders could offer complete reassurance.

Truman's apparent blunder brought into the open concerns already percolating in Whitehall. Approval for the Americans to base their B-29 bombers in Britain, given during the Berlin Crisis, had been founded on the calculation that the British would be an atomic power well in advance of the Soviets. Now that this assumption was demonstrably false, the realisation dawned that Britain had placed itself in the direct line of fire in a future atomic war. The decision had been taken in March 1950 to maintain this presence in the United Kingdom, though by the summer and without any clear say-so from the British Government, the B-29s had been armed with atomic bombs. Naturally enough, worries were expressed among the CoS and by Bevin that Britain might have little say if the United States decided to use the atomic bomb. After all, even if the Soviets' estimated stockpile of ten atomic bombs could not be delivered across the Atlantic, they could be dropped on London with relative ease. Nothing had been done to resolve this issue before the Korean War broke out. Therefore, when Attlee flew to Washington in December, he was not so much seeking clarification of Truman's recent outburst, which had already been obtained – though some need for activity was felt necessary to allay public concern – but looking for agreed general principles on any decision to use atomic weaponry.[53] Bevin had expressed a particular anxiety that the Allied position had been weakened by Truman's unguarded words and that unlike during the Berlin Crisis, when the Russians had really believed the atom bomb might be used against them if they went too far, loose talk had eroded this advantage.[54] To the consternation of State Department officials Attlee's personal rapport with the President, coupled with his negotiating dexterity, elicited a private agreement between the two leaders that Britain would be consulted before America considered using the bomb. After some pressure from Acheson, however, who preferred the verb 'inform' to 'consult', Truman declined to put this in writing on the homespun

ground that 'if a man's word wasn't any good it wasn't made any better for writing it down.' Attlee had to make do with what amounted to
a personal undertaking over consultation which it was recognised
would lapse when Truman left office. Although the Prime Minister
expressed his satisfaction with this outcome to the House of Commons on his return, Bevin pertinently wondered whether 'from [the]
public point of view or from that of action in the future, does not this
leave us just where we are now?'[55]

Agreement on how best to bring an end to the war was equally elusive. Although Acheson's acceptance that it must be fought to a
conclusion, should not overflow into Chinese territory and that negotiations would have to be set in motion were everything that Attlee
wanted to hear, the Secretary of State remained opposed to permitting Beijing to occupy Formosa or have a seat on the Security Council
and wanted concessions to await a reversal of the UN's military fortunes. Worse, he was inclined to talk vaguely of a 'limited war' against
the Chinese which might involve economic harassment – or, it was
feared, something rather more vigorous. At root was a crucial variance over the spur for China's intervention in Korea, involving some
modification of each of their earlier positions. To the British it was
'in essence a Chinese and not a Russian enterprise. The Americans
are wrong if (as they do) they think otherwise.' Acheson and his State
Department colleagues 'were convinced that the Chinese were acting
in complete agreement with the Russians and neither could nor would
pursue an independent line.'[56]

None the less, Attlee left Washington buoyed up with what he believed had been achieved and, especially, that throughout the talks 'we
were treated as partners, unequal no doubt in power but still equal in
counsel.'[57] There was a view in the Foreign Office that, compared to
the other Western Europeans, Attlee's mini-summit meeting with Truman had 'put us back in the position of leadership'.[58] Opinion was less
sanguine amongst the Prime Minister's political colleagues and Labour Party supporters. Dalton's information was that there was growing
dissatisfaction with the Government's international policy amongst rank
and file Party members who 'did not want war with Russia ... thought
Attlee hadn't been strong or outspoken enough at Washington, and
generally feared that we had become a satellite of USA and lost our
independence and were being dragged into a war.'[59] Indeed, it is difficult to see much justification for Attlee's optimism. He and Truman
had agreed to stand firm in Korea despite the military débâcle which

Chinese intervention had wrought. But Attlee had hardly touched ground in London before anxieties surfaced that the Americans had really not made up their minds what to do and maybe intended to pull out and engage China in a limited war, possibly with the Nationalist Chinese as proxies. Both sides agreed that MacArthur was a dangerous nuisance, though Acheson had done little other than shrug his shoulders to Attlee over this. Only an ambiguously temporary concession had been forthcoming on the vital question of the use of the atomic weapon and Washington was to continue to rattle the bomb at its own convenience for the rest of the war. Otherwise, as was pointed out in the Foreign Office, 'we appear not to have convinced the Americans of the need to make a serious effort to reach a political settlement with the Chinese and not to have shaken them in their intention to undertake some form of "limited war" against China. If matters are left like this, it seems inevitable that the United States at least will be drawn into war-like operations against China.'[60]

In the face of such meagre results, Sir William Strang, the Permanent Under-Secretary at the Foreign Office, attempted early in the New Year to analyse the British position. His conclusion was that:

> we have no alternative but to work with [the US]. For us to join the Soviet bloc would be unthinkable. The establishment of a neutral or independent European bloc, manoeuvring between the Soviet Union and the United States, has been repeatedly examined and as often rejected ... Though the Americans often behave as though our views and interest were of little regard to them, in the last resort they know they must rely on us. This strengthens our position in dealing with them ... Our problem is to deflect the Americans from unwise or dangerous courses without making a breach in the united front. This is not an easy operation, but then, whatever some people might think, diplomacy is not one of the easier professions. What it calls for above all things is patience.[61]

The latest 'dangerous course' was Washington's determination at the end of the year to present a resolution to the UN condemning China as an aggressor, coupled with economic and possibly even military sanctions aimed at China. This went against what Attlee believed had been agreed at his meeting with Truman, stretched the veneer of UN legitimacy to cracking point and risked provoking a futile war with China in which the greatest losses would be to British interests in Southeast Asia. To prevent this, or the prospect of demoralised GIs being withdrawn from the peninsula (for the Communist forces were still advancing) with calamitous consequences for Western prestige, diplomacy was brought into play in the shape, first of all, of a proposal for a cease-fire and, when this was rejected by the Chinese, a Commonwealth-backed plan for an end to hostilities followed by a wider Far Eastern settlement. In the face of this, the Americans reasserted their determination to continue the war and were persuaded to hold off their condemnatory resolution. Strang was quite right. The Americans, with some irritation, now played along because they needed the fig leaf of the UN and the British backing which supported this. Further Chinese advances in January induced Acheson to plead with the British that 'now that the Chinese were south of the 38th Parallel the whole principle of collective security depended on our willingness to declare China an aggressor. It was essential that Britain and the United States should be able to act together on this. On our joint action together with our friends depended the future of the United Nations and all confidence in the free world that aggression would be resisted.'[62]

After British delaying tactics failed and the Americans tabled their resolution at the UN on 20 January 1951, London took an even tougher stance. A Foreign Office communication to Washington condemned 'highly coloured political pronouncements', coming from MacArthur and others, and America's 'high pressure methods' in its 'urgent need of the United Nations as an umbrella to cover them in their Far Eastern policy'. This had been approved by Kenneth Younger, Minister of State at the Foreign Office, whilst Bevin was hospitalised as his heart disease approached its terminal stage. Younger had been critical for some time of the Government's failure to stand up to the Americans: 'For many months now we and other friendly governments have been subjected to insistent United States demands that we should join them in a course of action, the implications of which we could not fully see and the necessity for which we did not feel.' The US, it was declared, had made few concessions other than to offer temporary postponements leading to doubts:

> whether the United States really desire a settlement, or whether they are not rather spoiling for a chance to hit back on China by any means at their disposal, reckless of the consequences to others, prompted mainly by mortification over the failure of their policy

towards China. The pressure which they have been applying will undoubtedly result in an open split in the United Nations. It seems that they are even prepared to risk the loss of the United Nations cover rather than diverge from the course on which they have apparently set themselves.[63]

This straight talking had some effect. Although it had now been lodged with the UN, the vote on the condemnatory resolution was put on hold and concessions were offered in the form of a restricted list of proposed sanctions against China. But this vigorous line was not to every British taste. A Cabinet meeting on 25 January provided a triumph for those, such as Younger, Dalton and Aneurin Bevan, who wanted Washington to be put in its place and its UN resolution rejected. It was a short-lived victory. Their case was undermined by opposition in the Foreign Office to a vote which would put Britain in the same lobby as the Soviet Union and from pro-Americans in the Government, such as the Chancellor, Hugh Gaitskell, who threatened resignation if the Cabinet decision was carried through. The hardliners were further isolated by the fact that France, Australia, New Zealand, Canada and South Africa were won over by American concessions. On the 26th Attlee reversed the earlier decision and it was agreed to vote in favour of a modified resolution.

British influence, indeed, the very cohesion of the British Government over the extent to which their views might be pressed on Washington was approaching its limit. The retraction of the decision to oppose the condemnatory UN resolution signified the beginning of the ascendancy of an approach which made patient persuasion a hallmark of Britain's Cold War relationship with the United States. To Gaitskell the issue was 'the division between those [in the Labour Party] who believe it their duty and the right policy to follow opinion in the Party which certainly is pretty anti-American, and still rather pacifist, and those who do not attach a great deal of importance to this, even politically'.[64] The Chancellor's line was duplicated by Pierson Dixon of the Foreign Office, who also happened to be the Chair of the Russia Committee and who laid out his own rationale in rather more disconsolate terms than earlier supplied by Strang. Dixon argued that opposition to the US 'rests on the supposition that only by digging our toes in can we seriously influence American policy, the underlying thought being that the Americans have just as much need of us as we have of them and would therefore change their pol-

icy if they were convinced that we were not with them.' This was not
the case in the Far East where 'they are prepared, and indeed determined, to go there own way'. Where interdependence did exist was in
the West. But, Dixon's argument went, Britain could only influence
American policy in the Far East by threatening to reconsider its policy of opposition to Communism and the USSR and its support of
Atlantic defence; and 'clearly we are not prepared to go to those
lengths.' The conclusion drawn from this rather excessive proposition was that Britain had no muscle to flex at all. Thus:

> if we cannot effectively change American Far Eastern policy, then
> we must ... resign ourselves to the rôle of counselor and moderator.
> We have already had considerable effect in this rôle. But we should
> accept the disagreeable conclusion, in the end, that that we must
> allow the US to take the lead and follow, or at least not break with
> them. It is difficult for us, after several centuries of leading others,
> to resign ourselves to the position of allowing another and greater
> Power to lead us.[65]

And painful, one might add, to have to come to terms with the need
for such servility.

Certainly, benefits accrued from following the American lead. A
glance at a summary of (the somewhat negative) British aims in Korea drawn up three weeks after the war had begun – to assist the US
in bringing operations against aggression in Korea to a successful
conclusion; to localise the conflict and prevent it from developing
into a world war; to obviate an open breach between China and the
Western Powers and to convince the US to direct its policy wholly to a
solution of the Korean problem rather than the related issues of Formosa and China – indicates that these were all, in the end, achieved.[66]
But much was to be lost on the way. China's performance in the war
enhanced its prestige in Asia and, in the short term at least, did what
the British had hoped could be avoided by drawing the PRC and
Moscow together. Moreover, in trying scrupulously to avoid the charge
of appeasing the Russians, the British came close to falling into this
trap *vis à vis* the Americans. The evolution of a more active American
policy in the Far East had been welcomed as an improvement on the
previous situation, when the fear had been that the Americans had
'neglected and are neglecting the Far East, and that unless and until
they can be moved from their inertia, the rest of us will all be in very

acute danger'.[67] But it was not long before British influence in the area was not being buttressed so much as ousted. Hopes of a Pacific Pact to match the Atlantic Alliance and which might include India, Pakistan and the lesser countries of Southeast Asia as well as Britain were thwarted by an Australian initiative in February 1951 which had produced a defence arrangement between Australia, New Zealand and the United States by the end of the year. This ANZUS Pact, though generally consonant with Whitehall's defence objectives and therefore reluctantly accepted, had the decided disadvantage of excluding Britain. 'It could be said', the British complained to the Australians, 'that we were being supplanted by the Americans in a vitally important part of the Commonwealth and that we were withdrawing from one of our major obligations and responsibilities'.[68]

Given Britain's precarious over-extension and the inflammatory international situation, the remedies of the professional diplomats that benefits lay in assuaging her chief ally were understandably persuasive. But forthright resistance to American policy, when it seemed necessary and when practised, was not without some success, suggesting that subservience was not necessarily the only way to win concessions from Washington. In the end, British aims in Korea prevailed less through deference than out of a basic contiguity in British and American aims. Neither country gave much thought to the freedom of Koreans and both perceived their actions there as necessary to avoid a more general landslide of Communist aggression. This agreement on fundamentals, however, when coupled with Britain's inclination towards submissiveness, produced a tendency to gloss over significant divergencies of approach between the two and this usually worked in favour of Washington's way of doing things. For instance, precisely *how* their central purpose was to be achieved frequently divided the two allies. Apart from the aberration of late September 1950 when Attlee and Bevin pressed for the unification of the peninsula beyond the 38th Parallel, at which point the British were pacing rather than guiding the Americans, the British favoured a negotiated settlement probably leading to a return to the *status quo* before North Korea attacked. American policy, especially when MacArthur was in charge of UN forces, but even after he was relieved of his command in April 1951, tended to seek the unification of Korea by military means. The British failure effectively to engage this variance between them meant that the frightening prospect of conflict spilling beyond the peninsula and escalating into an atomic conflict remained a recurring nightmare up to, and even beyond, the armistice.

Similarly, American resistance to a negotiated peace laid bare the difference between the two over the conduct of what was technically a UN operation. The British had always seen the UN as a forum for Great Power co-operation which would work towards a peaceful settlement of disputes and with the ancillary function of enhancing Britain's status as a Power of the first rank. Over Korea, they were faced with an American tendency to view the UN as a 'police organisation' to 'frustrate international crime' with the inherent dangers of further dividing the world into armed and hostile camps, and with the UN being transformed into a part of a Western system of collective security and the consequent secession of the Soviet Union and the Communist bloc from the system. This propensity was encapsulated in the American insistence that China should not be given UN representation. Though fully aware of these hazards, the British determination not to fracture relations with the US meant that there was little they could do to derail what were privately dismissed as 'the stupidity of American tactics' over China or to resolve an anomaly in international affairs which was to exist for 30 years.[69] At the same time, the performance of the UN in Korea gave it, and to Britain within it, a persisting image as the tool of American policy.

Britain's reward for this conciliatory stance was an increased American contribution to the defence of Western Europe. This was not an inconsiderable gain. European security remained the first British concern. The ominous parallels between what was happening in Korea and what might happen in a divided Germany, reinforced by reports in September 1950 that the military police in the German Democratic Republic were being equipped to be capable of attacking the Federal Republic, increased the nervousness over what Moscow might do next. In November, when pressure from Washington for British rearmament and doubts in the Labour Party about Britain's part in the war were both intensifying, Attlee told the Cabinet that 'if we were to withdraw our support for US strategy in the Far East, the US Government would be less willing to continue their policy of supporting the defence of Western Europe.'[70] Bevin felt the same. Strong opposition to the US, he warned Attlee, might lead them to become disillusioned with collective security which would be 'disastrous' to the United Kingdom.[71] This tended to overlook the fact that the security of Europe was a principal consideration for the Americans too. No-one seemed to question whether an Administration which went to war ostensibly for a corrupt regime in Seoul would easily abandon more compatible democratic governments in London and Paris. An obvious signal that it would not was provided by the fact that for some time Bevin had been trying unsuccessfully to persuade the US to station significant numbers of troops in Europe to ensure that they would be involved from day one of the fighting should a Soviet invasion come. It was events in Korea which finally brought this about. Between 1950 and 1953 American fears for the security of Western Europe prompted them to increase their forces there from two to six divisions. NATO was also expanded and given an integrated structure with an American commander in overall charge.

Though the Americans might regularly threaten a return to isolationism, they never came within an inch of doing so. It was, however, a useful tool in exacting what they saw as a reasonable cost. As a *quid pro quo* for their own efforts in Korea, Washington expected Britain and the other Western Europeans to increase their own defence expenditures. A month after the North Koreans crossed the 38th Parallel, the British Government did indeed announce an extension of national service by six months to two years and a three-year programme of defence spending amounting to £3.6 billion – an increase of £400 million. In September, however, Washington curtly informed their European allies that their exertions were 'below American expectations'. A further month on, a British application for significant financial aid to support their programme (calculated at £550 million), and over which they believed they had received assurances from the Truman Administration, was rejected as 'far beyond anything that the United States had contemplated' and was almost halved. By the end of the year, the Cabinet had accepted an American proposal that Washington's support for rearmament should be shared between the European NATO states. The British managed to persuade themselves that, at least, this looked rather less like a demeaning return to dependence on American charity. But the following spring brought the news that, because of the then quite robust state of their economy, the formula devised for sharing aid meant that the British were unlikely to receive any financial support at all. Meanwhile, the Cabinet had revised its rearmament programme upwards in January to £4.7 billion. Robert Hall, a chief economic adviser to the Government and a protagonist of rearmament on the pessimistic basis that even if Korea did not bring on the next general war: 'something will', claimed to have been influential in this. He revealed in his diary that 'the present defence programme was largely pushed on to the [Government] Departments and the Cabinet and the public by a few people' – amongst whom Hall included himself.[72] Though this exaggerated his own influence, it also provides an interesting indication of a quite widespread reluctance to go down the route of increased defences plus a reminder that even eminent economists may be distracted by political considerations. The truth is that Attlee had been the victim of further pressure from the Americans at his meeting with Truman in December and had succumbed to it. Behind his capitulation lay the obsessively anxious mantra that the Americans would lose interest in the defence of Europe if they were not heeded. The CoS added their pennyworth too, arguing that Chinese intervention in Korea had increased the risk of a widespread war 'to the extent that all possible steps, short of general mobilisation, should be taken to increase our defence preparedness'.[73]

The implications of following America's bidding over rearmament had been spelled out to Bevin by Oliver Franks at the end of September 1950.[74] In essence, Franks said that because of ERP the British 'had won [their] economic independence and seemed likely to be able to keep it', but that 'the aggression of the North Koreans has radically altered this picture'. The cost of raw materials for rearmament would upset the balance of trade and weaken the pound and cause suppliers of raw materials to demand payment in dollars with Britain 're-entering the vicious circle from which we had just escaped'. Politically, the position of partnership with the USA, just being attained, was likely to be lost and – using what had by now become a well-worn metaphor – Britain put 'back in the European Queue, as in 1947, one of the countries helped by the United States'. This was already evident to Bevin. His early illusions that defence planning would be 'built on a Commonwealth-USA basis, an English-speaking basis' were dashed by American insistence that the European NATO members' defence progress be viewed as a whole. The Foreign Secretary could only impotently protest that 'Great Britain was not part of Europe; she was not simply a Luxembourg.'[75]

It is hardly surprising that as the war proceeded, a feeling grew in Labour constituencies of being 'not at all sure that we ought to have gone into Korea'. More generally, doubts began to be raised whether the public at large would accept the defence increases now being mooted and the efforts of both the IRD and the Russia Committee were deployed to 'bring home to our people the true nature of the

Soviet regime' so that they would 'accept the need for rearmament and all that implies'. Bevin himself now privately claimed that 'he had never been in favour of going into Korea' and put it down to 'one of the PM's little slips' whilst he himself was incapacitated with illness.[76] Indeed, the balance sheet for Britain of her entry into the war suggests that the reflex response to the North Korean invasion of the South had not necessarily been the appropriate one. True, a line had been drawn, appeasement of aggression renounced and, in the end, South Korea was saved. But Korea had never appeared on any list of vital areas to be defended until after the war had begun. Only then did the JIC argue that defeat there would have a knock-on effect elsewhere when the Soviets felt strong enough to advance. This intelligence, it was admitted, was 'based on very slender evidence' and, as noted above, contrasting voices suggested that Stalin was merely exploiting the advantages of a local situation.[77] What was more, the expectation had been that success would be earned cheaply by token support of the Americans. When this had proved not to be the case, the British reaction was to attempt to negotiate their way out. But it was too late. The British had welded themselves tighter to a demanding and difficult partner who proved essentially impervious to the British point of view no matter how politely presented and who, by their attitude to China and their insistence on preparing themselves to wage a war against the Soviet Union in Europe or anywhere in the globe, escalated rather than damped down international tension.

Britain's major concern, the danger to Europe, was increased – if it was increased at all – more by what the Western Powers were doing in Korea than as a result of new initiatives from Stalin. European anxieties, plus an obsession that failure to go along with the Americans in the Far East would result in a return to isolation, blinded the British to the reality that Washington's interest in the defence of Europe was not based on altruism, but on the risk to themselves should the resources of the Continent fall into Soviet hands.[78] The decision to cave in to American persistence over an increased commitment to rearmament brought the anxieties which troubled significant sections of Labour from the grass-roots to the Cabinet Room. These had been simmering in the conscience of Aneurin Bevan since August 1950 and exploded with his resignation as Minister of Labour the following April over the introduction of health service charges to offset some of the cost of rearmament. It proved a turning point in the postwar history of the Labour Party, marking the point where the consensus in the Party over the proper route to socialism broke down. The bitter divisions which ensued helped keep Labour out of office for the next 13 years. But much more was at stake than the health of the Labour Party or even of the nation. Bevan's departure from the Government, though couched in terms of resentment over fees for teeth and spectacles, was really about the confrontational foreign policy being pursued under the influence of Korea and Britain's following on American coat-tails. More significantly, Bevan was concerned about the economic impact of the scale of rearmament which the Government had approved. In the short term, at least, he was right to be so. As Oliver Franks had predicted, the demand for raw materials inaugurated a significant deficit in Britain's balance of payments and another dollar shortage, which was to reach crisis point by the second half of 1951. Worse, rearmament acted as a brake on a fragile economic recovery at the worst of times. A conglomeration of structural and social reasons may be put forward to explain Britain's halting economic performance during much of the latter part of the twentieth century. But, as Peter Hennessy has pointed out, 'there are powerful reasons for supposing our best hope for the kind of postwar economic miracle enjoyed by so many western European countries was scattered in fragments in the committee rooms of Whitehall, on the hills above the Imjin in Korea and along the Rhine in Germany as British occupation forces were rearmed in readiness for a Stalinist assault.'[79]

# 4

# INNOVATORS, 1950–56

After the dizzying reversals of military fortunes of the first ten months, the war in Korea became deadlocked from the summer of 1951 when peace negotiations were begun. An armistice, which was not to be signed for a further two years, brought an uneasy truce to the peninsula with the frontiers of the two Korean states more or less where they were before the conflict had started. Viewed in the light of the full span of the Cold War, this first international 'hot' encounter may be seen as a kind of equivalent of the Battle of the Marne in 1914. An offensive had been repelled. Neither side had the capability to produce outright victory – or, in the case of Korea, one side backed off from using its devastating force for fear of what might follow. Each now settled down to a process of attrition, reinforcing its front-line weak points, strengthening its redoubts and engaging in the occasional peace-feeler or even tactical offensive either to prohibit potential enemy success or in the hope of grasping a new salient. Aside from the awesome consequences of a general war, the difference was that 40 years on from 1914 the struggle was truly world-wide. After Korea no-one could doubt the Cold War as a central factor in international relations or, as the CoS had concluded in 1950, its global character. A 1952 PUSC paper, examining what its authors considered would be a 'long and arduous' process of reaching an accommodation between the two camps, envisaged that once global equilibrium had been finally achieved, the outcome would be that 'between the two spheres of influence will lie a "no-man's land"' including Finland, Eastern Germany and substantial parts of Asia.[1]

As we have seen, working with the Americans in Korea brought mixed blessings to the British. Keen to have the US act as a barrier to Communism in the Far East and enthusiasts of the military build-up in NATO, they nevertheless nurtured an overdeveloped trepidation that with American attention now attracted to that part of the world, they would run out on their commitment to fight in Europe. (In fact, during his first year as President, Eisenhower made it plain to his own defence advisers that he regarded the prevention of the Communisation of Western Europe as a *sine qua non* of American foreign policy.[2]) At the same time, the British found themselves having to restrain a recurring excess of zeal on America's part to extend the Asian conflict. Moreover, the suspicion grew in London that the West had allowed itself to be tied down in the wrong place. A year after the war had begun, the CoS noted that 'while the United Nations' forces under American leadership are fighting in Korea – an area of small strategic importance – the much more important areas of Indochina and Malaya are being defended piecemeal in isolation by France and the United Kingdom respectively'.[3] Anthony Eden, back at the Foreign Office after the Conservative victory at the General Election of October 1951, took a similar view. 'The war in Korea', he told the US Secretary of State, John Foster Dulles, 'was a strategic mistake which would have to be corrected as soon as possible. There was ... no point in our first eleven being held down on a barren peninsula by the enemy's second eleven ...'.[4] What the standoff in Korea from the summer of 1951, together with the return of a Churchill Premiership, did allow was some opportunity for the British to take stock of their position in a world fighting a Cold War.

An early foray in this process was provided by a review of 'Future Policy Towards Soviet Russia' conducted by the Permanent Under-Secretary's Committee of the Foreign Office which was completed in January 1952.[5] In some ways the PUSC's report was a re-hash of the analysis which had characterised George Kennan's 'Long Telegram' of March 1946, with its stress on the Kremlin's opportunist expansionism based on an ingrained sense of insecurity and with Communist ideology superimposed upon a determination to pursue Russia's long-standing interests. Like Kennan before them, the Foreign Office planners accepted that Moscow's proclivity to expand could be curbed by determined opposition. Six years on from the 'Long Telegram', the restoration of Western economic stability, the creation of the Atlantic Alliance, and with some signs of the emergence of embryonic defence systems for the Middle East and Southeast Asia, allowed a greater sense of optimism that a *modus vivendi* between East and West, to end what officials called 'the present state of uneasy absence of war', could be achieved. Certainly, it was a process of incremental easement in international relations which the PUSC envisaged. This would be arrived at 'by negotiating settlements, each one probably local and limited in character, which would improve the Western position and which might be expected to lead cumulatively to a general stabilisation' and was 'likely to last decades'. An equally interesting aspect of the PUSC's analysis raised the notion of the 'rollback' of the Soviet empire and the 'liberation' of Moscow's satellites anticipating, in some ways, the rhetoric of the Republican Administration which was to come to power in the USA in January 1953. Under this heading the possibility was raised of fomenting trouble in the satellite states with the object of detaching them from the Soviet bloc or covert action aimed at specific weak points in the Communist Government machine. The former was rejected as impracticable. It was too risky in that it might run the danger of war if it touched insensitively on Soviet 'sore spots', such as Germany and Iran, which could result in a hostile counteraction. It would also be counter-productive if it merely cemented the cohesion of the Soviet bloc and destroyed the prospect of a future settlement. This took a step beyond the position currently held by the IRD (which was supported in Cabinet) that the experience of undercover operations during the war had demonstrated the potential hazards of any premature encouragement of subversive activities within the Soviet Empire itself. But what both the PUSC and the IRD had in common was a shared anxiety to moderate any indications from Washington suggesting impatience to pursue such avenues.

The extent to which the PUSC review influenced the new Foreign Secretary is uncertain. Central aspects of the Foreign Office paper – the desire to maintain Britain's world power status, the need to restrain American enthusiasm for reckless activity against the Communist world and the necessity to husband carefully Britain's own deteriorating resource base – were quite compatible with Eden's thinking which he displayed in an important memorandum on 'British Overseas Obligations' in June 1952.[6] More particularly, Eden was to amplify the PUSC's view of narrowing the gap between NATO and the ANZUS Pact so that 'the Soviet *bloc* would be virtually contained by a series of defensive groupings extending round the world.' The specific impetus for Eden's *tour d'horizon* was, as so often, another economic crisis accelerated, if not prompted, by the massive rearmament programme which had come in the wake of Korea. The Chancellor of the Exchequer, R. A. Butler, in his first Cabinet paper in October 1951, gloomily informed colleagues of 'a balance of payments crisis, worse than in 1949, and in many ways worse even than in 1947'.[7] A mixture of elation at returning to office and a Cabinet mindset that assumed some kind of rerun of the last Churchill Government hampered attempts to get to grips with this deepening emergency. One Minister noted that the country was run by 'a team of … very able and in some cases brilliant men … and led by one of the greatest figures in the long history of the country. But, somehow, it doesn't really work.' The tendency for Churchill and his colleagues to see their difficulties as a kind of return to the dark days of 1940 was perhaps understandable, 'except', as one pointed out, 'that we are all 12 years older.'[8] The 'great figure' was, in fact, 78. This may go some way to explaining why Butler's insistent message that cuts in defence expenditure, then running at almost 10 per cent of the nation's GNP, must play a significant part in the drive for economic rectitude had only meagre results. Though his premise – 'on which we are all agreed' – was that the Labour Government's defence programme 'was based on assumptions about American aid and the strength of our economy which have since been proved false', the Treasury's struggle to contain defence expenditure was to continue until Churchill's retirement and beyond.[9]

Eden's projection of British foreign policy, whilst it acknowledged that the British economy was overstretched, rejected any precipitate withdrawal from the Government's major overseas commitments. To do so, Eden argued, was likely to damage Britain's economic and trading interests further. It was also a matter of status for 'once the prestige of a country has started to slide there is no knowing where it will stop.' As an alternative, the British people might be rallied to a greater productive effort, which would allow wider external responsibilities to be sustained in order to avoid seeing 'their country sink to the level of a second-class Power, with injury to their essential interests and way of life of which they can have little conception'. This kind of condescension has led some to detect in the formulation of much postwar British foreign policy the determination of an arrogant ruling elite to hang on to the traditional foundations of authority which were, as Eden himself put it, 'inherited from several hundred years as a great Power'. One commentator has gone so far as to suggest that the Cold War was 'almost a blessing' to British policy-makers in that it provided justification for clinging on to an otherwise insupportable influence.[10] Maybe this was a subconscious ingredient in Eden's overview. Yet Eden, like Bevin before him, tended to see it the other way around. The good fortune was not Britain's, but the West's in that self-interested, imperfect and over-exerted though it might be, British power was a benign and necessary force in a half-world under siege standing between the United States and Russia, 'two unwieldy prehistoric monsters floundering about in the mud'.[11] Any retreat by Britain risked a corresponding advance of Soviet power and Eden made it clear that his primary concern was that 'the Russians would be only too ready to fill any vacuum created by a British withdrawal.'

The trick, the Foreign Secretary believed, was, whilst ruling out any British retreat from major obligations, to convince other friendly powers to share their burdens. This would involve the construction of defence organisations in the Middle East and Southeast Asia drawing in appropriate local states, as well as members of the Commonwealth who 'enjoy the fruits of the rearmament efforts of the free world without making commensurate contributions.' These would be linked with the Atlantic Pact – 'the heart of the defence of the British Isles' – to which German forces should be added. The fundamental task, however, was 'to persuade the United States to assume the real burdens in such organisations, while retaining for ourselves as much political control – and hence prestige and world influence – as we can.' This was not a novel proposition. The desire to mask and sustain Britain's over-extended power had played an important part in British thinking before the First World War and had re-emerged in more straightened circumstances during the Second – when Eden had been Foreign Secretary – in the shape of the creation of a World Organisation which would project Allied co-operation into peacetime and prop up British authority. It was also an expansion, in a climate of worldwide Cold War, of what Bevin had obtained for Western Europe in 1949. Eden took a realistic view of the probable American reactions to their taking on new obligations. They would be hesitant, they would, as always, be suspicious of propping up British imperialism, but 'being heavily committed to the East-West struggle they would not readily leave a power-vacuum in any part of the globe but would be disposed, however reluctantly, to fill it themselves if it was clear that the United Kingdom could no longer hold the position (as they did, for example, in Greece).'

There were, nevertheless, hurdles which Eden's shrewd game plan glossed over. Success in shifting the burden to the United States, as he was fully aware, would be dependent on demonstrating that Britain was itself making the maximum effort. How was this to be done whilst, at the same time, reducing resource expenditure which was inexorably pushing Britain into the second class? As Adamthwaite has pointed out, Eden's strategy 'seemed to imply that Britain should continue to overstrain her economy so as to satisfy the Americans that we were still a powerful and worthwhile ally.'[12] Added to this, the transfer had to arise 'gradually and inconspicuously' without causing fissures between the Western allies which would only give comfort to the Communist bloc. With the Anglo-Saxons already at loggerheads over American pressure for a European Army aimed at reconciling the Europeans to German rearmament, the recognition of Communist China and continued strain between the two over aspects of the conduct of the conflict in Korea, this was likely to prove a tall order. Another related problem lay in wait. What if the US chose to fill a niche in an area of strategic or economic importance to Britain in advance of a British decision to move out? Given Eden's temperamental aversion to equating smoothing over cracks in the Western Alliance as implying British docility to her stronger partner, there was plenty of scope here for inter-allied friction. In the meantime, however, in an almost contemporaneous paper to Eden's, the CoS provided some reinforcement for the Foreign Secretary's assessment.

The Chiefs' 'Global Strategy' paper, prepared for the Defence Committee of the Cabinet and finalised on 17 June 1952, was prompted, as was Eden's analysis, principally by pressure for economies in defence spending. There were resonances too of a visit the CoS had made with Churchill to Washington in January 1952 which had left them all in awe of the increased atomic firepower of the United States and the American's capacity to deliver it. The trip was probably a contributory factor in inducing the Chiefs to upgrade the significance of nuclear weapons in preventing and, in default of this, of winning a war against the Soviet Union. Like Eden, the Chiefs started from the assumption, stated more bleakly than he was inclined to do, that 'the Free World is menaced everywhere by the implacable and unlimited aims of Soviet Russia.'[13] However, the development of a formidable American stockpile of atomic weapons and the lack of any effective defence against an atomic air attack meant that 'for Russia the best opportunity for using war as a means of furthering her aims has already passed.' As with the PUSC before them, the CoS drew the implication that 'the Allies must face the prospect of a prolonged period of Cold War waged by the Russians, their satellites and the

Chinese, with great intensity and ingenuity.' The CoS position on how to emerge victorious from this long haul also complemented Eden's closely – bringing German armed forces into the defence of Western Europe, organising, with the Americans and the Commonwealth, defence organisations in the Middle East and extending the 'Truman policy of containment' to Asia. It was, however, the Chiefs' increased emphasis on the atomic deterrent which broke new ground and which seemed to offer the tantalising possibility of a reduction in the burden of the defence budget.

The CoS were alive to the possibility that overspending risked a ruined economy which would be merely 'to play the Communist game and to present Russia with a bloodless victory'. In their view, both the United States and NATO were too wedded to a cripplingly expensive and outmoded expansion of conventional forces to meet the Soviet threat – a NATO agreement earlier in the year required Britain to provide just under ten divisions to the defence of Western Europe over the next two years. The deterrent value of the atomic bomb had been recognised by the Chiefs since the end of the war, but with American B-29 bombers which were stationed in East Anglia now atomically armed, they were sharply conscious of the vulnerability of the British Isles to nuclear attack.[14] The attractions of the development of a British atomic armoury were that defence costs could be reduced and, by bringing it home to the Soviets that 'atomic attack would be swift, overwhelming and certain', provide the best assurance that a hot war would not be engaged. It would also offer the best chance of winning an atomic war if it came.

Inevitably there were complicating factors. Because they judged that significant conventional forces would still be required to meet and deflect Cold War challenges and to fight and win, what came to be called, 'broken backed' warfare, which they were persuaded was likely to follow an atomic strike, and with the Army and Navy Service Chiefs particularly reluctant to see the status of their own Service downgraded, the CoS felt unable immediately to offer radical cuts in spending. What they did propose was an extended rearmament programme covering eight rather than three years. Even this was put forward with an emphatic warning that it 'can be undertaken only by incurring real and serious risks. These risks are only justifiable in the face of the threat of economic disaster.' Though holding out the prospect of cost-effective defence in the long run, the Chiefs' appraisal was disappointing to those seeking urgent remedies for Britain's economic difficulties and set the scene for months of Cabinet skirmishes over defence cuts.

But the real significance of the 'Global Strategy' paper was that it took a further stride towards a policy of deterrence founded on what would soon be termed 'massive retaliation'. As the Chiefs revealed an abridged version of their paper to the Americans during the first part of 1952, it seems likely that their thinking had some influence on the adoption of a similar deterrent strategy by the Eisenhower Administration after 1953, though there is some debate over this.[15] If this was in fact so, the Americans were soon ahead of the game with the British running to keep up. At the time of the 'Global Strategy' paper, London's atomic capability was zero. A test detonation of a British atom bomb did not occur until the following October. The first operational bomb was not available to the RAF until a year beyond that and the V-bomber (Valiant, Victor and Vulcan) force needed effectively to deliver them would not begin to come into service until 1955. Until then, deterrence depended entirely on the USA. Indeed, even as the CoS were deliberating, the world was on the threshold of a colossal leap in destructive capacity. Britain's newly achieved atomic power status in October 1952 was almost immediately overshadowed by American testing of a thermonuclear explosion in November. The Russians detonated their own 'intermediate' thermonuclear weapon the following August.

The Chiefs fully acknowledged that because of cost the American deterrent would always outclass the British. Even so, assumptions demonstrated in contiguous discussions of the 'Global Strategy' paper were centred on the understanding that deterrence *could not* be left to the United States alone. If deterrence failed, the advantage in Europe in a conventional war would be with the Soviet Union. If Britain was to be victorious in a future East-West conflict, it would have to be atomic. Moreover, if Britain was to have any chance of surviving an initial atomic onslaught so as to fight a 'broken backed' war, a first strike atomic attack on Soviet long-range bomber bases in order to reduce the atomic destruction to the United Kingdom would be necessary. The Americans should be assigned the task of attacking Soviet urban and industrial areas. The corollary of this was the need for intimate strategic co-operation with the United States. This held a further implication. Churchill returned from his visit to Washington in January 1952 convinced that the certainty of Anglo-American strategic collaboration in a future war depended upon a display of Britain's own efficacy in implementing atomic ruin.[16] The Chiefs too were adamant that Britain should speedily develop its own stock of atom bombs, without which influence over American policy in both the Cold War and in a possible hot war was bound to deteriorate. Here was another variant of the catch which lurked in a policy of 'burden sharing'. To entice others to take the strain, Britain had to stretch further.

Where this kind of thinking would lead may be illuminated by briefly looking ahead to the Churchill Government's decision in 1954 to develop a British hydrogen bomb. To the familiar supporting arguments of deterrence against Soviet aggression and the augmentation of British influence and prestige, new considerations were now added. The destructiveness of the new weapon meant that a nuclear stockpile could be acquired more rapidly and more cheaply than the atom bomb allowed. There was also the melancholy possibility that with the dawning likelihood that the United States might soon be as vulnerable as Britain to nuclear attack, which might wipe out major cities, the Americans would be less enthusiastic about defending London. This further underscored arguments for an independent British deterrence.[17] A more immediate British apprehension was that a Republican Administration in Washington might seize upon its existing nuclear advantage and opt for a preventive war. 'Will the Americans be prepared to wait', Churchill mused, 'or will they force the issue? Will they wait until, either by their own skill or by treachery, the Russians have learned the secret of the hydrogen, as they have of the atom, bomb?' Lord Salisbury, Lord President of the Council in Churchill's Government, felt that 'by a curious paradox, during the next few years the danger to the peace of the world came from America, not Russia. Russia knew that she could be attacked with terrible power by America, with no power of retaliation (except in Europe). America knew that for an interval of some years, she herself was safe. She might be tempted or provoked into rash action.'[18] A leap in American capacity for destruction thus made it even more imperative for the British to restrain their transatlantic partner.

The Labour Government's experience in Korea had amply demonstrated how difficult it was in practice finely to control their more powerful partner. After a cease-fire had come into operation in the summer of 1951, the British were mainly concerned to conclude an armistice in that uncongenial theatre and redeploy their forces. Truman and Acheson were in less of a hurry and were interested in British and Commonwealth troops remaining in Korea even after an armistice to provide security for the future good behaviour of the Communist bloc. They also wanted a clear warning to be given at the time of an armistice that any breach of it by Communist forces would lead to military and economic sanctions against China.[19] The Churchill Government, like their Labour predecessors, saw this as too provocative and preferred a more general statement about future aggression. They too were fearful that an economic blockade of the Chinese coast, which the Americans proposed if an armistice was broken, would merely precipitate a wider conflict. Though the British were to continue to act as an occasional brake, American policy went its own way, bombing power stations on the Yalu river in June 1952 and removing the United States' Navy from the Straits between China and Formosa in February 1953 without bothering to consult London. Eden's propensity was to resist either succumbing to American demands or accepting their surprises without protest, but he was hampered by a Prime Minister who saw Anglo-American relations as the linchpin of British policy. Also, until January 1953, he had in Acheson a counterpart who felt unable for domestic-political reasons to be conciliatory over Korea and who was therefore apt to issue threats that without British acquiescence over American policy, there would be 'no NATO, no Anglo-American friendship etc'.[20] What change there was after Truman and Acheson were replaced by Eisenhower and John Foster Dulles tended to be for the worse. British attempts to moderate the American position and criticise their apparent reluctance to reach an armistice were taken in Washington as a lack of understanding of American constraints and a disposition to 'adopt a carping tone, which came ill from a country making only a small contribution to the Korean struggle'.[21]

Despite this unpromising setting, the basic tenet of Eden's 'British Overseas Obligations' paper – transferring British burdens surreptitiously to the 'friendly' shoulders of the United States (and others) – remained the template which guided his foreign policy. An important element in this was the construction of a series of interlocking security groups in which, as with NATO, US involvement was anticipated. Again, the signs remained unpropitious. Both Eden and the CoS in their respective 1952 papers restated the earlier British position that, because of its oil and its potential as a base for striking back at the USSR, the defence of the Middle East held an importance second only to that of Western Europe, especially in the event of war. Churchill felt the same and hoped pragmatically (and maybe with some nervousness) that his highly-strung Foreign Secretary would 'meet the Americans over China, which really does not matter to us. Then they in turn might meet us about Egypt or Persia, which matter a lot. After all, what Conservative in England is in favour of Chinese Communists?'[22] Nevertheless, because the Americans looked upon the Middle East with some reproach as essentially a British colonial concern and lacking the same regional cohesion as Western Europe, they were reluctant to be drawn. The Korean War brought some change in American thinking, accentuating their perception of a global danger and increasing their understanding of the pressures which the British were facing in that area. In the early months of 1951 the Truman Administration stepped up economic and military aid to the region and in May began to work with the British on a Middle East Command (MEC) to co-ordinate the defences of the area.

The core of British difficulties in that part of the world, however, remained nationalism rather than American aloofness. Fanned enthusiastically by London during the First World War in order to preserve Britain's interests in the Middle East from the Turks, the French or any other potential rival, this force was now an increasing irritant to the British themselves. Of course, not all the Middle Eastern states were opposed to some form of co-operation with Britain, but this only served to intensify interstate rivalry between those prepared to collaborate and those who viewed the collaborators through a nationalist prism as the puppets of imperialism and made the construction of common defence arrangements more elusive. Egypt remained the focal point of British concern and, more particularly, the Suez Canal which ran through it and where by right of the 1936 Anglo-Egyptian Treaty, Britain was permitted to station protective military units. 'The Canal', Eden told the Cabinet in July 1952, 'is of more importance to the world today than ever before' and a stoppage of free traffic through the Canal would have a 'disastrous effect' on British trade and especially on oil imports.[23] Churchill too tried to sell the message, especially to the Americans, of the significance of the Canal to all, and not just to Britain.[24] In a speech to the US Congress in January of the same year he admitted that Britain could no longer bear the whole burden of the Suez Canal, but stressed that 'we do not seek to be masters of Egypt. We are there only as the servants and guardians of the commerce of the world.'[25] Behind these statements was the uncomfortable half-realisation that Britain was being squeezed out of Egypt. Under Labour an attempt had been made to reconcile the demands of Egyptian nationalism with Britain's need to protect her economic and strategic needs and an agreement seemed to have been arrived at in 1946 for the evacuation of British military from the Canal Zone to take place by September 1949, with the option of reactivating the military base if Egypt or her immediate neighbours were attacked. But this had foundered over Egypt's claims over the Sudan and was not ratified. In October 1951 – just as Churchill and Eden were returning to power – the Egyptian Government unilaterally abrogated the 1936 Treaty which was once again being renegotiated.

The advantage of a Middle East Command to the British – to consist initially of Britain, America, France, Egypt, Turkey, Australia, New Zealand and South Africa – was not only that it would lay the foundations for a regional defence system but, because it was envisaged that it would replace the 1936 Treaty and that MEC forces would man the Suez base instead of those of the United Kingdom, it would encapsulate in one initiative a neat solution to fighting the Cold War, coping with Britain's overstretched commitments and dousing the hostility of Arab nationalism. The mortal blow was delivered by the Egyptians, shortly after their abrogation of the 1936 Treaty, when they made it clear that they would not co-operate in a MEC until differences with the British had been settled. Despite these depressing circumstances the British, with the support of the Truman Administration, pressed on with the MEC proposal until early 1952. After a brief lull, Eden picked up the idea again, though the intention was not now to set up a fully-fledged military command system, but a planning and consultative body. As an indication of this modification, the proposed association was now termed a Middle East Defence Organisation (MEDO). Despite the Foreign Secretary's evinced confidence over achieving this, especially after a military coup in Cairo in July 1952 appeared for a short time to inaugurate a more accommodating government, a MEDO too was to be abandoned a year later for much the same reason as the ill-fated MEC – the refusal of the most significant state in the Middle East to join it.

The reluctance of Washington to back British aspirations in the Middle East has often been taken as a principal reason for their failure.[26] Churchill and Eden clearly believed that firmer American support and a willingness to shoulder concrete responsibilities would have resolved their difficulties. Others shared this feeling that the Americans' 'usual foolish impetuosity' made them 'not very friendly' to Britain in the region. This might be rationalised on the ground that what was at work was 'not ill-will, but inexperience', though there were those who were not prepared to be so generous and saw the Americans 'undermining the British and French empires as hard as they can'.[27] No doubt the attitude in Washington was frequently unhelpful and became increasingly so when Dulles took control of the State Department in 1953, bringing with him a regenerated fervour to avoid association with British 'colonial' views and to pursue a more independent policy in the Middle East.[28] From the point of view of Western security in the Cold War, Dulles's approach was wrong-headed and for such a zealous opponent of world Communism, almost perverse. Notwithstanding her colonial paraphernalia, Britain still had loyal friends amongst the Middle Eastern states and there was sufficient distrust of the Soviet Union amongst the others to suggest the existence of a basis for an anti-Communist system which the United States would find harder to build on its own.

Nevertheless, until the Suez issue was defused somewhat in 1954, the primary impediment to British policy in the region was bound to be Egypt rather than the United States. As Eden had put it in his 'British Overseas Obligations' paper in the summer of 1952: 'the dilemma is that until we can come to an agreement with Egypt no effective international defence organisation for the Middle East can be established; and so long as there is no settlement with Egypt and no international defence organisation we are obliged to hold the fort alone.'[29] It may well be that the British were guilty of a failure to associate Egypt and other Middle East states in a leadership role seeing them as subservient conduits for the preservation of their own authority.[30] Yet Eden, for one, showed sensitivity to the Egyptian position, insisting that what he had in mind 'was not a plan to substitute for the British occupation a military occupation by an international force. It was a plan for establishing a Middle East Defence Organisation in which Egypt and the other countries of the Middle East would be associated with ourselves, the Americans, the French, the Turks and the Commonwealth countries concerned in planning and organising the defence of the Middle East as a whole.' In the 'more practical' climate in Cairo which he sensed after the overthrow of the Egyptian monarchy in July 1952, Eden was even prepared to consider whether a base in Egypt was absolutely essential to the defence of the Middle East, in part because to remove it would reduce a fundamental source of tension between the two countries.[31] (The decision was actually taken in December 1952 to transfer British military headquarters in the Middle East from Egypt to Cyprus.)

In his attempts to resolve the intractable problem of Egypt, Eden discovered that his room for manoeuvre was limited. In the immediate term he was faced with Egyptian demands for the evacuation of troops at a time of mounting violence against British citizens living and working in Egypt and whose lives had to be protected. The unofficial view emanating from the Prime Minister's Office that 'we should sit on the gippies and have a "whiff of grapeshot"' and 'if it meant letting the British communities in Alexandria and Cairo be massacred that could not be helped' might reflect Churchill's robust approach to the Suez problem, but it was not a position which the Foreign Secretary had yet arrived at.[32] The apprehension in the Cabinet, which Eden shared, that 'what happens here (in Egypt) will set the pace for us all over Africa and the Middle East' and that 'there is a serious danger that the Middle East will slip away from us' should be set against the downgrading of the Middle East in the CoS 1952 'Global Strategy' assessment as an important theatre in the Cold War.[33] Though it was still judged vital to defend the region if war came, the fact was that there was no direct threat from the Soviet Union on that front, whereas the Cold War had taken on a 'violent and aggressive form' in Indochina, Korea and Malaya. Logic increasingly suggested that in the face of continued pressure for military cuts, the Middle East was where these might now do least damage. This mirrored a growing consensus among policy-makers, including even a reluctant Churchill, that the Suez base was no longer an unqualified asset to Britain. In October 1954, to howls of disgust from certain sections of the Conservative Party, Eden concluded an agreement over Suez involving the withdrawal of British troops by June 1956, but with the right to return if the Canal became or threatened to become part of a war zone.

The resolution of the Suez base issue in 1954, as well as being one of the minor triumphs of a year which witnessed Eden operating at the height of his powers, also signified a further reassessment of Britain's Middle East policy. Stalin's death in March 1953 released some optimism that a fighting war was even less imminent. In the wake of the dictator's demise came an armistice in Korea and also troubles inside the Soviet Empire, especially in East Germany, as the Stalinist grip relaxed.[34] Should war nevertheless occur, the development of the hydrogen bomb was judged by the CoS to have transformed the way the war would be played out. The Soviet Union would now be so damaged by a thermonuclear attack at the outset of a war that a resolute Soviet attack southwards would be unlikely and could be effectively held by using forces based beyond Egypt. Attention was now transferred to the prospect of building a defensive bloc coalescing around the more pliable states of Iraq and Jordan. Behind this shield, improved Anglo-Egyptian relations would provide further political stability in the region as well as serving British economic interests. Attracting Egypt into this defence organisation now assumed a lower priority. In some ways it was an inventive adaptation to new circumstances and allowed confidence to spring that, out of the wreckage of the MEC/MEDO failure, there might emerge a sturdy defensive system free of Anglo-Egyptian animosity. What was more, when in July 1953 Dulles declared his intention to construct a defence organisation in what was called the 'Northern Tier' of the Middle East from Pakistan to Turkey, new British thinking seemed sufficiently compatible with Dulles's own as to entice them into assuming it would allow deeper Anglo-American collaboration and thus Britain's burden-sharing. This was a miscalculation. Dulles was attracted to a 'Northern Tier' precisely because he had experienced the deep hostility to the British in Egypt on a visit there in the spring of 1953. His response was to distance himself from this source of friction and construct a defence system which excluded them both. Indeed, a less systematic version of this approach had already been demonstrated by the United States' exasperating unwillingness to support the British in their tortuous Suez negotiations or to persuade Egypt to join MEDO.

It may be that British progress towards a new direction in the Middle East was more opportunistic than this and that they were pressed forward less by a coherent urge to construct a defensive system than by an immediate need to renew the expiring Anglo-Iraqi treaty, which would secure RAF bases in Iraq and embrace the lapsing treaty within a wider defensive umbrella. Carried along by the Iraqis and Turks, each of whom vied with the other to bask in the glow of Western approval, the British in April 1955, this view suggests, joined an Iraqi-Turkish arrangement which became the foundation for what was to be the Baghdad Pact (Pakistan and Iran were later to join). According to this scenario, the British were simply sucked into 'a second best solution' to a MEDO. If this was the case, difficulties with Egypt provided a strategic rationale for the new policy. It must also have been unusually comforting for the British to have Middle East states pressing for association rather than stonewalling or stoning them. It was true, as Eden's Middle East specialists pointed out, that without Egypt a northern defence system might look a little thin. But this consideration did not seem a drawback to Dulles's plans, which also disregarded Egypt. The irritant for the British was that Dulles continued to set his face against adhering to a British dominated group. As Eden was later to complain, the American Secretary of State's Middle East policy was confusing and erratic. He chose, for instance, to ignore the advice of his own specialists that Britain was 'our strongest and most reliable ally' who, in return for support of the American position in the Far East, should be buoyed up in the Middle East 'to avoid finding ourselves trapped in the unwelcome role of mediator between native regimes and Great Britain.'[35] It was all very well for the Americans to draw the lesson that it was best to avoid giving the impression of too close association with Western sponsorship. But the Middle East states which provided the core of the Baghdad Pact – Iraq, Iran, Pakistan and Turkey – *welcomed* Western backing and the state which did not, Egypt, was regarded as something of a maverick even in the Islamic camp. Moreover, American excuses for not joining the Baghdad Pact on the ground that that they could not provide a commitment to Arab Iraq for fear of offending pro-Israel opinion in the United States hardly stood square with Dulles's envisaged inclusion of Iraq in his own notion of a 'Northern Tier'.[36]

Over one problematic Middle Eastern issue some comfort could be taken in London that a converging approach between themselves and Washington did eventually develop. When, in May 1951, a crisis had broken out in Anglo-Iranian relations after the Iranian Prime Minister Mossadeq nationalised the Anglo-Iranian Oil Company (AIOC), the Labour Government had been tempted to use force to retrieve their installations at Abadan refinery, but had been dissuaded from doing so by the Truman Administration. During the summer of 1952 the diaries of the Conservative Housing Minister, Harold Macmillan – who had a highly developed interest in foreign policy matters – were peppered with references to the 'half crazy' Mossadeq.[37] Macmillan's ire was exercised by a vision of the potentially grievous economic and political consequences to Britain which the Iranian coup threatened. In the first place, the flow of dollar-free oil from Abadan was disrupted presenting serious problems for Britain's balance of payments and contributing significantly to Butler's problems when he entered the Treasury at the end of 1951. Politically, Mossadeq's action might tempt others to act with similar peremptoriness towards the Suez Canal or generally serve to reduce respect for Britain in the region. At the end of 1952 Macmillan observed that the Saudis were 'making trouble' for the British. 'We are', he noted, 'treated with scant courtesy – all, of course, the result of Abadan.'[38]

Because the crisis interrupted the export of Iranian oil it had also seriously disrupted Iran's own economy, giving rise to fears in the United States of a drift towards Communism. With this in mind, Washington now urged London to find a resolution to the problem and contemplated offering aid to Iran so that it often seemed to the British that the Americans were more concerned to avoid offending Mossadeq than themselves. A not unrepresentative view was that 'the Americans are behaving badly to us. They are, of course, pretty vain and anyone can blackmail them by threatening to go Communist.'[39] Working on the latter assumption, MI6 began to jockey for a resolution to the Iranian matter and, after 1953, found a willing listener in Eisenhower who also happened to have a fascination for clandestine operations. This was gratifying to the extent that Mossadeq was removed by an MI6/CIA inspired coup, Operation Boot, in August. British rights within the AIOC were reasserted and Iran soon became a staunch member of the Baghdad Pact. But these were not unalloyed dividends. Despite Dulles's attempts to brush aside British worries that there might be 'certain "smart boys" who thought that the US might profit from the dispute between the AIOC and the Persian Government' this is precisely what occurred.[40] The monopoly which Britain had enjoyed in the AIOC before May 1951 was reduced to a 40 per cent control – American oil companies also took 40 per cent. Also, although MI6 had planned and prompted it, the action against Mossadeq ended up as an American rather than a British affair. At the time of the plot Eden (who was anyway inclined to be more fastidious over clandestine operations in Iran than was to be the case with Egypt three years later) was out of action through illness and with Churchill more or less incapacitated following a stroke, 'the CIA and US dollars were the most important factors.'[41] What was also apparent, of course, was that the British were ultimately dependent upon the vagaries of American policy.

The truth was that Britain's commercial and strategic interests in the Middle East significantly outweighed those of the United States. In the Far East, however, the reverse was true. The worry for the British in Asia was that American 'trigger-happiness' might inaugurate a fighting war. From the American perspective, there was an inconsistency in the British position. When some of the details of the CoS 1952 'Global Strategy' paper were revealed to them, they complained that whereas 'in Europe [the British] wanted the maximum deterrent used to show that war would not pay; in Asia [they] refused to consider the blockade of China and the bombing of internal communications, the threat of which was the maximum deterrent to China.' Although the British accused their ally of being 'governed more by emotion than by reason' and did not rate sufficiently highly the likelihood of Russian intervention if China was blockaded, the American position was not devoid of logic. [42] It was in Asia that fighting wars already existed and though the contests in Korea and Malaya were being contained the situation in Indochina, where the French were clearly in difficulties and with Beijing giving reinforcement to the Vietminh, was deteriorating. In comparison, the front in Europe was a model of stability. NATO had been strengthened, its members were rearming and Acheson, in September 1950 in the wake of the outbreak of hostilities in Korea, had made the reasonable suggestion that the West Germans be allowed weapons to reinforce the front-line defences of that continent.

In order to distinguish the principal threads in Britain's conduct of the Cold War at this stage, we must now follow the conjunction of these two ostensibly unrelated factors – the proposed rearmament of Germany and the degenerating position in Indochina. Taking the German question first; what had seemed simply pertinent to Acheson had an explosive impact on the Western Europeans who were appalled at putting arms into the hands of a nation which twice in 40 years had succeeded in dominating the continent by military force. It was also an embarrassment to the French whose recently found desire for intimate economic co-operation with the Federal Republic of Germany in a European Coal and Steel Community was predicated upon preventing a repetition of German militarism. In their attempt to avoid so obvious a gesture of distrust towards their new partners as a straight refusal over German rearmament, the French complicated matters further by suggesting that an armed Germany be confined within a European Defence Community (EDC) and regulated by a supranational European Ministry of Defence. The British had been pondering favourably on the prospect of bringing Germany into the defence of Western Europe since the late 1940s, but no British Government, either Labour or Conservative, could stomach the loss of authority over their armed forces which the EDC now implied. Yet the French (and the Belgians and Dutch) seemed determined against arming the Germans in any other way – though the former too would come to have second thoughts about a loss of control over their own defence. All the British felt able to do in these circumstances was fully to support the creation of an EDC, whilst abjuring any commital to joining it themselves. Increasingly irritated by this turn of events, the Truman and then the Eisenhower Administration sought in turn to cajole the Europeans into co-operation or to threaten to abandon them. The dreary epic of the EDC strained relations between the Western Powers for almost four years until the summer of 1954, when the French destroyed their own invention by refusing to ratify the treaty which would set it up, and presented the NATO members with such a real danger to their solidarity that Eden found himself simultaneously attempting to construct new regional defence organistions whilst he laboured to preserve the existing European system from disintegration.[43]

This thorny issue was part of Eden's inheritance when he returned to the Foreign Office in 1951. He was also faced, as we have seen, with another persisting difficulty in American reluctance to establish formal machinery for politico-military consultation in the shape of regional defence systems outside the NATO area.[44] This included Asia as well as the Middle East. However, by 1953 it was obvious that the West was in difficulties in Indochina. Despite significant material aid from the United States, war-weariness in France and the successes of the Vietminh suggested that the alternatives to a significant reinforcement of the French position in Indochina were either a negotiated settlement or military defeat. Britain's position was at first to encourage the French to greater military exertions. But early in 1954, with the French desperately searching for an exit from their difficulties with as much honour as they might preserve, the British emphasis switched towards negotiation.[45] The vehicle which Eden eventually alighted upon for this was a conference of the major Powers. A high-level conference had the added attraction of providing a possible arena for promoting burden-sharing via negotiations with the Americans for a system of collective defence in Southeast Asia. A proposal from Eisenhower to Churchill on 4 April, 1954 for a 'coalition of nations which have a vital concern in the checking of Communist expansion in the area'[46] seemed superficially to coincide with Eden's long-term objectives and 'could remove the anomaly of our exclusion from AN-

ZUS and contribute to the security of Hong Kong and Malaya'. As one Cabinet Minister privately mused, 'properly handled we may get great advantages. So far we have no American guarantee of any kind for our Eastern interests – Hong Kong, Malaya etc. We are not members of ANZUS (which is very shaming for us). Now there is a chance of getting a sort of Far-Eastern NATO.'[47]

Another good reason for a 'Far Eastern NATO', so far as the British were concerned, was that it would enable them to keep a close eye on the United States and prevent the Americans from taking any reckless action in that part of the world which might lead to a more general conflict.[48] This, of course, was a lesson learned in Korea and was to be reinforced when, in 1955, Eisenhower appeared ready to back Nationalist China's possession of the islands of Matsu and Quemoy to the point of atomic war against the PRC. It soon became apparent that over Indochina too Washington was liable to act rashly. Because of the distasteful probability that Communist China would be present, Dulles was only reluctantly manoeuvred towards Eden's objective of a conference on Far Eastern issues by the prospect of settling the future of post-armistice Korea (not Indochina) and expected, as a *quid pro quo*, that the French would now put the EDC treaty, which had been signed as far back as May 1952, to the National Assembly for ratification.[49] This coincided with Eden's wishes. Part of the reason why the French had been so dilatory over ratification of the EDC treaty was a concern that with their own armed forces tied down in Southeast Asia, the Germans would dominate any integrated defence arrangement in Europe. Eden's growing interest in a conference embraced the possibility that it would be one which would discuss Indochina *as well as* Korea, thus giving the French some prospect of an acceptable escape from their Southeast Asian morass. He also shared with Dulles hopes that the French, in return, would be more amenable over the EDC. The converse, the British thought, was that if the present French government was not helped out of its difficulties in Vietnam, it would be replaced, in the whirligig of French domestic politics, by one which would entirely abandon the EDC project. Agreement was eventually reached for a conference of interested Powers to meet at Geneva in April 1954 to discuss the future of Korea. Indochina was only latterly placed on the agenda. It may be going too far to suggest that the summoning of the Geneva Conference 'had little to do with the Cold War in South East Asia and everything to do with the Cold War in Europe.'[50] Though the EDC might have been intimately tangled up with the French predicament in Indochina, the quenching of the highly combustible situation in Southeast Asia was an increasing imperative and Eden embarked on the road to Geneva believing that 'the best hope of a lasting solution [to the Indochina question] lay in some form of partition.'[51]

In the weeks preceding the conference the French situation had become so parlous that the Americans were increasingly ready to talk of 'united action' between the Western Powers to settle the Indochina problem. The British chose to define this as a broad collective security approach, making it clear that they wanted to see discussions towards a NATO-style system follow a clarification of the international scene at Geneva. It soon became evident – and confirmation of London's worst fears over American impetuosity – that what Washington had in mind was common *military* action, either threatened or real, to end Beijing's material backing for the Vietminh. Dulles's hard-headed view was that before any security organisation became permanent, its prospective participants should first prove their mettle by issuing threats backed by force to China. Indications that this was, indeed, what the United States were driving at had been inherent in Eisenhower's suggestion to Churchill on 4 April (three days, incidentally, before the President referred publicly to the 'domino theory') of a Southeast Asian coalition in that he had also intimated that 'appreciable' British ground forces were not envisaged by Washington. Eden picked up this nuance and was quite clear what the Americans were after when he met Dulles in London a week later. But, by accident or design, he failed to get it across to him that, whilst Britain wished to see a collective security arrangement, they did not envisage its immediate use as an instrument to browbeat China.[52] When the British put the brakes on Dulles's attempts to construct a coalition to fit his own model, the Secretary of State believed he had been deliberately deceived by Eden and relations between the two were to be soured by this at Geneva and beyond.[53]

On 26 April, a matter of days before the Geneva Conference was due to open, relations in the Western camp reached crisis point. News began to filter through that in a major set-piece battle around their garrison at Dienbienphu the French were heading for a calamitous defeat. In the eyes of the Americans this would be catastrophic for Vietnam and the whole of Southeast Asia. It would mark the end of France as a great power and thus have implications in Europe and also in Africa. Dulles's reaction was to reassert the need for joint military action with air strikes around Dienbienphu to relieve the French and, even when the realisation dawned that such drastic measures could not save the situation, to urge a scheme for collective action by the USA, the United Kingdom, France and the Philippines for intervention in Vietnam and possibly against China. If Eisenhower was to obtain the approval of Congress, British support was considered essential. 'We are', Eden's Private Secretary noted, 'much pressed by the dilemma. If we refuse to cooperate with the US plan, we strain the Alliance. If we do as Dulles asks, we certainly provoke the bitterest hostility of India and probably all other Asiatic states and destroy the Commonwealth. Also, a war for Indochina would be about as difficult a thing to put across the British public as you could find.'[54] This exaggerated British difficulties. Unlike its Labour counterpart in June 1950, the Churchill Government had no intention of following the Americans into another Asian adventure.[55] The consensus was that the Americans' was 'an amateurish plan' aimed to obtain an 'emotional response' from the French which would be rejected by the House of Commons, the Commonwealth and the Asian states.[56] Eden and the Cabinet's view was that the West's negotiating position would be enhanced if the Chinese were left unsure of what might be done to help the French and, despite his sensitivity to accusations at home of 'Munich', once at Geneva, Eden set out to work for a negotiated settlement based on partition.

One result of all this was that Eden's personal relations with Dulles (which, like his relations with Acheson, were seldom cordial) entered a further deep trough. At the Conference Dulles oscillated between trying to convince the British and the French (who were especially susceptible to such persuasion out of desperation to save face and possible influence in Indochina) of the need for wider armed intervention in Indochina and denying that this was his intention. In fact, when pressed, it was evident that the Americans had no operational plan to intervene. Not surprisingly, the widely held view in London was that an attempt to find agreement at Geneva was hampered by 'the uncertainty and essential insecurity of American policy'. Macmillan's more forthright opinion was that 'Dulles is crooked. He says one thing to one man and another thing to another.'[57] It may well be that the Secretary of State was playing a devious game, urging military action upon his allies without expectation that they would comply. In this way, the Europeans and not the Eisenhower Administration would receive the obloquy for appeasing Communism. Certainly, some

on the British side had the feeling that Dulles's emphasis on the necessity for Britain's approval for military action made them the
'whipping boys' for the failure of this to materialise. The pressure for
air strikes around Dienbienphu was also, no doubt, part of Dulles's
bid to stiffen French resistance in negotiation.[58] But there was more
to it than cool calculation. Dulles was clearly 'in a fearfully excited
state' over the situation at Dienbienphu and the Chairman of the US
Joint CoS also seemed to be 'obviously raring for a scrap', suggesting
that the American game was something other than poker.[59] Most likely, Dulles's twists and turns were the mark of an Administration divided
over the best way to deal with the problem of Indochina and with its
uncertain policy conducted by a figure who, at the best of times, was
liable to speak with a vagueness which could make his thoughts im-
penetrable.[60]

Eden's course proved the wisest. His skill and determination prevented a Conference which included resentful Americans, dejected
French and confident Vietnamese – who captured Dienbienphu on 7
May, the day before the Conference began to examine the Indochina
situation – from entirely collapsing. 'If it had broken up ... ', Eden
confided at the time, 'we would have been in World War Three by
now.'[61] Possibly, though this would have depended not only on whether
the Americans were serious about military intervention, as they probably were, but also whether the Soviet Union and China would have
thought Vietnam worth the risk of retaliation and therefore atomic
war. One close observer, at least, doubted whether they were.[62] This
is not to deny that the potential for a greater conflagration was entirely absent. But Eden, justly fêted as 'the King of the Conference',
needed others to assist him in defusing this possibility. Such aides
existed: Molotov fearful of atomic war; the Chinese anxious to appear statesmanlike during their first strut across the world stage; and
a new French Premier, Pierre Mendès-France, who came to office as
the Conference was unfolding on a ticket of finding a rapid solution
for the French in Indochina. Eden's achievement is that he kept his
eye on the ball he was playing; an acceptable negotiated settlement
based on partition followed by arrangements for a regional defence
organisation.

The outcome of the Conference, (which, incidentally, made no
progress whatsoever over its ostensible purpose, Korea) was that the
independent states of Laos and Cambodia were carved from Indochina and Communist Vietnam was divided from non-Communist along

the 17th parallel. After Geneva negotiations began which were to lead
to the setting up of a Southeast Asia Treaty Organisation (SEATO)
the following September made up of Britain, the United States, Australia, New Zealand, Thailand, the Philippines and Pakistan. Neither
of these outcomes had an air of permanency. No final treaty emerged
from Geneva, but only a series of Accords which the United States
sullenly agreed not to disturb by force.[63] As for SEATO, it failed to
attach to itself the formal military arrangements associated with NATO
and was hampered by antagonism towards it from the two major neu-
tralist Asian states, India and Indonesia. Even so, the British took
satisfaction over what had been achieved 'in spite of American "ham-
handedness"' and over Eden being 'the central figure and Britain the
leading country in the Geneva Conference. This is good, because so
unusual.'[64]

At the point when it seemed that a 'Far Eastern NATO' might be a
possibility, Eden was faced with the serious prospect of the collapse
of the real NATO. As we have seen, the Geneva Conference had been
summoned with half an eye to persuading the French to ratify the
EDC Treaty, which would thus create a European Army and allow a
controlled form of German rearmament. Since formulating it in 1950
the French had, in fact, become increasingly nervous of their own
proposal and tried to put the onus for its success on the British in a
series of attempts to entice them towards a more intimate arrangement with the EDC prior to French ratification. Eden's persistent
stance, identical to that of the preceding Labour Government, was to
associate Britain with the EDC short of joining it and to work for its
success whilst preparing a viable alternative should it fail. The French
sense of discomfort at the possibility of being locked into a European
Army with the Germans and without the British was real enough. So
too was their associated fear that, with the bulk of their forces engaged in Indochina, Germany was likely to dominate the EDC. But
they were also procrastinating. At root, as some realised at the time,
was that 'in most countries the European movement had been an in-
tellectual movement of the few', that 'Frenchmen are only just
beginning to realise (with a shock) what is involved in "Federation"'
and that 'when it came to the point, a European Army where German
Generals ordered about French troops, and where the great French
army (the finest in Europe) had to be merged in a European force,
took a lot of swallowing.'[65] When, in 1954, 'the great French army'
was routed by the Vietminh at Dienbienphu, Mendès-France was

unwilling to throw his weight behind such a divisive issue and the EDC Treaty was rejected by the French National Assembly on 30 August.

Though half-expected, the French action nevertheless sent shock waves through the NATO Powers. France was in danger of being isolated from her partners, in particular the Germans who felt a slight to their equality by the long-awaited *dénouement*, and for a second time Dulles publicly warned that the United States might have to 're-appraise' its policy towards the defence of Europe. The winner from this Western European disarray appeared to be the Soviet Union, with NATO in tatters and the possibility of the Federal Republic of Germany drifting into neutralism. There was even suspicion of French collusion with the Soviets and that 'many of the five [sic] EDC powers suspect [Mendès-France] of having wanted to sabotage EDC all along, and even of having made a deal about it with Molotov at Geneva, in return for the Indochina agreement.'[66] The bickering scene was set for another personal triumph for Eden and what has been termed 'the high point of British cold war/European diplomacy.'[67] Ten days before the National Assembly vote, Churchill had expressed the fear 'that if everything fails, the Americans may be forced to "agonising re-appraisal" (Dulles's phrase) resulting in "peripheral defence" and all that this implies' and that the 'EDC in itself is not important. NATO is the effective instrument. Even a modified EDC could help. If EDC fails we must make a supreme effort to "re-cast" NATO.'[68] This incorporates a concise summary of what Eden intended and ultimately achieved in the setting up of the Western European Union (WEU). Via this solution, Germany's rearmament was supervised by her alliance partners by bringing her into the 1948 Brussels Treaty as a preliminary to her entry into NATO – 'using the Brussels Pact on the basis of a European box inside the Atlantic (NATO) box', as Macmillan described it.[69] At the same time, Eden gave a commitment that British armed forces would remain in Europe so long as there was a threat to the security of the Continent, with escape clauses that this might be revised if Britain was faced with either an economic or overseas crisis. He had always been prepared to go this far and what he now waved before the Europeans 'was merely a more definite and succinct statement of Britain's intention than had been contemplated under the terms of Britain's association with the EDC.'[70] The real significance of Eden's salvaging of the wreckage of the EDC was that it was – literally – a confidence-trick. Providing a reassuring boost to allied partners in turmoil. No doubt too, fear that the West's disorder would only give succour to the Soviets made everyone in the Western camp – even the French – more disposed towards a 'NATO solution' of German rearmament.

Eden's success saw him lauded as the man who 'saved the Atlantic alliance'. Macmillan, who had never liked the 'federalism' of the EDC and who was another in the still lengthening list of those to claim credit for the WEU solution, believed it 'a great triumph for us' and 'a real pleasure to see England leading Europe'.[71] And so it was. Eden had done more than manoeuvre the West out of a crisis that threatened its most substantial collective security system. He had enlarged that system and by paving the way for West Germany's entry into NATO, he had banished immediate fears of German neutralism and given the West's most formidable Cold War structure almost its final shape before the collapse of the USSR. (Spain was to join in what was to be the last decade of the Cold War.) In this way, he underpinned and completed what Bevin had begun in 1949. The tide of opinion was in Eden's favour, but it is to his credit that he pulled the final arrangement together (despite unhelpful interventions from Churchill and Dulles) by a tireless round of complex negotiations in London, Bonn, Brussels, Rome and Paris and in the concluding nine Power conference at Lancaster House.[72] Some have been less magnanimous. It has been suggested, for instance, that Eden's fear that 'the whole Western alliance may collapse', that 'French negative policy would result in driving Germany into the arms of Russia and the US into "fortress America"' pressed Eden towards a solution which the Americans had by this time come to view as inescapable, and that he therefore found himself unintentionally playing out Washington's policy for them – an ironic twist to burden-sharing.[73] What this ignores is the fact that the Americans had always wanted the EDC and had not only been 'hopelessly wrong all through', but also remained firmly attached to the idea even after the French had rejected it.[74] Dulles made it obvious that he did not much care for the WEU proposal and 'complained that the Brussels Pact had no supranational features [and] that this is what had interested the US.'[75] But he was forced to admit that he had no better alternative to offer or 'at any rate he had not thought of it'.[76] The fact is that the Americans had not come up with an alternative to the EDC and the British had.

Implicit in the British method of conducting the Cold War – standing firm against Communist encroachments and constructing, with those willing to help take the strain, interlinking defence systems as a back-up – was the eventual necessity for dialogue. It was the line taken by the PUSC in 1952 and by Bevin before that. Eden too viewed the erection of a position of strength as the prelude to an eventual East-West accommodation to be reached through diplomatic intercourse. 'You cannot expect', he told Churchill, 'to get anything out of people if you won't speak to them.'[77] To set one's face against such exchange would not only have been a tacit admission of the permanency of East-West tension. It also risked, in a nuclear age, the intensification of rivalry, whether by purpose or error, to unimaginable proportions. Vanity, the esteem of being the focus of world attention, no doubt added a piquancy to Eden's proclivity for negotiation. It also happened to be, by all accounts, his *forté*. Churchill shared his Foreign Secretary's belief in the value of talking with the enemy. As he put it, over dinner in Washington in the summer of 1954, in a phrase which would gain immortality in a revamped form: 'meeting jaw to jaw is better than war.'[78] Before and during the 1951 General Election campaign, Churchill had spoken publicly of his desire for a 'parley at the summit' (an original use of the word for a top-level meeting) to ease Cold War tensions and inaugurate a *détente* in East-West relations through conversations at the highest level.[79] Once he was Prime Minister again, Churchill did little at first to move this idea along. In part, this was due to opposition in Whitehall and in Washington to broad talks on non-specifics which might unrealistically raise popular expectations and merely provide fertile ground for Soviet propaganda. More precisely, there were apprehensions that even the mirage of agreement with Moscow would increase French procrastination over accepting the EDC. However, with the death of Stalin in March 1953, Churchill's intention to talk with the new collective Soviet leadership gained a second wind. With signs emerging from Moscow that Stalin's successors also seemed interested in reducing tension over Korea and maybe over Germany, Churchill's mind turned towards the possibility of a unified and neutralised Germany as the basis for an East-West security pact which would bring *détente* to a troubled world.[80]

Persuasive arguments to douse the Prime Minister's enthusiasm were not always easy to muster. After all, the Foreign Office line on eventual accommodation with the Kremlin under Stalin had been based on the need for gradualism so long as the Communist regime existed 'in its present form'. Indeed, even though Churchill's ardour sprang partly from the self-absorption of a man determined to have his last major political initiative endorse him as the world's peace-maker, it was a position which basked in the glow of idealism and was founded on a sincere wish, which millions shared, to rid the world of the international stresses which might lead to nuclear annihilation. This may account for some of the ambivalence which frequently debilitated those who tried to dampen Churchill's enthusiasm for summit level negotiations. Eden, for instance, who was the greatest antagonist of Churchill's proposed summitry, was, on the other hand, 'very keen' himself to take up a suggestion from Churchill at the end of March 1953 of an Eden-Molotov meeting now there was a new climate. To the dismay of his advisers, who saw room for Russian divisive tactics, the Foreign Secretary was eager enough to set this up without consulting either the United States or any of the NATO states. It was presumably not an unimportant consideration to Eden that it would be he, not Churchill, who would be in the limelight and it took the pleas of Evelyn Shuckburgh, his private secretary not to 'go whoring after the Russians' who had 'been kicking us in the stomach for five years' to change Eden's mind.[81]

In May, and with Eden out of the way following a gallstones operation, Churchill grasped the initiative again. In a Commons speech on the 11th, delivered without informing the Cabinet, he urged a conference 'on the highest level' between the leading powers 'without long delay'. The ensuing flurry was sufficient for Eisenhower (who, like the Foreign Office, preferred talks on precise topics and had little taste for negotiations between Heads of State) to suggest to Churchill a tripartite meeting with the French (who claimed annoyance that the Prime Minister's initiative would cut across EDC ratification) at Bermuda. As so often, however, the reaction to Churchill's proposal was ambivalence. Returning from his convalescence, Eden remarked privately that Churchill's speech 'though brilliant – was dangerous, and if pressed too hard, might be fatal'. His own policy, he believed, 'of sustained pressure on Russia and the building of strength in Europe' was proving successful.[82] Macmillan had his own initial forebodings that Churchill's speech might mean that Central and Eastern Europe might be '"sold out" in a super Munich' and declared in the privacy of his diary that 'I shall *not* stay if we are now to seek "appeasement" and call it peace.' Later, however, he told the American Ambassador (who also at first had declared Churchill's speech 'great stuff ', though a month on thought it 'a mistake') that 'it was a world event of great importance. Nothing could put us or our policy back into the pre-May stagnation. It was on the move. We must learn to steer among icebergs.'[83]

Churchill, however, had the Captain of the *Titanic*'s disdain for icebergs. Temporarily incapacitated by a stroke on 23 June which prevented him from going to Bermuda, he was forced to witness the dilution of his idea of a summit meeting into Foreign Minister-level conferences on specific issues, which were arranged to meet at Berlin (on a German peace treaty) in January/February 1954 and Geneva (on Korea and Indochina) in April/July. His dour opinion was that 'this will be an age of continuous and more or less ineffective conferences.'[84] Three discernible imperatives drove him forward on his mission to promote a summit. There remained the genuine desire to bring peace in the face of the awful power of the hydrogen bomb over which he was increasingly given to brood. He was not alone in this. The nuclear fallout from American thermonuclear explosions in the Pacific between March and May 1954 caused world-wide protests against such tests and there was deep unease amongst the political leaders in the USA and the USSR over what these latest weapons spelled out for the future of humankind.[85] For Churchill, a summit tackling these developments would provide the final triumph of his political career. On a more directly personal level, but no less compelling, was that the prospect of a summit would provide counter-arguments to those who wished him to retire. He could not, his reasoning went, deal effectively with the Americans and the Russians if he was a 'lame-duck' Premier on the point of leaving office. Others suspected another factor. By the summer of 1954 Macmillan was 'persuaded that Churchill is now quite incapable – mentally, as well as physically – of remaining Prime Minister. Like many men who have had these strokes, his judgement is distorted. he thinks about one thing all the time – the Russia visit and his chance of saving the world – till it has become an obsession ... He has forgotten what barbarians the Russians are ... '[86] The suspicion that age and infirmity had robbed Churchill of a sense of proportion over the value of a possible summit had, in fact, existed well before his stroke. Ten months earlier Eden, as impatient heir-presumptive and therefore perhaps not always a reliable witness on such matters, thought that Churchill 'was now the wreck of a great man – a tragic wreck of one of the greatest men in our history.'[87] Underneath this was apprehension over what damage he might do if he ever got to a summit. 'He is, of course',

Macmillan averred, 'physically and mentally incapable of serious negotiation. In Washington or Ottawa, among friends, they tolerate the endless repetitions and the frightful waste of time, out of loyalty and respect. (Although Eisenhower did say to Eden "I don't understand how you do any business at all.") But with the Russians up against him, he would, of course, be absolutely lost.'[88]

For whatever reasons – idealistic, personal or medical – Churchill in the summer of 1954 continued to act out his obsession. First of all, to the irritation of Eden who believed that discussions on Indochina were at a critical stage, he engineered a Washington meeting with Eisenhower during the recess in the Geneva Conference. Whilst in Washington in June he obtained a surprising general endorsement from the President (who only recently at a rescheduled meeting with the British and French at Bermuda in December 1953 had declared the post-Stalinist government in the Kremlin to be 'the same whore underneath'[89]) for a meeting between Churchill and Malenkov (supposedly the leading figure in the Kremlin). Eisenhower even hinted that he might participate in it himself so long as it took place in London. The President's unexpected *imprimatur* was accounted for in the Foreign Office on the ground that 'Eisenhower passionately wants to be asked by the Queen for a State Visit to London, there is the simple explanation of his rather light references to the matter. It will not be for the *beaux yeux* either of Malenkov or of Churchill that Eisenhower may come to London, but for the Queen's!'[90] Having received some sort of blessing from the President (though not from Dulles[91]), Churchill, returning to Britain aboard ship and safe from either Cabinet or President, proceeded in the middle of the Atlantic to send a telegram to Molotov sounding out a possible meeting with Malenkov.

Churchill's wiliness almost brought his Government down. In Foreign Office eyes a high-level meeting would risk all kinds of mischief from the Russians. They would only try to separate London from Washington, and demand concessions over nuclear weapons and agreements which would wreck the EDC and possibly NATO.[92] Eden, who was afloat with Churchill, must accept some responsibility for failing to stand up to the Prime Minister. In Macmillan's view, Eden should have threatened to resign unless the Cabinet or the President was informed – though this would have been dangerously risky at this stage in the Geneva talks. As it was, the power of the Prime Minister's personality and, once more, the abiding ambivalence towards Churchill's final ambition again disarmed opposition. Eden, 'shockingly treated' according to Macmillan, 'allowed the PM to overwhelm him, partly with the strength and partly with the weakness of his appeal. he was absolutely determined; nothing would shake him; he would go alone; if his colleagues abandoned him, he would appeal to the country, who would support him. All this from strength. It was his last passionate wish – an old man's dream – an old man's folly, perhaps, but it might save the world.'[93] Some saw ambition rather than a noble docility in Eden's bearing. Shuckburgh, until recently his private secretary, was 'seething with contempt for him', believing he had entered a 'disgusting bargain' on the basis of 'this is the only way of getting rid of the old man.' The end result was that 'we are under the dictatorship of an old dotard, pandered to by the miserable A[nthony] E[den].'[94] Lord Salisbury, Lord President of the Council and stand-in Foreign Secretary when Eden was indisposed, was less vitriolic but hardly less judgmental. He was 'shocked' that Eden had given way to Churchill. Salisbury was told that 'he had a long tussle, but the old boy looked so old and pathetic, he hadn't the heart to say no.'[95] Probably the fairest verdict is that which blamed 'all [Churchill's] colleagues for not standing up to him – in fact applauding him to his face and then abusing him behind his back.' On this evidence, Macmillan was picked out as 'playing the dirtiest double game.'[96]

The Cabinet, which Churchill met on his return to dry land, was already facing a crisis over the outcome of the Geneva Conference, with the Americans threatening to boycott the second half of the Conference thus providing uncertainty over whether they would accept the inevitable compromise solution which would arise. There was also serious backbench opposition to the recent agreement over the Suez base. Into these choppy waters the Prime Minister insouciently dropped 'his second bomb. He told us that the decision had been taken to make the hydrogen bomb in England and the preliminaries were at hand.'[97] Astonishingly, the mood of crisis evaporated. Salisbury was the only senior Minister to threaten resignation (apart from Churchill himself, if he did not get his way), though if this was acted upon it was thought likely to create an avalanche of resignations and so bring the whole Government down. Salisbury's threat seemed bound up with the outcome of the Geneva Conference – if it was acceptable to the Americans, then they would accept an Anglo-Soviet Summit and he would acquiesce – compounding the pressure on Eden to pull off a success. And so it turned out. But it was the Russians who finally let Churchill – and his Government – off the hook. An anti-American statement from the Kremlin at the end of the Geneva Conference suggested wedge-driving tactics on Moscow's part and gave pause for thought. When this was followed up by a suggestion from Molotov of a meeting of Foreign Ministers (ignoring the Prime Minister's earlier invitation), Churchill was able to withdraw his offer of a 'top level' meeting, saving both face and Government.

By the end of the summer French rejection of the EDC, which made Western disunity too transparent for any meeting with the Russians to be contemplated, and an official visit by Attlee to Moscow, which Churchill confessed had 'taken the bloom off the peach' of any trip by him, marked the effective end of the Prime Minister's personal efforts to minimise the effects of the Cold War.[98] In April 1955, he reluctantly resigned in favour of Eden. In some ways his fixation was an embryonic vision of the *détente* which marked summit meetings over the next two decades.[99] Certainly, it was more inspirational and dramatic than an accommodation process 'likely to last decades', which was all that was on offer from the Foreign Office. A recognition of the validity of Churchill's concept, that the Cold War was not a permanency and that negotiation might produce an acceptable *modus vivendi*, had contributed to the equivocal attitude of Eden and others to the old man's dream. Even as Churchill was about to retire, Eden had begun laying the ground for a summit which would take place in Geneva in July 1955 and the ex-Premier was to remark mischievously 'how much more attractive a top-level meeting seems when one has reached the top!'[100] The rationalisation of this *volt face* in the Foreign Office was that with the EDC a dead issue and the capacity for Soviet disruption emasculated by the legerdemain of the WEU, the West was now negotiating from a sounder base. 'All the complicated questions involved in the new European settlement have been miraculously solved', Macmillan asserted.[101] Yet only a year earlier, opponents of summitry had argued the opposite view that the apparent thaw in the Kremlin after Stalin's death was due to 'the success of our own constant pressure and increased strength'.[102] That the Geneva Summit took place at all made it something of a milestone in the Cold War. But the fact that not much of substance emerged from it was grist in another form to those who questioned whether much could be obtained from the Russians at high-level talks. Probably, they were right. Assessments based on Soviet documents suggest that Stalin's foreign policy remained intact after his death and that the Kremlin's 'peace front' was a ploy to capitalise on Western discord over the EDC. This was complicated by the struggle for power taking place amongst the Soviet collective leadership. Malenkov, the Politburo member on whom Churchill placed most hopes, does appear to have been sympathetic towards the idea of a summit. Ironically, he was, in the summer of 1954, already a broken reed and any thoughts he might have had of meeting the Western leaders were overruled by Khrushchev, the rising star.[103] But neither Churchill (who did not get his summit) nor Eden (who did) could have known any of this for sure. Ultimately, it was less the *idea* of a summit which was unattractive to those who argued against it between 1953 and 1955 than the horror of a summit conducted by a decrepit Churchill. This was not quite fair for he was not blind to what was required. At Bermuda in December 1953 he had 'advocated what it amused him to call his policy of "Double Dealing". This he defined as a policy of strength towards the Soviet Union combined with holding out the hand of friendship.'[104] The truth was that no one any longer trusted Churchill's judgement and that 'all of us who really have loved as well as admired him, are being slowly driven into something like hatred. Yet we know that illness has enormously altered and worsened his character. He was always an egoist, but a magnanimous one. Now he has become almost a monomaniac.'[105]

Were Eden's methods of combating the Cold War more successful than those he had helped deny Churchill? In the short term; yes. The pattern which he had set for the foreign policy of the United Kingdom in his 1952 'British Overseas Obligations' paper, and to which he remained essentially faithful, produced notable achievements. Arrangements over Korea and Egypt consolidated the position of Britain and the West. More spectacularly, his penchant for piecemeal diplomacy defused the possibility of hot war over Indochina and laid new foundations for the Atlantic Alliance when his tireless attempts to breath life into the EDC had failed. SEATO, the Baghdad Pact and an enlarged and resuscitated NATO held out the possibility of hemming in a predatory Soviet Union across the globe. Moreover, this was done ostensibly as an independent associate of the United States and he was resistant to Churchill's blandishments for a more intimate Anglo-Saxon partnership to curb Communist expansion. Perhaps more remarkably, he was impervious to American pressure for more vigorous action in a part of the world where their interests were more considerable than those of the British. 'We are', Eden averred, 'no less aware of the dangers of Communist expansion in South East Asia than they are' but 'we have and are entitled to have, our own ideas on how best this can be done.'[106]

It is an impressive, but flawed prospectus. Whereas Churchill might well be criticised for living in a past where Britain could still mould affairs to suit its interests, Eden recognised that the world had moved on. Yet, paradoxically, he too sought an essentially undiminished British influence. His attempts to conjure away evidence of decline involved a further contradiction. Britain might attempt to ease its world-wide burdens onto American (and other) shoulders, yet the necessary distraction whilst this took place meant picking up other responsibilities. In practice the process meant that: Germany was re-armed, but the deal involved additional British commitments to Western Europe; the evacuation of the Suez base was finally negotiat-ed, yet this only nudged the search for a Middle East defence system further to the north and resulted in greater acrimony with Egypt; SEATO added to British obligations in Southeast Asia and defence spending was not significantly reduced at all. This raises the question of how long sleight of hand could disguise reality which, indeed, had already begun to cast a harsh light on his achievements in the Middle East and in Southeast Asia. The CoS, for instance, considered that rivalry between its member states and the lack of a coordinating com-mand structure made the Baghdad Pact a mediocre obstacle to Soviet encroachments. They also held similar reservations about SEATO.[107] For a short time, none the less, Eden's mastery of the international scene distorted his view of Britain's, and his own, ability to direct events.

The longer term success of burden-sharing was also impeded by the personal failings of the conjurer himself. Determination to stand up for British rights against the arrogance of American power sailed close to the Churchillian perception that nothing much had really changed. There was a risk too of estranging those from whom favours were expected. As it was, Eden's reputation for dispassionate calcula-tion shared uneasy quarters with more febrile responses causing him to fret over whether Britain's chosen partner was any less predatory than their common opponents. This was not an unreasonable assump-tion, though under stress it was liable to be given exaggerated expression. At Geneva he was willing to believe that, as well as sup-planting the French in Indochina, the Americans 'want to replace us in Egypt too. They want to run the world.'[108] The danger always lurked that burden-sharing could slither into asset stripping. Mingled with this was the recurrent problem of Eden's temperamental inability to work harmoniously with those he found uncongenial, whether it be Chamberlain, Mussolini, Acheson or, in the end, even Churchill. When he finally achieved the office of Prime Minister, his attempts to prove himself in the complex context of the Middle East provoked a collision with two more personalities who were distasteful to him – Dulles and Nasser. A brew was thus concocted which was to destroy both Eden and his strategy for managing Britain's part in the Cold War.

# 5

## DEDICATED TO *DÉTENTE*, 1956–63

On 26 July 1956 the Egyptian leader, Colonel Nasser, in response to
the withdrawal of Anglo-American funds for the construction of the
Aswan High Dam, announced the nationalisation of the Suez Canal
Company. The ensuing crisis culminated in an Anglo-French invasion of Egypt at the end of October. International outcry and financial
pressure from the United States led to a cease-fire on 6 November
and unconditional withdrawal from the Canal Zone in December. The
Suez Crisis was a complex affair. Many in Britain, Eden included,
believed that the Canal in potentially hostile hands spelled ruin. An
essential purpose, described by Macmillan, now Chancellor of the
Exchequer, was 'to humiliate Nasser – or there will be no oil to put
through the Canal'. As the crisis developed this was expressed more
shrilly: 'We *must*, by one means or another win this struggle ... *without
oil and without the profit from oil*, neither the UK nor Western Europe
can survive.'[1] At its most extreme, therefore, the Suez affair was driv-
en by a sense of a life or death struggle being played out between
Britain and the forces of Arab nationalism as manifested in the per-
son of the Egyptian leader, Colonel Nasser. The troubles of those
who held such views were compounded by being faced with an American Administration which, perhaps reasonably, did not share a sense
of acute danger and, less appropriately, for much of the crisis acted
duplicitously. Eden's persistent denials that Suez had been bungled,
'except, I suppose in failing to estimate that the Americans would
take the lead against us', was more than just self-serving rationalisation.[2] Dulles reproduced his line in schizophrenic policy statements
which he had practised at the Geneva Conference. In mid-crisis Eisenhower allegedly expressed the view to Macmillan that 'he was sure
that we must get Nasser down', though the difficulty here is that in
relaying this encouraging information to Eden the Chancellor, with

his own eyes on the Premiership, may have been being deceitful too.[3] For good measure, the crisis was also managed by a Prime Minister whose renowned diplomatic sagacity abandoned him under the strain of ill-health and whose desire to restore a wallowing domestic esteem lured him into decisions which would leave his reputation irretrievably sullied.

It was also a crisis about the Cold War. British self-interest in preserving their own presence in the Middle East was inevitably bound up with keeping the Soviet Union out and, immediately before the onset of the crisis, the CoS were sure that 'Russian interference in the Middle East has increased the instability of the area', whilst the IRD of the Foreign Office warned of Soviet penetration of Africa using Egypt as a 'bridge'.[4] Shortly after the withdrawal of British troops from Suez, Eden expressed the view that 'but for the events of this autumn Russia and Egypt would have been able to move at their own time and on their chosen objectives, and we would not have had long to wait. This [i.e. Suez] at least puts their plans in disarray.'[5] It had been felt for some time that a combination of social conditions and nationalism in the Middle East might easily throw up a credible 'fifth columnist' acting as a conduit for Communism. Nasser's decision in September 1955 to obtain arms supplies from the Soviet bloc seemed to some – Macmillan, Shuckburgh, as well as Eden – to enhance his candidature for such a role, though the first British instinct had been to buy him off by offering credits for the Aswan Dam.[6] Some of the American ambivalence before the crisis, as in distancing themselves from the Baghdad Pact, and then during it was due to their inability to make up their minds which was the worst scenario for the Middle East, American contamination with European 'imperialism' or Arab nationalist fervour subverted by world Communism. The signs are that 'what Dulles and Eisenhower were looking towards was American influence replacing that of the discredited colonial Powers.' Thus Suez 'was the climax of the [American] policy pursued since 1953. That it also removed a Prime Minister who refused to let British interests suffer simply to win nebulous American "goodwill" was a bonus ... This is not to say that the Americans designed matters this way, any more than that they designed them so Eden would fall, but when events put the attainment of these things in Eisenhower's lap, he took full advantage ...'[7]

There is plenty of evidence which points in this direction, though it may be that certain American attitudes were conditioned more by a visceral resentment of the British than carefully calculated policy and such an interpretation probably overstates the slickness of the diplomacy of the man Macmillan was wont privately to call 'dunderhead Dulles'.[8] What looks to be the clearest indication of a dedicated policy of American hegemony in the region, the declaration of the Eisenhower Doctrine in January 1957, which offered military and economic assistance to those Middle East states which felt threatened by Communism could well have been no more than a frightener aimed at Moscow which shortly before the Suez cease-fire had threatened Britain and France with rockets. Though there had been little direct connection between this intimidation and the collapse of military intervention in Egypt, Soviet 'atomic diplomacy' was obviously disconcerting to the West and one lesson from this for the British was that 'our recent experience over Suez ... brings out the danger if we were ever to leave our nuclear protection to the United States alone.'[9] More significantly, it seems that the Soviet leadership itself believed that it really was Soviet nuclear muscle which had helped win the day in Egypt and over its own rebels in Hungary. Such confidence may have supported it in the pursuit of more perilously adventurous foreign policies over Berlin and Cuba in the early 1960s.[10]

Britain continued to play a part in meeting these later challenges. But it is difficult not to see Suez as a turning point in the British contribution to how the Cold War might now be played out. No-one disputes the celerity, supported by the Foreign Office and the CoS, with which Macmillan, Eden's successor from January 1957, added balm to soothe the bruising which Suez had given to Anglo-American relations. But before 1956 the British had been junior, though far from sleeping, partners in this association. In their conception of how the struggle should be engaged they were frequently innovators. Many of what were to become the received idioms of the early Cold War – globalism, domino theory, nuclear deterrence, containment, *détente* and summitry – could claim to be British conceptions, though they may have failed to register the copyright to the precise terminology. Borrowing a cliché from the world of postwar technology, Britain was capable of remarkable invention, but others outpaced them in their application. Suez provided a further lurch in this general direction. Washington continued to place great importance upon British support, but something had been lost and politico/strategic creativity tended to become the domain of the Americans (though *détente* and summitry were to remain British preserves for a while longer) with the minor partner becoming more obviously the subservient accomplice – a position which Bevin, Eden and even Churchill had each in their own ways sought to evade. Of course, this demotion was on the cards anyway. From the early 1950s successive governments had grappled with a deteriorating economic performance and a recognition that defence expenditure was unaffordably high, as well as diverting too much skilled labour from export production. Even without the trauma of 1956, this made some retrenchment of Britain's world position difficult to put off. But Suez joined Munich in the British psyche as an indelible and recurring indicator of a world which had changed to their disadvantage.

One assessment of Suez argues that it encapsulated the failure of the British governing élite and that better leadership and resource management might have stopped or decelerated decline. As an exemplar of Britain's policy-makers being wise after the event, this critique alights on the ruminations of an ex-Foreign Office Permanent Under-Secretary, made seven years after Suez, that British interests might best be served by 'reverting to the style of diplomacy which we had employed up to the eighteenth century. This method consisted in essence of the weaker power playing stronger powers off against each other in its own interest, and putting its weight where it could see an advantage for itself ... We ought to continue to work with the United States but not to be subservient to them and not to be above some exploitation of events in our own national interest.'[11] This is not a bad sketch of what Eden had, in fact, tried to achieve. Suez, however, undermined the chances of success of his version of a policy of burden-sharing, the last, if slender, hope of any serious equality of contribution to the conduct of the Cold War. Eden mistakenly anticipated similar support over Suez, similar to that which Britain had been ready to provide in areas where she had no principal concerns, notably in the Far East. In making this assumption Eden, one of his biographers has suggested, displayed 'an attitude to the Anglo-American alliance, based on equality, to which no American government had felt it necessary to subscribe since perhaps 1943. That the United States was not prepared to treat its leading ally on the same basis she expected when the roles were reversed may have been irritating – even unfair – but it was a fact of international life and Eden had had plenty of time to assimilate it.'[12] But Eden was not blind to British inequality and that he was colossally wrong-footed over Suez was less a mark of his failure to recognise the 'facts of international life' and more a miscarriage of his method of coping with it and a misjudgement of the sway the weaker associate might have over the stronger.

Macmillan, whom the ex-Premier believed, like Dulles, had double-crossed him over Suez, had a not dissimilar approach to international relations to that of his discredited predecessor. He considered, as did Eden, that he had special talents to bring to diplomacy and was just as determined to keep a firm control over the running of foreign policy. Selwyn Lloyd, whom Eden had chosen as a cipher to replace what he regarded as Macmillan's over-zealous stint as Foreign Secretary ten months before the Suez crisis broke, was kept on. The Ambassador in Washington, Harold Caccia, an old wartime crony, frequently reported direct to Downing Street, by-passing the Foreign Office. There were other similarities. Eden's embittered reproach that Macmillan's government 'seems content to tag along as the 49th State, though this American government cannot run the other 48', overlooked the parallel with his own line of enticing American support in order to buttress British influence and to pursue British objectives.[13] But there were important differences in style and in emphasis. Macmillan's assiduous restoration and maintenance of the ties with the United States, first with Eisenhower and then with Kennedy, has been universally hailed. It was indeed a triumph, not least for the Prime Minister's ability to charm two generations of the American governing classes which, notwithstanding his own brand of allure, Eden was never capable of doing. Also, Macmillan's strategy of what he liked to call 'interdependence', harboured hopes of more intimate collaboration with the Americans than his predecessor had worked for, though their aims of maintaining a significant British voice in the world were comparable. In a rather later position paper on British policy for the 1960s it was affirmed that 'by exerting the strongest influence we can over our allies we can, in concert with them, maintain a better status than we can hope to have on our own.' This was pure Eden. The corollary of the study, that 'we may have to be more ready to subordinate [British interests] to the general interests of the West in order to carry our friends and allies with us' was not and represented the Macmillan variation.[14]

'Interdependence' was to have an intermittent appeal in Washington, but it was really recycled Eden for a post-Suez world, for if Suez had demonstrated anything it was that at a critical moment fundamental British policy was contingent upon the attitude of the United States. As added reinforcement, Britain's persisting economic difficulties, knocked further askew by the haemorrhage of dollar reserves at the time of Suez, meant that maintaining her world-wide commitments, as well as keeping up with the military technology as a central player in the Cold War, proved an unsustainable burden. Essentially what 'interdependence' came to mean was that the Americans should back Britain's overseas interests where this seemed to suit the common cause against Communism, whilst providing much of the hardware for the British to remain a nuclear Power. In this way, Britain would have the trappings, though not the reality of authority. Macmillan was, more or less, content to play along with this in a mock world-weary patrician style that had an appeal in Washington, especially if he could also stage-manage the occasional summit meeting to suggest that Britain still had a leading position in the international hierarchy. And, for much of the time, he had the aplomb to carry off with some conviction a sensation that British authority remained largely undiminished. His Premiership provides a remarkable episode in the lengthy and continuing history of the Anglo-American relationship, whether regarded as uniquely 'special' or otherwise, and helped prolong the hallucination of British power. In the shorter and more specific history of the Cold War, however, Macmillan's stewardship of British foreign policy merely marks a caesura between the mirage of influence and the decline into Washington's useful acolyte.

That there existed little inclination in Washington to provide a prop for British interests where these did not coincide with those of the United States was demonstrated quite soon after Suez. The lesson came in, of all places, the Middle East. That such instruction was necessary casts serious doubt on the opinion that it was Eden who was 'the last British Prime Minister who believed ... that Britain was still a world power, only temporarily weakened by the impact of the war years' or that Eden's Middle East diplomacy 'reflects the illusions of a passing age.'[15] His successors had their delusions too. Suez, of course, had to a significant degree been about the British perception of the economic and strategic significance of this part of the world for themselves. The crisis had not changed this and Macmillan was eager both to restrict the influence of Nasser and the advance of Communism in the region – sometimes taken to be the same thing. The restoration of friendship with the United States during 1957, which will be dealt with later, and Washington's fear of Moscow's intentions in the Middle East encouraged Macmillan to believe that, only a year after Suez, there might be the possibility of 'a joint Anglo-American plan for the whole Middle East area'.[16] Worries about the advance of Communism did indeed produce some convergence between London and Washington, but not as much as Macmillan appears to have wished. Both Powers were concerned over political upheavals which emerged in Syria during the summer of 1957 and seemed to favour the Soviets and which, to British eyes, Nasser was behind. But, despite blandishments from Macmillan, Washington shied away from military intervention. Even so, there was a sufficient meeting of minds between the two over what what was happening there to allow Macmillan to see it as a 'key to a great new venture' in the Western partnership.[17] What seemed at the time to be an associated military coup in Iraq in July 1958 undermined British influence with – so far as they were concerned – the big fish in the Middle Eastern pool, shattered the Baghdad Pact and threatened to spill over to neighbouring states.

Eisenhower's decision in July to send American troops into the Lebanon to prevent what was misjudged to be Communist/Nasserite/Iraqi penetration of that state tempted Macmillan to think even more in terms of a new order for the Middle East imposed by London and Washington acting in concert which would hold back the Russians, eliminate 'Nasserism' and expunge the shame of Suez. There was some co-ordination of Anglo-American plans for intervention in Lebanon but, as it turned out, the American desire to send strong signals to the Soviets of their intentions in the Middle East, decided them to move in alone. Later the same month British paratroops, in an attempt to prevent the turmoil from spreading, landed in Jordan. There is evidence to suggest that the Jordanian crisis was exaggerated by the British in their eagerness to be part of American action in the Middle East. If this was so, American endorsement of the British operation turned out to be lukewarm. What was more, in a kind of inverted echo of earlier events in Korea, nervousness that British forces might be trapped in Jordan prompted Macmillan to ask for American ground support. This did not materialise and British forces withdrew under the umbrella of the UN. Though his sequence of events was publicly hailed by the British Government as evidence of a revived association between the two Western Powers, what had happened in Lebanon and Jordan 'may properly be characterized as coincidental and contemporaneous than combined and concerted'.[18] Eden, grinding his own personal axe on the sidelines, complained that 'the Americans are at it again ... and we let [them] do just as they like. We shall soon have nothing left in hand East of Africa. Of this I am sure. American policy will ruin us. Nobody cares.' But Macmillan noted too that American Middle East policy 'seemed to be becoming all the time more fitful and uncertain.'[19]

A possible alternative to bowing to the capriciousness of the United States had already begun to beckon. Although the British had kept their distance from the negotiations between the Western European states for a Common Market which were to culminate in the Treaty of Rome in 1958, concern over the impact that such an organisation could have on the British economy had prompted investigation in Whitehall of a looser Free Trade Area which might be constructed under British auspices. There were also Cold War anxieties about what the Western Europeans seemed intent upon. With some states inside the proposed European Economic Community (EEC) and others, like Britain feeling unable to join, the development appeared potentially divisive and advantageous to the Soviets. On the other hand, there was a recognition that an economically powerful and rearmed Federal Germany, if not tied into to some closer European association, might be tempted to play off East against West.

Suez inevitably energised such thinking. Eden himself mused that one outcome of the débâcle was that Britain might have to work more closely in future with the Europeans.[20] Selwyn Lloyd, with the aid of his Foreign Office advisers, came up with something more specific in the form of a radical proposal which he presented to the Cabinet as his 'Grand Design' on 8 January, 1957.[21] This held two basic assumptions. The first, obviously induced by recent events, was that there were only two great Powers in the world – the USA and the USSR. Second, Britain's economic debility meant that she could not, on her own, match these two Powers. Though she would shortly have the hydrogen bomb, 'Britain cannot by herself go the whole distance. If we try to do so we shall bankrupt ourselves.' An alternative to opting out of the nuclear club altogether was, it was argued, to pool research, resources and skills with the other members of the Western European Union – which also comprised the states heading towards an economic Common Market. This would result in an association 'almost as powerful as America and perhaps in friendly rivalry with her'. Lloyd went out of his way to make it clear that he did not intend a revival of Bevin's 'Third Force' idea and that he envisaged it as a group within NATO. None the less, if this path was followed, Lloyd argued, the WEU could become a third great Power, the cost of defence would be spread amongst Britain's European partners and influence in the

Middle East and in Africa would be strengthened. It would also in-
sure against American withdrawal from Europe whilst the Federal
Republic of Germany would be bound more tightly to the West.

In different circumstances, this bold and considered scheme for
'sharing our defence burden with our friends in Western Europe' might
have appealed to Eden. But he was absent from the Cabinet discussion and presented his resignation as Prime Minister the following
day.[22] As it turned out, the 'Grand Design' was rejected in favour of
revitalised co-operation with the United States. It is not difficult to
see why. Lloyd's proposal, refreshingly iconoclastic in hindsight, must
have seemed to its audience a premature recipe for British retreat as
a global Power and a distasteful fusing of Britain's purpose and identity with the Western Europeans. On a more practical level, the United
States was likely to be hostile to the proliferation of nuclear arms
which the 'Grand Design' envisaged and fears were raised that, in its
annoyance, Washington might hinder British acquisition of uranium
from Canada and South Africa. The Cabinet chose therefore to continue to lean on the United States, even if this cut across commitments
only recently given to the Europeans. Macmillan was also absent from
the Cabinet discussions of the 'Grand Design', though his lack of response when Selwyn Lloyd returned to the argument in May – by
which time Macmillan was Prime Minister, highlights that at this point
Macmillan was not a Europeanist.[23] Indeed, by then, he was pursuing
a direction quite contrary to the 'Grand Design'.

In April 1957 the British Government defaulted on its commitment to the Western Europeans, given by Eden during the setting up
of WEU three years before, and reduced British troops stationed in
Germany by 40 per cent as a result of which, Macmillan acknowledged, the French were 'bitterly hostile' and the Germans 'rather
sore'.[24] This was one outcome of a review of British defence policy
instigated by Macmillan and published in April by the new Defence
Secretary, Duncan Sandys. The defence White Paper also ended con-
scription from 1960, cutting back the size of Britain's armed forces
by 300 000 emphasising instead a reliance on professional contin-
gents to uphold Britain's presence in the world. The package included
reductions in the size of the RAF's Fighter Command and the surface
capacity of the Navy. Britain's authority in future would rest on her
nuclear capacity to hit back destructively – what Dulles had chris-
tened 'massive retaliation' in America's similar 'New Look' defence
programme. Sandys's review was founded on assumptions which, as

we have seen, had crystallised well before Suez that nuclear weapons had made total war less likely and it was part of the continuum of the CoS 1952 'Global Strategy' paper and successive appraisals of defence, including an assessment in 1957, which took it as a given that a war involving NATO would be both global and nuclear. The other side of the equation, that 'in our defence programmes generally we are doing too much to guard against the least likely risk, viz., the risk of major war; and we are spending too much on forces of types which are no longer of primary importance' was one which the Chiefs were more reluctant to get to grips with.[25] Lloyd's 'Grand Design' was one solution to this dilemma. The Sandys review, on the other hand, sought a more orthodox path to a root and branch reduction of defence expenditure which would free industrial resources for non-military use without loss of international authority. It represented something of a triumph too for the current rather blithe assumption that the H-bomb 'is terribly cheap, really'.[26] In line with this, Macmillan wished to cut costs by further concentration on Britain's nuclear deterrent and the paring down of other defence commitments below the level required to prevent all-out war. Put another way, 'Britain would commit as little to Europe as it could get away with politically and continue to spread its forces thinly around the globe.'[27]

The difference between 1957 and earlier British attempts to cut their coats from less cloth was that Macmillan now installed an abrasive Minister of Defence in office, backed with new decision-making powers which liberated a predilection to overrule the different perspectives and the vested interests of the CoS who were, in any case, poorly placed to resist after the Suez débâcle. Sandys had also taken the opportunity to clear his proposed changes, which had obvious ramifications for the effectiveness of Western defence as a whole, with Dulles on a visit to Washington in January before entering the fray with the CoS. For good measure, Macmillan repeated the process at his first meeting as Prime Minister with Eisenhower in Bermuda in March.[28] In April Macmillan was able to reassure the President that the ensuing Defence White Paper (published on the 4th) had gone very well, though this naturally omitted to mention the extraordinary animosity which had arisen between Defence Minister and CoS which, on one occasion, descended to physical blows.[29]

A vital consideration underlying the Sandys reforms was that Britain was about to explode its own thermonuclear device. This, it was anticipated, would give continuing credence to an independent deterrent as well as providing weight in discussion with the Americans. There were, none the less, two looming drawbacks to this token of British might: first, the vulnerability of the delivery system of the V-bomber force to hostile attack when on the ground and to enemy defences once airborne; and second, the already escalating development costs. When he was Chancellor of the Exchequer, Macmillan had demonstrated a keenness to make short cuts in Britain's possession of a more credible deterrent by contemplating the possibility of persuading the Americans to site the latest advance in defence technology, intermediate range ballistic missiles (IRBM), in Britain while her own missile, Blue Streak, was being developed. At the same time he sought to co-operate with the US in the research and development of nuclear armaments.[30] The trials on a British thermonuclear weapon, which took place in May 1957 off the coast of Malden Island in the Pacific, appeared to provide Macmillan with important leverage with the Americans, demonstrating the UK as possessors of advanced nuclear technology and within a year of his Premiership, to his own surprise, both his objectives had been achieved.

During Macmillan's meeting with Eisenhower at Bermuda in March, the President repeated an offer made to Sandys in January to place 60 American intermediate Thor missiles in Britain with joint-control over their use. The Thor missiles would allow Britain an up-to-date nuclear striking capacity five years before her own IRBM, Blue Streak, was due to be off the drawing-board. On the debit side, there were those who believed the Government had rushed headlong into a deal, which magnified Britain's position as a prime bulls-eye if hostilities broke out, without capitalising fully on the bargaining chips this offered. There were those too who considered the Thor to be technologically dubious. This tended to be the favoured argument of some of the military who wished to strike back at the hated Sandys. The old friendship and respect between Eisenhower and Macmillan no doubt helped smooth the path towards all of this, as did the latter's powers of persuasion. Dulles, however, was rather less easy to appease. Though embarrassed by accusations from Sandys when he was in Washington that he had mislead Britain during Suez, he did not attempt to deny it.[31] Nevertheless, he continued to snipe and apparently told the West German Chancellor, Konrad Adenauer, that 'Bermuda was a failure' and that 'the British had no foreign policy and were finished.'[32] He also complained to others that Sandys's cutbacks meant that 'the British [are] outdoing us to adopt the theory to

treat any aggression as giving rise to massive retaliation.'[33] It goes
without saying that the Americans did not act out of charity. Nor do
Dulles's remarks suggest that they were particularly impressed by Britain's progress as a nuclear power. Given the British reduced
contribution to NATO and French jaundice after the Suez experience, they took the road they did principally from their own concerns
over Western defence. Added to this was Washington's desire to spread
their own mounting defence costs and to deploy the existing short-
range missiles in bases from which they could target the USSR.
Macmillan departed the Bermuda Conference in some elation, though
what clear-cut advantages he had earned for Britain is uncertain.

The outcome of a further meeting with Eisenhower in Washington
in October was different. The Soviet launch of the first Sputnik satellite on 4 October faced the Americans with the alarming possibility
that Moscow now had the capability, which Washington did not yet
possess, of launching nuclear warheads on an inter-continental ballistic missile (ICBM). It was a stunning development. The shock to
the USA of this peril to their own cities, Macmillan believed, was akin
to the impact of Pearl Harbor and Dulles's policies, he noted with
evident satisfaction, 'are said to have failed everywhere'.[34] He now
urged another meeting with the President, causing one American official to note that 'Mr Macmillan has found himself, possibly
unexpectedly, dealt a remarkably good hand.' 'Without desiring to
appear unduly cynical', it was observed, 'I think that the request by
Mr Macmillan for the meeting constitutes the supreme effort by the
British to regain their wartime position of exclusive and equal partnership with the United States. To the attainment of this objective,
they have tossed to the wolves their partner in their Suez adventure a
year ago, France, with a cynicism which I doubt the French will easily
or quickly forget.'[35] At the Washington meeting Eisenhower offered
to persuade Congress to bring an end to the restrictions of the Mc-
Mahon Act over the sharing of nuclear information. This and the
Bermuda offer of American missiles were signal developments and
the implications for the supposed 'special relationship' – no other
nation was offered such advantages – has not gone unnoticed by com-
mentators. Of the two, the former had the greater significance and
there was less criticism over obtaining an exchange of nuclear information and materials than over Thor. Without this concession, 'Britain
would have been unable to make use of the weapons systems which
the United States was prepared to supply' and from the early 1960s

'the links with the United States penetrated deeply into the realm of design and production of warheads.'[36]

At the close of his first year as Prime Minister, Macmillan could be forgiven for believing that 'interdependence' had real meaning. Reeling from the jolt of Sputnik, the Americans seemed especially ready during his visit to Washington in October to go along with his call for a 'marriage of heart as well as worldly goods' and the 'hope that agreement could be reached on this broad concept of working together since he was satisfied that in the world today no nation can now live alone.' Dulles's downbeat conviction 'that we were in a psychological crisis in the world' made even the cantankerous Secretary of State receptive to Macmillan's suggestions which seemed to 'give us an opportunity and a peg for constructive action' and he toyed with the idea of a joint 'declaration of interdependency'. Even so, the American view remained hard-nosed and Dulles's advisers suggested 'responding affirmatively in our own interests ... with our eyes open to the risks we are taking and we should certainly ask in return from the British such quids as they have at their command'. [37] The communiqué at the end of the conference, whilst making reference to 'interdependence', revealingly had the more opaque title of a 'Declaration of Common Purpose'. Meanwhile, the unenviable job of juggling with the semantics of what 'interdependence' might mean in practice was given to the Foreign Office. Its inescapable, if contradictory, assumption was that the partnership was based on 'two Powers of very unequal resources' that 'Britain in its relatively weak position, is already greatly dependent on United States support.' What, it was decided, 'interdependence' boiled down to was a 'constant effort to increase the degree of Anglo-American interlocking ... in order to make it as difficult as possible for any future American administration to go into reverse'. Again, this was really a post-Suez version of what Eden had tried to accomplish. That it was currently working in Britain's favour owed everything to a new and quite precise turn of events which were unlikely to last. As officials noted, the mutual dependence of the two states 'has been one-sided, for at bottom we have needed the United States more than they us, but the balance has been at least partially restored by Russian technological advances which have made American bases in Britain (and elsewhere) essential to the home defence of the United States.'[38]

An opportunity to exploit this tilt of fortune came over Berlin. During his first year as Prime Minister, Macmillan observed to Eisenhower that in the struggle against Communism 'there is a continual change in tempo and the spotlight seems to come now in one place, now in another. Some years ago it was all on the Far East, and then it changed to the Middle East.'[39] This was true, though Germany, the crucial arena at the heart of the most vital Cold War theatre, remained a potential flashpoint throughout the Cold War. The perpetual fear, shared by both West and East, that German militarism might reappear to cause havoc in the world became particularly acute in Moscow during the late 1950s with the growing economic prosperity of the FRG, West German rearmament and entry into NATO. Overtures for a reunited, neutralised Germany which came first from Stalin in 1952 and then from Beria in 1953, when the latter was making a play for the mantle of the late dictator, fizzled out. These were essentially tactical moves aimed either at disrupting the EDC or gaining advantage in the Kremlin's post-Stalinist in-fighting. The fact was that, despite the superficial attractions of German reunification, few viewed the prospect with any authentic enthusiasm. A reunited Germany, both sides feared, would either slip into their opponents ambit or play off East against West. Therefore, as Selwyn Lloyd put it, 'everyone – Dr Adenauer, the Russians, the Americans, the French and ourselves – feel in our hearts that a divided Germany is safer for the time being. But none of us dare say so openly because of the effect on German public opinion. Therefore we all publicly support a united Germany, each on his own terms.'[40]

An ultimatum from Khrushchev on 27 November 1958, which sparked off another, four-year long, crisis over the status of Berlin, was premised on the continuation of a divided Germany. This gave the Western Powers six months to leave West Berlin. Failure to comply would lead to a separate peace treaty between the USSR and the German Democratic Republic (GDR), with the East Germans taking over from Moscow control of all access routes into the city. Behind this was the threat that the West should recognise the legitimacy of the GDR, which they had refused to do since its inception in October 1949, or risk a new blockade when the East Germans took over the entry points into Berlin. Khrushchev's motives were complex, but a significant ingredient was Soviet apprehension over the economic strength of the Federal Republic and the pull it might be able to exert upon the much weaker GDR and even on Poland and Czechoslovakia. Behind this, with the prospect of NATO being 'nuclearised' by American short-range tactical missiles under Eisenhower's 'New Look', were fears over the control the FRG might eventually have over those weapons sited on her own territory. There was also the old fear that the West was intent upon pushing Germany eastwards. A part of Khrushchev's aim therefore was simply to loosen the West's grip on Berlin by pressing for the recognition of the GDR and the demilitarisation of the city. Another important result would be the weakening of West Germany's position on reunification and the possible insertion of a wedge between Germany and her allies. On another level, Berlin was merely a convenient pressure point for Khrushchev to obtain general concessions from the West. One indication of this, and an explanation of the attenuated nature of the crisis, was the extension of the ultimatum deadline, four times in all, whenever tensions seemed too high or if it seemed to the advantage of the USSR to do so. At this point too, though this conviction was to waver, Khrushchev did not believe that the West would press the Berlin question to the point of war. Britain and France, he judged, did not favour German unification whilst the Soviet development of Sputnik and the hydrogen bomb meant that 'America has moved closer to us – our missiles can hit them directly.'[41]

'Summiting', Selwyn Lloyd wrote, 'is an occupational weakness of any incumbent of No. 10 ... Since the war, Winston was the principal advocate. Eden disapproved when Foreign Secretary, but not when PM.'[42] This was a swipe at Macmillan. Like his predecessors, the Prime Minister had an eye on his present and future reputation as peacemaker as well as a genuine desire to ease international tension. To these were added Britain's post-Suez vulnerability in a world of increasingly sophisticated and deadly weaponry and a feeling that summitry was a way of burnishing Britain's tarnished world standing. The possibility of a summit had been on his mind for some time, but when articulated, it had met the same coolness from Cabinet and White House as had Churchill's earlier proposals. The crisis over Berlin provided a new opportunity, particularly following a public suggestion of a top-level meeting made by Khrushchev in December. As the Americans remained uninterested, Macmillan jumped at the chance of going to Moscow alone. This was not well received in Washington. Dulles considered the Prime Minister's chief motive was propaganda for the General Election due at the end of 1959. Adenauer thought this too. Both were correct, though Macmillan was driven by nobler purposes as well. Washington's reaction to the Soviet ultimatum was to make contingency plans to force a way through the autobahns to Berlin if they should actually be blocked. But the development of nuclear weapons and arsenals had made such brinkmanship much more of a potential danger than in 1948 and Macmillan was eager neither to push Khrushchev into a corner from which the Soviet leader could not retreat nor, his other expressed fear, to let matters drift towards war as in 1914. He did not believe that Berlin was worth atomic devastation and was tempted to wonder if, until the routes to Berlin had indeed been blocked, there was even a crisis at all, doubting 'whether we can make the question of whether Russians or East Germans approve the bills of lading or punch the railway tickets into a *casus belli*. What matters is whether civil and military supplies actually reach Berlin.'[43]

This was a commonsense approach. There is, however, room for doubt whether his enthusiasm for putting this to Khrushchev in direct talks was the wisest course. The visit to the Soviet Union which took place in February 1959 was to earn him plaudits at home as the first Head of a Western Government to do so since the Cold War had begun. This was part of the exercise. But he also attracted the irritation of the Americans and, maybe more significantly in the long run, his Western allies in the process. Some of this exasperation, no doubt, sprang from jealousy at Macmillan's stealing the limelight. Though there was also a fear that in the Communist lair the British might give away too much. This may not have been an unjustified concern. Courted, insulted (over Suez) and snubbed in turn, the British contingent appears to have been tempted to avoid complete humiliation by stepping beyond the agreed Western line by raising the prospect of recognising the GDR.[44] Other leaders meeting the Soviets, notably John F. Kennedy two years later, were submitted to similar rough treatment, though inducing British ministers to scud across ice in a wicker basket seems to have been a unique form of indignity.

By narrowly eluding a diplomatic catastrophe the visit was able to make some contribution to Macmillan's election victory in October 1959. It is sometimes contended that his efforts in the Soviet Union earned him a postponement of the Soviet deadline for the settlement of the Berlin problem, though the length of the ultimatum was, as already noted, always singularly elastic. Nothing else on the urgent matter of Berlin was resolved and a later American evaluation which judged Macmillan to have 'made a lone wolf journey to Moscow and returned with an empty sack' seems about right.[45] It has been put forward in support of Macmillan's 1959 venture that 'if the same spirit had been shown by Eisenhower and de Gaulle early agreement over

Berlin and East Germany ... might have been reached', though what kind of arrangement this might have had to have been is open to question.[46] It is true that the Foreign Office was aware that Khrushchev's demands contained a strong element of bluff and the Americans, French and Germans were more inclined to call this than were the British.[47] But the Western decision to defend Berlin in 1948 meant that an inordinate amount of prestige rested on the future of the city and any retreat now, without clear gains, would provide a notable propaganda victory for the Russians. Nor was there any indication from the Soviets of a desire for a settlement other than on their own terms. An eagerness for face-to-face discussion, as Macmillan's earlier criticism of Churchill's *détente* efforts had noted, dangerously skirted abandoning negotiation from strength – what the old man himself had called 'Double Dealing'.

The Berlin issue dragged on at Khrushchev's whim for a further two years, reaching an ominous peak on 26 October, 1961 when American and Soviet tanks came muzzle to muzzle across Checkpoint Charlie – an entry to the Soviet Sector of Berlin which, since August of that year, was part of a barrier of concrete and barbed wire erected across the city to staunch the haemorrhage of East German workers heading for the West. Two old hands at Cold War diplomacy, Frank Roberts at the Moscow Embassy and Dean Acheson acting as an informal adviser to the Administration in Washington, had each predicted that 1961 would see a more forward Soviet policy over Berlin. When this materialised in the form of Khrushchev's raising of the Berlin Wall (after some prompting by the Poles and East Germans) it did not shift the British view that only nuclear war could prevent the Russians from strangling West Berlin if they chose to do so and that, despite the rhetoric, West Berlin was not worth a holocaust. With Kennedy now in the White House, the British noted a more perceptible willingness than Eisenhower had evinced to negotiate over Berlin, though the new Administration also drew up contingency plans for another airlift and the distribution of fallout shelters for US citizens. This tended to cut across Macmillan's prevailing preference for some compromise over Berlin based on a larger military disengagement in Central Europe. Despite Macmillan's assertions to the contrary, an impression was left in Washington – as well as in Paris and Bonn – that if the crunch came over Berlin, the British would not resist the Russians.[48]

The stage which the Prime Minister envisaged for a settlement of the Berlin question was another summit with Khrushchev. Part of the propellant was Macmillan's acute sense of History which encouraged him to think in wider terms of nineteenth century-style international system-building as a bolster to British prestige. Though he privately mocked de Gaulle as 'Rip van Winkle' who 'talked about the "Concert of Europe" and seemed not to have realised what has happened to the world since the end of the Second War', Macmillan had his own delusions.[49] During his first year as Prime Minister he had expanded to Dulles upon co-ordinating 'the free peoples on a scale not yet seen'. He doubted that 50 or 60 years on 'we would be still existing in our separate and independently sovereign relationship. We must unite and use our assets effectively or we will lose them all.'[50] This kind of collaboration seems to have been in his mind as a way of resolving the volatile situation in the Middle East during 1958. More generally, he was inclined to invoke the notion of summit meetings as a sort of revival of the post-Napoleonic Congress System and as 'a more or less continuous or permanent Conference – adjourning for long periods and reassembling for new work, with Ministers attending from time to time, and officials (Ambassadors, etc.) working on committees and reporting to Ministers. Such a Conference, or Congress would in itself "relieve tensions".'[51] The process might also, through accretion, produce a final *modus vivendi*. His meeting with Khrushchev in February 1959 merely reinforced this attachment to the vision of summits grandly gathering in successive capitals each year.

Eighteen months after his visit to Russia Macmillan had to face up to the collapse of his hopes for a new Congress System and a corresponding consolidation of de Gaulle's notion of a 'Concert of Europe'. His verdict after the Russia trip that business could only be effectively done with Khrushchev at a wider summit was, in itself, a part-admission of British impotence. And there was always the danger that the United States, brushing aside British *amour propre*, would elect to handle East-West tensions without reference to lesser allies. This seemed about to occur when in September 1959, to the Prime Minister's dismay, Eisenhower, who had thus far steadfastly resisted pressure for a summit, invited Khrushchev to visit him at his Camp David retreat. Macmillan's Russian visit could be credited with opening this door, but, of course, once it was ajar, the British risked finding themselves left out in the cold. As it turned out, and to the great relief of Macmillan – 'who by now was prepared to go anywhere at almost anytime so long as he had a summit to go to' – the Eisenhower-Khrushchev conversations cleared the way for a Heads of State meeting which was scheduled for Paris on 16 May, 1960.[52]

The Paris summit turned out to be a humiliation for Eisenhower, but a personal disaster for Macmillan. The interception of an American U-2 spy plane by a Soviet rocket in the heart of Russia, with some irony on May Day, doomed the summit before it began. Khrushchev, characteristically overplaying his hand, demanded an abject apology from Eisenhower when the two arrived in Paris. It was not forthcoming and the summit was prematurely brought to an end. Though Macmillan was annoyed at the Americans for permitting such sensitive intelligence operations so close to the date set for the summit, the reality was that Britain was intimately involved with the USA in aerial reconnaissance over the Soviet Union. Less famously than the U-2, another spy plane, an RB-47, was also shot down by the Russians over the coast near Murmansk after the Paris meeting. This had, as the Soviet Government knew, taken off on its mission from RAF Brize Norton and continued a process of Anglo-American collaboration in aerial intelligence gathering which had existed since Attlee's first Government and continued under Churchill.[53] Since 1948 the RAF had extended its electronic intelligence operations over Communist territory using bases in Germany, Iraq and Honk Kong to listen in to Soviet and Chinese signals traffic. In 1952 British pilots in American planes – presumably with Churchill's authority – penetrated Soviet airspace as far as Moscow on a potentially provocative photographic reconnaissance mission. At the Bermuda Conference in March 1957 Macmillan had agreed that U-2 flights could operate from British bases and by the end of the decade some U-2 missions had British pilots.

For Macmillan the failure of the summit meant the postponement of any chance to negotiate a settlement of the Berlin issue, the disappearance of any 'thaw' in East-West relations which his visit to Russia may have helped to induce, a deterioration in his relations with Eisenhower who believed the Prime Minister had not provided him with sufficient support in Paris and a corresponding cooling in the 'special relationship' which Macmillan had done so much to re-establish. British impotence when confronted with the power games of the Superpowers was thrown into high relief. Most significantly, Macmillan's hopes for a international system based on summitry was in ruins. Though he was to continue with half-hearted attempts to orchestrate a further summit meeting, 1960 witnessed the last Four Power meeting until the Cold

War was almost over. His private secretary later recalled that 'I never saw him more depressed ... this was the moment he suddenly realised that Britain counted for nothing.' 'We have', Macmillan himself told the Queen, 'fallen from the summit into a deep crevasse.'[54]

But British problems ran deeper than this. Macmillan's dejection coincided with the augmentation of two other perceptible developments which threatened to undermine further Britain's position as a major player in the Cold War. These were: the rapid technological development of nuclear weapons; and the emergence of an international power-base in Western Europe – de Gaulle's 'Concert of Europe' – as a latent alternative to Britain's own. Macmillan had always been concerned that Franco-German moves towards developing a European Economic Community were politically disadvantageous to Western Europe during the Cold War. One motive for the British proposal for a Free Trade Area (FTA) in Europe as an alternative and associated structure to the EEC was Macmillan's concern that these divisions would only rebound to the advantage of the Kremlin. 'It depressed him', he said to the French once their opposition to a FTA had become clear, 'to feel that the French Government had decided that Sparta and Athens must quarrel. The Russians were getting stronger all the time and here was the free world voluntarily weakening and dividing itself. History would regard this as the crowning folly of the twentieth century in Europe.'[55] Such admonitions had no impact on the French or Germans whose 'axis', if anything, was strengthened by Macmillan's reaffirmation of the Anglo-American relationship and dismay at his gallivanting in Moscow. By the time of the failed summit, the EEC had been set up and was beginning to look like an economic threat to Britain. What was more, the United States was clearly in favour of the EEC and wanted Britain to join it rather than invent complicating alternatives. This raised the nightmare of Washington deciding to work more closely with the six countries of the EEC than with Britain. Shortly after the collapse of the Paris summit, a Cabinet Committee noted that the EEC 'may well emerge as a Power comparable in size and influence to the United States and the USSR ... We should find ourselves replaced as the second member of the North Atlantic Alliance and our relative influence with the United States in all fields would diminish.'[56]

These accumulating considerations decided Macmillan during the early months of 1961 that Britain must apply for membership of the EEC. The key to success was de Gaulle. Persuading the French President was likely to be difficult and it was recognised that some form of inducement would be necessary. One which Macmillan had had in mind since 1959 was a half-turn back to the rejected 'Grand Design' of Selwyn Lloyd by offering the French a nuclear partnership with Britain coupled with an informal tripartite (US-British-French) ascendancy within NATO.[57] Whether this was likely to have been persuasive, whether de Gaulle believed that Macmillan *had* offered a nuclear deal only to renege upon it and whether this belief influenced his decision to veto Britain's application to join the EEC in January 1963 are all open to speculation. What is certain is that the climax of negotiations for Britain's entry synchronised with a point when the theory of Anglo-American 'interdependence' came glaringly into question. The American Thor missiles furnished to Britain following the Eisenhower-Macmillan talks in Bermuda in 1957 were intended as a stop-gap until Britain's own ground-launched IRBM, Blue Streak, and air-launched missile, Blue Steel, were in service. By the end of 1958 this development had come under serious attack with the then Chancellor of the Exchequer, Derick Heathcote Amory, calling for the cancellation of Blue Streak on the ground that it was likely to cost around three times the original estimate of £200 million. Amory's doubts were brushed aside by both Sandys and Macmillan. By early 1960, however, the CoS had also come out against Blue Steel and Blue Streak on the basis of their vulnerability to attack and they were finally abandoned. In March, Eisenhower agreed as an alternative to sell Britain the air-launched missile, Skybolt, to which the British could fit their own warheads. Given an unrestricted choice, most in Whitehall would have opted for America's planned submarine-launched missile, Polaris. Skybolt won through partly because it was seen as a way of extending the life of the obsolescent V-bombers but also because Britain did not have the submarines to accommodate Polaris and because of the American strings attached, which would mean that its acquisition would involve linking the British deterrent to NATO. Macmillan, none the less convinced himself that he was given the option to take up Polaris should Skybolt, which was still in the development stage, not come up to scratch.[58] As part of the deal, the United States was permitted to build a base for Polaris in Scotland and construct an early-warning radar system in North Yorkshire.

By the end of 1962 this arrangement had gone badly wrong. This was partly bound up with the emergence of the Kennedy Administration at the start of 1961. Despite early misgivings over how he might relate to a man 20 years his junior, Macmillan managed to develop a very solid rapport with the new President which was to stand the Prime Minister in good stead. Macmillan's apprehensions were understandable, not least as some of the warmth of the relationship which he had worked hard to foster with Eisenhower had already palpably disappeared before the change in Administrations. Also, the British were now faced with a new generation in office which included Dean Rusk, the Secretary of State, and Robert McNamara, the Defence Secretary, neither of whom were particularly Anglophile and who, moreover, looked with some distaste at Britain's nuclear pretensions. Faced with advancing Soviet nuclear strength, the White House under Kennedy drew back from the previous Administration's defence policy based on 'massive retaliation' as lacking subtlety and began to develop what was termed a 'flexible response'. This, amongst other things, implied an increase in conventional forces to permit action beneath the nuclear threshold. This coincided with a similar British retreat from reliance on the nuclear deterrent and the expansion of the conventional defence arm at the height of the Berlin crisis. The new American approach also embraced a determination to avoid being pressed into nuclear retaliation triggered by circumstances beyond Washington's control. Here US defence thinking meshed less well with the UK and with the Americans picking up on obliquely expressed British fears that if the crunch came in Europe, Britain's deterrent would be necessary to push a reluctant America into action. To the American mind, their new thinking argued the redundancy of the British independent deterrent. Additionally, there was the feeling that the resentment in Western Europe at Britain's privileged position, now regarded as an error of judgement by the Eisenhower Administration, was a justification for nuclear proliferation – actual in the case of France, potential in the case of the FRG.[59]

Increasingly, Washington's preference was for what was called a multilateral force (MLF) for Western Europe. One intention of this rather vague concept was that by providing the European NATO states with a fleet of surface vessels with armed Polaris missiles and with crews of mixed nationalities, it would allow them the illusion of a finger on the button even though the intention was that the ultimate decision would rest in Washington's hands. There was no obvious role for an independent British deterrent within an MLF and the strong view of the State Department was that the alternative of a simple Anglo-French ascendancy within NATO would be a divisive and com-

plicating factor. These signals could only have added to British unease as they hesitantly began to move towards European co-operation.
When it came in December 1962, Washington's decision to cancel
Skybolt, mainly on the ground of excessive cost but announced before consulting the British Government, was judged by many – and
not without some foundation – as merely a ruse 'to drive Britain out
of the nuclear business'.[60]

Macmillan, with his Foreign Minister (Lord Home), his Minister of
Defence (Peter Thorneycroft) and Solly Zuckerman (Chief Scientific
Adviser to the Ministry of Defence), arrived at a scheduled meeting
with Kennedy at Nassau in the Bahamas on 19 December in an angry
frame of mind, though some of this show of temper may have been
theatrical to thrust the moral responsibility of providing an acceptable replacement onto the shoulders of the Americans. Their
assumption that the 1960 agreement meant that Polaris was now au-
tomatically on offer was, indeed, over-optimistic. Kennedy's dilemma
was 'the complexity of the problem which appeared to involve grave
political risks for Mr. Macmillan if we should not help him, and serious risks for our own policy in Europe if we should help him too
much.' This meant giving the Prime Minister a hard time. Macmillan
had to endure three days of tough bargaining in which he refused an
offer that Britain share the further development costs of Skybolt or
to accept an alternative air-to-ground missile, Hound Dog, which
would not fit the V-bombers. In fact, Kennedy had already conceded
to his colleagues immediately prior to the Nassau meeting that his
bottom line was that the British should be offered 'appropriate components of Polaris missiles' on condition that they be committed to
an eventual multilateral force within NATO.[61] Thus Macmillan's
achievement at Nassau was not to obtain Polaris, which the Americans had already agreed amongst themselves to offer. His feat was
that, though the British missiles were to be 'assigned' to NATO they
would be released from this if Britain's 'supreme national interests'
were involved. This, coupled with the ambiguous phraseology of the
agreement, gave him ample scope for wriggling out of the disagreea-
ble concept of the MLF and maintaining the pretence of British
nuclear independence.

The cavalier manner in which the Kennedy Administration handled the cancellation of Skybolt can be put down to its preoccupation
with more weighty matters, given that the Cuban Missile Crisis had
reached its peak only two months earlier. But it also suggests that the

UK was seen as one of several American allies in a world where only the strength of a Superpower really counted. Conversely, Macmillan, against the odds, was given exceptional favours at Nassau. This echoes a dual pattern discernible during the more intense drama which had recently been played out over Cuba. Kennedy's intimate phone calls to Downing Street and the advice sought of the British Ambassador, David Ormsby-Gore, during that crisis are often cited as evidence of British influence at the moment when the Cold War reached its most terrifying climax. But this conferring must be seen more as an indication of a President with terrible responsibilities talking over half-made decisions with respected friends in order to draw encouragement rather than approaches from an ally seeking the approval of an equal partner. Though Washington conceded to British suggestions over relatively peripheral issues such as the publication of the photographic evidence of the Soviet missiles in Cuba this, alongside Foreign Office pernickertiness over the legality of the American blockade of the island, may have seemed to some in Washington a rather less forthright public stance – as also seemed to be the case over Berlin – than was, say, de Gaulle's. An overture by Macmillan to have the 60 Thor missiles based in Britain disarmed as part of a bargaining counter for the dismantling of the Soviet missiles on Cuba was not taken up. On the contrary, it would seem that during the crisis the RAF took its lead from the United States' Strategic Air Command putting the Thors and V-bombers in a state of readiness for action at 15 minutes notice. It is unclear whether the Prime Minister was fully aware of this, whilst Alec Douglas-Home, then Foreign Secretary, later admitted his ignorance. The British Government's specific approval, supposedly necessary as a 'fail-safe' measure, might well have proved academic had the critical moment arrived for, alarmingly, during an earlier wargame using the Thors, a screwdriver had apparently served as an effective alternative to one of the temporarily absent 'dual keys'.

On the diplomatic level there was a more transparent inclination to discount the British. Though Macmillan warned throughout the crisis against any deal with Khrushchev which involved a tit-for-tat dismantling of American missiles in Turkey for a removal of the missiles in Cuba, this was precisely what Kennedy did and the secret arrangement which Washington and Moscow eventually arrived at defused the situation. As Ormsby-Gore later admitted, 'I cannot honestly think of anything said from London that changed the US action

– it was chiefly reassurance to JFK.'[62] Maybe this was just as well. Urged on by 'the frightful desire to *do* something', Macmillan was initially inclined to advise invading Cuba 'and have done with it'- a phrase excised from a first draft of a letter to Kennedy, though it did appear in his first telephone conversation with the President during the crisis. Macmillan went on to add that 'in my long experience we've always found that our weakness has been when we've not acted with sufficient strength to start with.' We know that during the Cuban Crisis Kennedy had the Munich exemplar in mind. It may be that Suez too presented conscious lessons, spurring him on to finish quickly what he had begun – though not in the way that the Prime Minister advised. There was also a contemporary analogue. In both London and Washington the crisis was seen as a kind of extension of the Berlin contest and there was a frequent expectation that either some move would be taken there while attention was distracted in the Caribbean, or that Cuba would be used by Khrushchev as a lever to obtain concessions in Berlin. As it turned out, the mutual fright provided by Cuba helped dissipate tension over Berlin. Though by this time Khrushchev had, anyway, come to doubt both the passivity of the West if he should press ahead with a separate treaty with the East Germans and Moscow's ability to support the GDR during any economic embargo which might follow. As for Macmillan, possibly influenced by signs of alarm in public opinion, he soon moved away from pressing swift military action, though there was little he now suggested which the White House appears to have found helpful. The editors of the tapes on which Kennedy secretly recorded the deliberations of the Executive Committee of the National Security Council as it edged its way through those awful events suggest that it is 'obvious from these records that Macmillan and Ormsby-Gore became de facto members of Kennedy's Executive Committee, though we suspect that by October 26 [ the day on which Macmillan suggested immobilising the Thor missiles] Kennedy had become skeptical of the quality of Macmillan's advice.'[63]

This may have had some bearing on the fact that Nassau was not an agreement without strings. The British agreed to increase their conventional forces in NATO. Also, as we have seen, the missiles which Britain was to receive were to be 'assigned' to NATO, to be used for the defence of the Western Alliance except when Britain's 'supreme national interests' were at stake. As Macmillan commented, 'these phrases will be argued and counter-argued. But they represent a genuine attempt (which Americans finally accepted) to make a proper contribution to *interdependent* defence, while retaining the ultimate rights of a sovereign state.'[64] This was a patent attempt to square the circle and as so often with such efforts the result was sophistry rather than geometry. Macmillan was at pains to claim that interdependence was not a synonym for dependence and that, in his words, 'interdependence and independence were the two sides of a coin.'[65] This, of course, is a phrase often used as an analogy for opposites. But what Macmillan clearly meant was that a close harmony of interests existed between the two, though his sense of the expression was plausible in its strictest sense only at those moments when Britain could offer the United States a means of striking at the USSR which Washington otherwise did not possess. This was the position at the time of the 1957 Bermuda agreement when Thor missiles in East Anglia permitted the Americans to work to the *Time* magazine formula that IRBM + NATO = ICBM.[66] Five years on, with an obsolescent bomber force, outdated missiles and the prospect of soon having no practicable nuclear capability unless the United States provided them with one, the British had little but their aspirations to contribute. Moreover, as the age of the actual ICBM dawned a separate British capability seemed to Washington not only redundant, but dangerous. A basic flaw in the rationale of 'interdependence' was the assumption that having bases and warning systems in Britain was indispensable to the United States, as opposed to important. On their side, the Americans assumed that 'British motives are more political than military, for they must realise the additive factor to free world nuclear strength provided by their strategic force is at best marginal.'[67] What Kennedy recognised at Nassau was the continuing potency of the totem of nuclear capability to British claims to international authority and, on the narrower level, to Macmillan's own hold on political power. Though Kennedy was averse to an independent British deterrent, it was offered out of friendship for Macmillan and concern over the consequences of bringing his government down. At the same time, the agreement was hedged by references to an MLF and an offer, which de Gaulle rejected, of Polaris to the French too.

But, in the last resort, independence/'interdependence' was about control rather than construction. The British had long recognised their subservience to their greater partner in such matters. Early in 1956 American B-29 bombers had acted as delivery vehicles before

V-bombers were operational. Blue Streak had itself relied upon American technology. The crucial consideration was that, in the final analysis, the deterrent should be under an independent British *command*. Yet even before Nassau, Macmillan's private secretary doubted 'whether we could in fact use our deterrent independently.'[68] After Nassau a former Chief of the Air Staff wrote of the 'really appalling thought that a couple of Ministers and a zoologist can skip off to the Bahamas and, without a single member of the Chiefs of Staff Committee present, commit us to a military monstrosity on the purely political issue of nuclear independence – which anyway is a myth.'[69] Whose finger was on the button was bound up with questions of how war, hot or cold, might be contested. But, unlike ten years earlier, the British had neither the prestige nor the muscle to be innovators in this direction. The fact was that 'with the move to concepts of flexible response shaped by the state of parity between the superpowers Britain ceased to be a key player in the development of nuclear strategy.'[70] Macmillan's Ministry of Aviation, who 'found it difficult to feel complete confidence that the Americans will in fact deliver the missiles' suggested an alternative to reliance on the United States. This proposed offering to work with France as a *quid pro quo* for easing Britain into the EEC: 'if de Gaulle says "Yes", we shall be in the Common Market and we will have a truly independent deterrent. If de Gaulle says "No" we shall have to stretch our existing deterrent as far as we can and either hope for Polaris or make a new missile on our own.'[71] Whether de Gaulle might have been open to such persuasion is doubtful. When the chips were down, however, Macmillan chose to place his trust in the United States, giving de Gaulle the excuse for spurning Britain's application to join the EEC. The independent deterrent and a viable policy towards Europe which would preserve the preeminence of sound Anglo-American relations had each taken a buffeting. 'All our policies at home and abroad are in ruins', he confided despairingly to his diary.[72]

Macmillan's delusions over Britain's capacity to cut a major figure on the world stage had come to grief as surely, if not as publicly, as had Eden's. In the midst of this disarray, which was accompanied by deep domestic difficulties, there appeared something of a triumph. This was the Partial Nuclear Test Ban treaty of July 1963 which prohibited atmospheric (though not underground) testing of nuclear weapons and marked the start of a process of arms limitation and even *détente* which was to continue sporadically until the end of the

Cold War. Many regard this as Macmillan's most striking and influential achievement.[73] This requires some qualification. Though Macmillan's persistent application of pressure on the Soviet Union and the United States from 1959 until the Test Ban Treaty was signed seems undeniable, his initial attitude, with both the USA and the USSR jockeying to earn propaganda points by being first to ban nuclear testing, was to try to avoid any kind of restriction of tests until Britain had successfully exploded her own thermonuclear device and built up sufficient stocks. Like many others, Macmillan was prone to the contradiction of being so fearful of the sound of the last trump of Britain's influence in the world that it was prepared to risk doomsday itself. The detonation of an effective British thermonuclear explosion in a second set of tests in the Pacific in November 1957 (the earlier tests in May-June had resulted in an 'intermediate' explosion) and the revision of the McMahon Act the following summer put Britain in a more comfortable position. Indeed, the British Government was now keen for a halt to tests which would help freeze Britain's position in the nuclear hierarchy.[74] From this point on, it publicly espoused the swelling cause of test limitations. The latter was epitomised by the Campaign for Nuclear Disarmament (CND) which came into being in 1958 with its well-publicised annual protest marches to the atomic research headquarters at Aldermaston against the environmental damage caused by the fallout from atmospheric tests and the destruction of civilisation which nuclear weapons threatened as one international crisis succeeded another. Macmillan was ambivalent to the protesters. Some of the pacifist views of those whom he and Eisenhower referred to as 'long haired starry eyed boys' seemed honourable enough, though he considered others 'rather more sinister and hang about the Soviet Embassy more than I would wish.'[75] In any case, the edge which CND might give to the Labour Party suggested that the formulation of a clear policy of banning nuclear tests could bring political gains.[76] The arms race too, as Macmillan was fully aware, was a worry to many natural Conservative voters. But interest in arms control was not just political humbug and reflected a general growth in understanding of the damage exploding nuclear devices in the atmosphere could do, even when not being used in anger, and a recognition that, having helped create the monster, an attempt should now be made at least to try to tame it.

The crisis over Cuba not only increased public agitation against nuclear weapons, but initiated a change of attitude, first in Moscow and then in Washington, on which Macmillan was able to capitalise. The sticking point for Khrushchev was a refusal to contemplate inspection which the Kremlin equated with espionage. Kennedy's problems lay with the Pentagon and Congress, who saw no advantage to the United States in halting tests. In the end, Macmillan's powers of persuasion with Kennedy, fuelled by a desperate need for a political success as his domestic support unravelled, led to his suggestion of direct talks between emissaries in Moscow away from the official, but interminable and unproductive disarmament talks at Geneva. Khrushchev, for his part, was concerned with rapidly deteriorating Sino-Soviet relations and increasingly anxious to try to prevent China from becoming a legitimate atomic power. Agreement was arrived at in July, mainly by leaving aside the harder to detect underground tests and thus ruling out the need for inspection. It has been claimed that 'Macmillan laid the foundations for the ending of the Cold War by the initiation of summit meetings and the achievement of the 1963 test ban treaty.'[77] But Macmillan's summitry could hardly be called a success. Indeed, his attempts in 1963 to link arms limitation with a summit meeting came to nothing as neither Washington nor Moscow were interested. It is also open to question how much summit meetings did in the long-term to contribute to a conclusion of the Cold War. They may have provided opportunities for the slow process of mutual understanding. In this sense, they were arguably some antidote to a disposition to view East-West confrontation as the normal state of affairs, an attitude which owed something to the earlier stance, which the British had helped establish, that negotiation should take place from a position of strength. The standpoint of the summitry of the late 1950s and early 1960s, however, was more a fear of mutual mass destruction and, in any case, the pioneer was surely Churchill, or maybe Eden, rather than Macmillan.

In judging the test ban it needs to be recalled that it was a limited agreement, did not significantly affect the development of nuclear weapons and did not include either France or China – who both condemned it as a fix by members of the elite nuclear club. The final negotiations in Moscow were dominated by the American and Soviet delegates. Stated more baldly, 'the treaty would not have been signed … if it had not served the interests of the United States and the Soviet Union as perceived by their respective leaders.'[78] It has also been argued that such arms control agreements may have been counterproductive by undermining progress towards disarmament itself as unrealistic and even legitimising the arms race because the acceleration of arms production itself had not been banned.[79] Such qualifications to Macmillan's achievement may be excessively churlish and, perhaps, we should see his efforts as the last significant contribution made by Britain to the development of the Cold War. As Richard Crockatt notes, 'The Test Ban Treaty marked an important divide. It is hard to think of any instance after 1963 in which a British statesman played the role in US-Soviet relations which Eden did at Geneva in 1954 or Macmillan did in the test ban talks. Curiously, as the world became more multipolar and the blocs less rigid, the bilateral superpower relationship became more salient and more exclusive, at least as regards the nuclear issue.'[80]

# 6

---

# DEFEATING THEMSELVES, 1964–91

Perhaps, looking back, Macmillan's most perceptive contribution to how the West might win the Cold War lay in a judgement made in 1957, even as Soviet technology was in the ascendant with Sputnik circling the earth, that by pooling 'the efforts of the free world we can build up something that may not defeat the Russians but will wear them out and force them to defeat themselves.'[1] It was a theme of the Cold War as an economic contest to which he was intermittently to return throughout his Premiership. In early 1961 he warned the incoming President Kennedy that if the West did not continue to expand its economic strength then: 'Communism will triumph, not by war, or even subversion, but by seeming to be a better way of bringing people material comforts.'[2] For most of the period since 1945, however, governments in London were more absorbed with the ramifications of Britain's own economic fatigue. It is worthwhile noting at this point that Macmillan's attempts via the Sandys Programme had themselves failed to provide noticeable easement to Britain's economic burdens. The cost of the nuclear deterrent had not compensated for the reduction in conventional forces which were, anyway, decreased less than was anticipated when the crisis over Berlin suggested that further economies over the defence of Europe would be imprudent. Nor had Sandys's pruning suggested a commensurate lessening of Britain's overseas obligations. Arguments that retrenchment in defence expenditure was now a necessity were becoming more vocal amongst Liberals, the Labour Left and even amidst the wilder fringes of the Conservative Party. But such opinions were still viewed as eccentric and the received view was that Britain's part in world affairs was still a great one.

Coping with Britain's economic stagnation therefore survived as a particularly acute predicament for the Labour Government, which came into office in October 1964 determined to conserve the over-lapping objectives of the parity of sterling on international markets and a British presence throughout the world. Despite recent shrinkage, this presence remained real enough. The collapse of the Baghdad Pact following the Iraqi revolution in 1958 had precipitated a shift of emphasis from the northern tier of Middle Eastern states towards the attractions of the oil states of the Persian Gulf. In the early 1960s British defence interests principally rested south of a cordon stretching from West Africa to Singapore. Alongside bases dotted across the Mediterranean, Britain also had forces in Singapore, Aden, Hong Kong, Bahrain and Borneo. Ironically: 'it was a line which Attlee had suggested in 1946 in order to save money and avoid conflict.'[3] Notwithstanding the firmest of intentions, Labour found itself three years on presiding not only over a devaluation of the pound, but also a decision to withdraw all British forces east of Suez. As if to signify that Harold Wilson's electoral victory in October was little more than a parochial political turning point, it was accompanied, centre-stage, by the fall of Khrushchev and the detonation of an atom bomb by China. Even before these events, some recognition was emerging in the Foreign Office that the world was experiencing a 'sea change'. This was mainly put down to the impact of the H-bomb and meant that East and West were settling down to 'a sort of stagnant co-existence'. The implication for Britain, in this view, was the need to be ready efficiently to tackle 'brush fires' rather than major conflagrations in the world and that 'Polaris, the big aircraft carrier and the TSR-2 [a dual purpose reconnaissance bomber then being developed] are relics of an obsolescent politico/military strategy.' Britain's economic difficulties merely corroborated this.[4]

The Labour Government did not quite see the picture this way. Wilson returned from a visit to Washington in December 1964 jubilant that the Americans 'want us with them ... They want our new constructive ideas after the epoch of sterility. We are now in a position to influence events more than ever before for the last ten years.'[5] There was something in this, though not as much as Wilson's gushing optimism suggested. Armed since August by Congress support for the Gulf of Tonkin Resolution, the Johnson Administration was on the edge of deeper military involvement in Vietnam and welcomed any allied support in Southeast Asia. 'What the United States most required from Britain', McNamara told his British counterpart, Denis Healey, 'was the maintenance of the British policy of playing a world

Power role.' Better still, if there could also be, as Johnson put it, 'a few soldiers in British uniforms in South Vietnam'. Wilson's exhilaration aside, the desire to work specifically with a vibrant new Labour Government did not seem a paramount consideration in the White House. Anyone would do really. As Rusk made it clear, Britain was at the head of the line 'since France had cut back her commitments in South-East Asia and the Germans (for understandable reasons) had not come forward to play a world-wide role.'[6] Yet to be wanted, even by default, is something and it was a rare experience for the British to be enticed into Asia by Washington rather than castigated for being there. Indeed, this was the closest the two states had come to real 'interdependence', with the British able to offer what the US really needed since the agreement to deploy Thor missiles in the United Kingdom in 1957. It was not to last.

The worm in the bud for the Wilson Government was Britain's perennial economic weakness. A balance of payments deficit – approaching £800 million in October 1964 - which was to dog Wilson throughout much of his period in office and the familiar problem that 'defence is taking too big a share of our real resources in terms of foreign exchange, scarce types of manpower and load on the most advanced industries' was behind another radical review of defence expenditure inaugurated as soon as the Government took office.[7] If Britain was to continue to command world influence, then cuts in equipment rather than manpower would be easier to absorb. At the Washington meeting in December the Americans showed a readiness to pay an economic price for a continued British global presence, looking favourably upon a proposal from Healey for joint development programmes for military hardware and with the United States underwriting the most sophisticated and costly items. McNamara also suggested that development of the British TSR-2 bomber, 'in his opinion an expensive and nearly worthless project', should be dropped.

The British were also keen to peddle the idea of an Atlantic Nuclear Force (ANF) at the Washington talks as an alternative to the MLF. Healey's later recollection that the ANF was devised 'as a means of scuppering the MLF' does the former a disservice.[8] Wilson was as eager as Macmillan had been to distance himself from this side of the Nassau agreement and the proposition of an ANF, made up of a tripartite British, American and mixed-manned European nuclear force comprising air and seapower as well as missiles, made more strategic sense than the MLF which would be limited to an unwieldy and vulnerable multi-national surface fleet armed with Polaris. Given also that an assumption behind the MLF was that, in the long term, the American veto over the MLF's use of nuclear weapons would devolve to a consolidated European community, the ANF side-stepped the problem of proliferation whilst giving the European members of NATO the impression of having a greater influence over Western defence. The ANF also presented a particular domestic advantage for the British. The government had decided, despite an election pledge to renegotiate the Nassau agreement, to uphold the decision to buy Polaris. Renegotiation could now take the form of a British willingness to consider merging their Polaris missiles within the ANF and renouncing the right to withdraw, which had been obtained at Nassau, so 'putting ourselves on a par with the Germans as regards veto and control'.[9] On top of this, an American contribution to an ANF would attach them even closer to the defence of Europe whilst British resources were released for use elsewhere. This, no doubt, was attractive to the Americans who, according to Wilson, showed 'a gratifying readiness' to consider an ANF, though they did not commit themselves.

Wilson's attention was soon distracted from an ANF towards promoting a Non-Proliferation Treaty (NPT) to inhibit the dissemination of nuclear weapons. This was seen to have similar advantages for Britain as an ANF. It would choke-off nuclear proliferation in Europe, especially to Germany and crystallise an existing situation in which the British deterrent would be preserved. In the meantime it would divert domestic attention away from election promises over the renegotiation of the Nassau agreement and put Britain in the spotlight on the world stage. The difficulty was to persuade the Americans of the benefits of an NPT, particularly as the Soviet Union was opposed to discussing a treaty until the risk of a nuclear armed FRG was banished by the West's abandoning of the MLF. In turn, the Germans, who had a positive approach to the MLF, saw an NPT as discriminatory and possibly damaging to their non-military nuclear industry. That a Non-Proliferation Treaty was signed at all, as occurred in 1968, owed something to the energy, persistence and negotiating skills which Britain brought to bear to reduce the fears of participants and persuade them of their complementary interests. It was a modest British success and a complement to the work Macmillan had begun with the Test Ban Treaty. Similar reservations have to be made that, as with the test ban, the goad was self-interest and that without the eventual acquiescence of the Superpowers Britain's efforts would have been in vain. Indeed, five years on British influence was noticeably reduced. In contrast to the earlier experience

> there was no scope for dramatic initiatives to push the negotiations along. There was no David Ormsby-Gore in Washington with the President's ear. The close relationship between Macmillan and Kennedy was scarcely replicated by Wilson and Johnson. Britain was now much more evidently the junior partner forced to line up with the Americans, in public at least, and to work patiently and rather self-effacingly towards a treaty.[10]

When the Strategic Arms Limitation Talks (SALT) began the year after the NPT was signed, the British, for all their recent efforts, found themselves left outside of what were exclusively Superpower discussions.

For all his enthusiasm to make Britain's mark on the world stage and for collaborating with the United States, Wilson refused to be lured into providing physical assistance to the Americans in Vietnam. This, at first sight, might suggest a more independent attitude than his Labour predecessor had demonstrated over Korea 14 years before. On the other hand, Wilson was quite aware that whilst the American Administration harboured hawks who wished to pressurise Britain into active support, Johnson was not among the most avid.[11] Also, the British had little military slack to spare. The Malayan 'Emergency' which had troubled the Attlee and Churchill Governments had ended in 1955, but the British were now faced with protecting the new Malaysian federation from an attack from Indonesia. Moreover, joining the Americans would have been intolerable to the Labour left. The situation was further complicated by the fact that whilst the Foreign Office saw an identity of interest between Britain and America in the struggle to hold back Communist advance in Southeast Asia, they did not believe that the war in Vietnam could be won. Wilson's dilemma was that to tell Washington this and to offer to broker a negotiated settlement might open the possibility of being treated as a scapegoat by the Americans once defeat was a reality. To keep silent over Vietnam, however, was an irritant to the left of the Labour Party which sought condemnation of American actions. At the same time, Wilson was keen to have Britain act as intermediary in the conflict. The weakness of his position was demonstrated forcefully in February 1965 as the US began to step up their operations in North Vietnam. With the left of the Party incensed at his failure to condemn this escalation, Wilson felt he would be better able to answer criticism if he was seen to be in conversation with the Americans, though he made it clear to Washington that he would continue to back US actions. Persistent pressure for a Prime Ministerial visit to Washington for this purpose, but which the Americans felt would smack to the world of desperation, wore the President's patience paper-thin. 'I won't tell you how to run Malaysia and you don't tell us how to run Vietnam', he testily told the Prime Minister over the phone on 11 February 1965.[12] The parallels with Attlee's flight to Truman during the Korean war are interesting - but at least Attlee had made it to the plane.

Once the American bombardment of North Vietnam began in March as Washington's method of humbling Hanoi, Wilson's tendency was to hide behind the legal facade of Britain being the supposedly impartial co-chair (along with the Soviet Union) of the 1954 Indochina settlement, as either an excuse to withhold open support for US actions or, more enthusiastically, as the opportunity to play the part of conciliator (so long as it did not undermine the American position). This was a further source of vexation to the Americans. But the Prime Minister's ardour to be go-between was almost unquenchable and consummated by a series of initiatives in Washington, Moscow and even Hanoi to explore the possibility of ending America's deepening engagement. These were motivated alternately by attempts to take the heat out of domestic opposition to events in Vietnam and also to enhance the standing of the Government during three successive sterling crises which rocked the Government between late 1964 and the summer of 1966. In fairness, it did seem at times that there were practical gains to be accrued from supporting the US. Johnson let Wilson know that 'we will back you [against Indonesia] if necessary to the hilt and hope for your support in Vietnam.' Moreover, the British were dealing with a confused and divided Administration which, as a member of Wilson's Cabinet noted, 'don't want to pull out: but don't see a way out.'[13] Nevertheless, there existed the conceit, shown to be specious when Moscow and Washington took British attempts to mediate seriously only when it seemed convenient for them to do so, that London could actually influence events in Southeast Asia.[14]

The actuality, no longer a mere probability, that the Cold War was now a bi-polar conflict was clouded for a time whilst both participants attempted to live up to the spirit of the Washington meeting of December 1964. On the British side, during 1965 Healey scrapped expensive aircraft projects including the TSR-2, which was to be replaced by the American F-111. The following year the purchase of three CVA 01 aircraft carriers was cancelled at the same time as Britain's determination to maintain a considerable strategic capability east of Suez was affirmed, though carriers were the traditional backbone of this presence. For their part, the Americans increased their purchase of British arms and eased the cost to Britain of the development costs of Polaris and of aircraft bought from the United States. Over the 18 months following the Washington talks, the USA provided important backing as London looked for dollar support from the International Monetary Fund and Western banks to support the weak pound. Though there seems to have been no explicit agreement between the two governments that Washington would help prevent a devaluation of sterling in return for a continuing British presence east of Suez, this, alongside the fear that the dollar would be the next target for speculators if the pound was devalued, certainly energised the Americans. It was to prove futile. Deflationary economic measures openly strained the Government's trade union support which, in turn, caused the pound to wobble. American fervour to support sterling had already begun to cool as devaluation came to seem inevitable.

Under these pressures, Healey's decision in July 1967 to halve British forces in Malaysia and Singapore by the early 1970s and abandon these bases altogether in the middle of the decade underscored American misgivings. Nevertheless, this was not a premeditated step towards complete withdrawal from east of Suez. It was seen and publicly presented as a further step in the rationalisation of Britain's strained defence budget. The impact of the closure of the Suez Canal during the Arab-Israeli war of June and the decision to apply again for entry to the EC - which many believed would necessitate the devaluation of sterling in order to be successful - brought new pressures to long-term problems and on 18 November, despite a last-minute proposal from Washington to rescue the pound in return for British support in Southeast Asia, it was announced that sterling was to be devalued by around 14 per cent.[15] Further defence cuts were bound to follow. Even so, there remained sufficient resistance to fundamental change in Wilson's Cabinet that at first no radical reappraisal of Britain's global commitments was envisaged. As it turned out, the currency crisis crucially shifted the polarity of the Cabinet. Wilson himself, the most

fervent supporter of Britain's world role, was knocked askew by devaluation and was soon to face rumours of a leadership challenge. At
the same time, Roy Jenkins, made Chancellor in the wake of the emergency over sterling and long convinced of the necessity of a shift
towards Europe, was able to push through a programme of more urgent and penetrating reductions which marked a brusque conclusion
to Britain's overseas pretensions.[16] In January 1968 Wilson told the
Commons that all British bases in the Far East (except Hong Kong)
and the Persian Gulf would be run down by the end of 1971.

Here was an incontrovertible turning point. The fig leaf which had
obscured the threadbare British pretensions to globalism fluttered to
the ground. Oddly, as they had frequently been at the front of the
crowd which declared that the Empire had no clothes, it was a sight
almost as shocking to the Americans as to the British. In truth, it was
an inconvenience to them rather than a revelation. Not least because
of the intelligence-gathering value that British bases in Asia provided for Washington. Rusk accused the British Foreign Secretary, George
Brown, of betrayal and Brown himself believed that irreparable damage had been done to Anglo-American relations.[17] But the
ramifications ran deeper than disappointing the Johnson Administration. The decision to leave the Gulf and the Far East was not merely
an asylum from unacceptable defence costs or disengagement from
an outmoded attachment to Empire, it was evacuation from what was
acknowledged to be the principal fighting arena of the Cold War. A
briefing paper for Wilson's visit to President Johnson in December
1964 had made it quite clear that the main danger points were in the
Far East and Southeast Asia, that 'East-West conflict [is] stalemated in
Europe', that the West 'has in fact won the battle for Europe', and
that the present problems of NATO (a reference to difficulties with
the French) 'are the problems of a military Alliance that hasn't really
got a war to fight.'[18] 1968, therefore, was not just about shedding a
vestigial imperial past, but also a conscious, if largely reluctant, retreat from the most critical theatre of the ideological struggle which
had dominated international relations since 1945. In this sense, the
withdrawal from east of Suez marked an involuntary declaration that
Britain was no longer a major combatant in the Cold War in its global
form. Change was also apparent in other ways. Different emphases
on where best to make a stand against Communism had frequently
characterised the Anglo-Saxon Cold War partnership. But agreement
on fundamentals was now overshadowed by unshared distractions.

America was obsessed with Vietnam. Britain had other preoccupations crowding in – the economy, entry to the European Community, Rhodesia and Northern Ireland. These had only tenuous links, if any, with the Cold War. Of course, a guard had to be kept up in Western Europe via NATO so that smoldering threats were not rekindled in what remained the main pillar of British defence. But the American nuclear umbrella made this phoney rather than actual Cold War. The British deterrent remained to some a comforting insurance in case of default over this guarantee. It also served another purpose. Even after 1968, like the amputee who senses the ghost of the severed limb, there were those unable to dislodge a self-perception that, despite all that had been abandoned, everything remained the same. The deterrent was a necessary solace to a bruised, but – many were still able to convince themselves – largely undiminished standing.

In a curious way, the British were once again, albeit inadvertently, ahead of the game. The fright which the Cuban Crisis had given the world coupled with strains on the Superpowers' own economies, ushered in a period of international *détente*. British officials began to speak, though not always to act, as though the Cold War was a thing of the past and a state of affairs to which they were reluctant to return even after the invasion of Czechoslovakia by the Soviets and their allies on 21 August, 1968. Tanks in Prague, it was decided, was 'not the action of strong "expansionist" leaders, but of frightened men'.[19] This is not, of course, to say that *détente* rested on any example which the British might have set. The Superpowers' own preoccupations were central. The developing tension between the Soviet Union and China, intensified after the latter's atomic detonation in 1964, gave Moscow a strategic as well as an economic impetus to mend some fences with the West. Soviet discomfort, and the United States' own costly embroilment in Vietnam which accelerated adverse trends in the American economy, encouraged Washington to rethink the policy of non-recognition it had upheld towards China since 1949. At the same time, the Vietnam experience dislodged support for that other long-held maxim, containment. Also as the Americans increasingly sought from 1968 to extricate themselves from Vietnam, *détente* seemed a necessary preliminary.

Oddly, given their persistent approach throughout the Cold War to find an accommodation from strength with the Communist bloc, the British approach to *détente* was more cautious, even pedestrian, compared to other exponents of the policy during the late 1960s and 1970s. Naturally, the British were unable to match the drama of President Nixon's remarkable visit to China (February 1972) or his less striking, but noteworthy meeting with the Soviet leadership (May 1972). But even Britain's Western European associates exhibited a more positive and confident international profile during this period. This contrast was most signally demonstrated by Willy Brandt's reversal of the West German boycott of the GDR embraced by his *Ostpolitik* and also by the attempt of de Gaulle, and to a lesser degree his successor Georges Pompidou, to revive the much older 'special relationship' between France and Russia, which de Gaulle had tried to inculcate as early as December 1944 when he had visited Stalin in Moscow. Henry Kissinger's, Nixon's National Security Adviser, explanation for this was a draining of British self-assuredness, observing that 'with every passing year they acted less as if their decisions mattered.'[20] In a way, the Germans and the French were adopting the position attempted earlier by Churchill and Macmillan as the intermediary between East and West, another indication of Britain's abdication as *the* European Power. The Soviets themselves were happy to exploit this divergence.

When Alec Douglas-Home entered the Foreign Office following the Conservative's electoral victory in the summer of 1970, he encountered unfavourable contrasts made by the Russians 'between our own relations with the Soviet Union, which [they] implied were "stagnant", and the progress made in developing Franco-Soviet and West German-Soviet relations [and] ... that we were in danger of becoming the odd man out'. The preceding Wilson Government had been conscious too that in the absence of any concrete initiatives towards Moscow compared with the Americans, French and Germans, Britain 'ran the risk of being accused of rigidity and a lack of enthusiasm for a *détente* between East and West.'[21] It was an image which was hard to dislodge and, though alert to the obvious advantages in bringing an end to Cold War and for Britain to be seen to be attempting to do so, British policy-formers tended to view *détente* through a sceptic's lense. From this perspective the Soviet Union remained a state driven by Marxist ideology which had pragmatically embarked upon a calculated policy of co-existence, in order to cope with current economic difficulties and its rivalry with China, yet remained committed to weakening the West and expanding Soviet influence. The government of Leonid Brezhnev, a JIC report surmised, 'is grey, cautious, suspicious, nationalist to the point of chauvinism, but it is also persistent and, within a given framework, opportunist and capable of tactical switches that may take the West by surprise.'[22]

Circumstances conspired to accentuate the British lack of confidence which Kissinger had observed. NATO's conventional force imbalance in Europe and the expansion of the Soviet navy led British experts to see Russian *détente* initiatives as a passing phase. *Ostpolitik*, initially welcomed in London, increasingly came to be seen as an attempt by Moscow to draw the whole of Germany into the Soviet orbit. Apprehensions that the bilateral Strategic Arms Limitation Talks between the USSR and USA which had opened in 1969 might negotiate away Britain's American manufactured delivery systems added to this uncertainty. 'If ', one official noted in 1970, 'Western Europe eventually achieves a significant degree of political and defence cooperation, at that point a genuine *détente* in East-West relations could be valuable; but for the time being, we must expect that Warsaw Pact propaganda regarding European security and *détente* will be designed to change the balance of power in Europe to our disadvantage. So long as this remains the case, the need for wariness and caution is not likely to diminish.'[23] Indeed, it seemed that the more Britain was marginalised as a key actor in East-West relations and the less direct interest political leaders appeared to take in the *détente* process, the more policy was framed by the guarded views of bureaucrats in the Foreign Office.[24]

Other counsel was on offer, notably, dogged attempts by Sir Duncan Wilson, British Ambassador in Moscow between 1968 and 1971, to inject a more positive approach in Whitehall. In a series of far-sighted despatches drafted in an Embassy whose complement of staff was now quite small, reflecting the corresponding significance of relations between the two states, he cast doubt upon the predominating view in Whitehall of the Soviet Union as an ideologically driven monolith. In his view 'and that of all my senior political and economic staff ... in spite of all too much continuity in some aspects of policy, the Soviet Union is undergoing changes which may in the long or even medium term produce a different mixture.' He questioned whether Brezhnev was guided much in his conduct of foreign policy by Marxist-Leninist notions of the class struggle and treated problems on a pragmatic basis rather than acting as a standard bearer for revolution. One of these factors was that, technologically, the USSR was lagging behind the West, especially in computers. Britain, Wilson believed, needed to change the style rather than the substance of its policy. Instead of advertising its defensive posture against the Soviets and leaving contacts with Moscow to the French and West Germans, Britain should develop a greater dialogue with the Russians – as much on the level of 'town twinning' as governmental contacts – which in turn could lead to mutually advantageous commercial relations. His advice, more pertinent than he could have known, suggested the possibility of serious future economic difficulties and that 'a reasonably flexible response to current Soviet tactics ... does not involve serious risks for the West and could bring important dividends not only in trade, but in the longer term also in encouraging political and social change in Eastern Europe and the Soviet Union itself.'

This had little appreciable impact on the Foreign and Commonwealth Office (as it was termed after October 1968) or on the Secretary of State. 'I do not think', Douglas-Home asserted, 'that our current policies are of critical importance at present in the determination of how and by whom the Soviet Union shall be ruled.' What was more, 'there is nothing we can give the Russians which is comparable in value to them to the French partial withdrawal from NATO and the West German acceptance of the European *status quo*. Nor is Britain a super-power like the USA.' On a lesser, but revealing note, Walden, of the Eastern Europe and Soviet Department of the Foreign and Commonwealth Office (FCO) noted that his Department 'had always had reservations about "town twinning" arrangements' because of 'Soviet ability to use such contacts for their own purposes' and because of the 'danger of contagion.'[25] If anything, the British attitude towards the Russians hardened. In September 1971, as *Ostpolitik* reached a climax with a Quadripartite Agreement over access to West Berlin and which the Prime Minister, Edward Heath, sourly regarded as 'the best of a bad bargain', 105 members of the Soviet Trade Mission at the London Embassy were expelled from Britain under suspicion of espionage in a sweep codenamed Operation FOOT.[26] Early the following year, and with evident lack of enthusiasm, the British agreed to accept a long-standing Soviet invitation to convene an East-West Conference on Security and Co-operation in Europe (CSCE). To the FCO the conference was a means by which the Soviet Union would undermine the solidity of the West by posing as the champion of *détente* and extend what had already been obtained via *Ostpolitik* by consolidating further its own legitimacy in Eastern Europe (though, arguably, the muted reaction to the 1968 invasion of Czechoslovakia had already tacitly done this). The whole process therefore was cheerlessly embraced as 'inevitable rather than desirable, and our primary aim defensive'. Even though they were successful in widening the scope of the Conference before a final agreement was signed at Helsinki in August 1975, notably over the question of human rights, British mistrust of the process survived. In the immediate aftermath of the Helsinki Accords – usually taken as the highpoint of *détente* – the sombre assessment of Sir John Killick, Wilson's replacement in Moscow, was that 'it remains to be seen whether [the Cold War] is over, or has only taken new shape.'[27]

Not surprisingly then, during this period successive British Governments were preoccupied as much by defence as *détente*. Economic frailty, financial crises and a defence bill judged to be higher than the nation could afford had, as we have seen, moulded the decision in 1967 to limit Britain's defensive role predominantly to the NATO area. An emphasis on NATO, which was increasingly propounded in Government publications to be an arm of *détente* as well as defence, was enhanced by Denis Healey as Labour Minister of Defence from 1964 to 1970. It was the British who played a significant part in easing NATO through the crisis caused by de Gaulle's decision to pull out of the NATO command structure in 1966. This in turn appears to have spurred Healey to dodge between a growing American propensity to come out against first use of nuclear weapons, without which Western Europeans felt unable to sustain an attack from the overwhelming conventional Soviet forces based in Eastern Europe, and German eagerness for a policy of nuclear retaliation if the 'tripwire' of their eastern border was crossed with his compromise, agreed in the spring of 1967, for a graduated flexible response if Western Europe came under attack.[28] At the same time, Healey worked to create a platform within NATO, known as the Eurogroup, to co-ordinate European positions on defence. Enthusiasm for this was fuelled by proposals from Washington to Moscow, first suggested by President Johnson in early 1967, of arms limitation talks which, yet again, seemed worryingly likely to encourage the Americans to abandon their nuclear guarantee to Europe. Arms limitation was also a potential threat to Britain's own deterrent. Indeed, the eventual dawning of Britain's effective nuclear capability was surrounded by ironies. By the time the first British Polaris submarine was in operation in 1968, the military threat to Western Europe had significantly diminished. On top of this, the frightful notion of mutual assured destruction and the development of anti-ballistic missile systems capable of upsetting this balance of terror provided variable arguments for the Superpowers to begin to contemplate nuclear arms control. The official British stance was that this was in itself an additional incentive to keep their hands on their own deterrent and not get involved in too much *détente*. At the same time, the high running costs of nuclear submarines plus the fact that the Americans intended to replace Polaris in the early 1980s with the Poseidon sea-launched missile made it clear that Britain too would soon have to rethink options for its defensive systems. As if to underline Britain's already deteriorating position, Poseidon was a multiple, independently targetable re-entry vehicle (MIRV) with ten warheads to Polaris's mere one.

The Wilson Government, which had to square up to these issues in 1967, was conscious that contemplating the replacement of Polaris was December 1962 all over again. In making a decision not to seek Poseidon as a alternative, it was, as Wilson made clear to de Gaulle, 'Nassau in reverse'. High on Wilson's agenda was the need to win support for Britain's second attempt to join the EEC. But Wilson had no intention of throwing away Britain's independent deterrent. Though of minor significance in global strategic terms, it was valued both as a trigger to ensure American nuclear support and also a boost to Britain's voice within NATO. Wilson decided to defer any immediate decision, but instead to have researchers at Aldermaston investigate the possibility of a more effective warhead for the existing Polaris missiles. After 1970, the government of Edward Heath, after flirting with the idea of nuclear co-operation with France and following discussion with the Americans, also decided not to opt for Poseidon. By this time, the work at Aldermaston had come up with the possibility of a warhead which would not be a MIRV, but would have a greater penetrative capacity than Polaris and a more sophisticated ability to confuse enemy defences. The warhead was code-named Chevaline. In the spring of 1974 an inner group of the Cabinet of the newly returned Labour Government decided to adopt the Chevaline programme. The decision had little to do with strategy and more with the familiar desire to stay in the nuclear game. Chevaline had the perceived advantages that it was British and would not offend their (by now) partners in the EEC by asking favours of the Americans. Because it was not MIRVed it would not appear significantly to ratchet up the arms race. In any case, the Labour Government, in particular, was not disposed to publicise Chevaline in terms other than as an update of Polaris for fear of starting hares with the anti-nuclear supporters in the Party.

As suggested earlier, the British decision was made more complicated because of the developing sophistication of nuclear armaments. Consideration was given to the possibility of transferring to a Cruise missile system launched from either land, sea or air and, meanwhile, Poseidon was itself on the point of being outmoded by the Trident ballistic missile. The SALT II agreement, signed in 1979, seemed to pave the way for further arms reductions, which again raised the perpetual apprehension that the USA might be tempted to sign away its nuclear guarantee against an attack in Western Europe. How dangerous this might be was brought home during the latter part of 1977 with the deployment of Soviet SS-20 IRBMs targeting Western Europe. Over and above this, the expectation of both main British political parties seems to have been that, like Polaris, Chevaline would provide cost-effective defence. This was a major misjudgement. By 1977 the estimates for Chevaline had quadrupled and were expected to be around £1 billion by 1980. Retrospectively, senior members of the Labour Cabinet have expressed the view that the project should have been scrapped. In reality, reluctance to face a political row and to lose what had already been spent resulted in a political fudge until after the 1979 General Election.

Though turning points have a habit of punctuating Britain's postwar history, they remain a relative rarity and in terms of Britain's part in the Cold War, the advent of Margaret Thatcher to power in May 1979 was not one of these. For instance, the Thatcher Cabinet's decision in December 1979 to purchase Trident, after due investigation of possible alternatives, was the continuation of a development which the preceding Government had been groping towards. Having obtained the approval of senior Ministers, the previous Labour Prime Minister, James Callaghan, had reached a private, non-committal agreement with President Carter at a meeting of Western Heads of State at Guadeloupe in February 1979 that the US would look favourably upon the replacement of Polaris/Chevaline with Trident.[29] Admittedly, Thatcher's burgeoning friendship with Ronald Reagan after 1981 did mean that Britain obtained an updated version of Trident at a bargain price. Similarly, though the new climate in East-West relations persuaded the Callaghan Government to close the IRD in 1977, even before the Soviet invasion of Afghanistan in late 1979 inaugurated the 'new', or so-called 'second', Cold War, Labour statements, coloured by Moscow's opportunistic involvement in Mozambique, Angola and South Yemen from the middle of the decade, had already begun to adopt a more cautious note towards *détente*.[30] Of course, the Foreign Office, for which ironically Thatcher had little time, had always been sceptical. Her view that 'the Cold War itself had never really ended, at least from the Soviet side: there were merely variations of chill' was well represented in King Charles Street and echoed Sir John Killick's earlier opinion that 'the phrase "peaceful co-existence" as used by the Russians is a fraud and should be exposed as such.'[31] Undoubtedly, *détente* on both sides was tactical with each manoeuvring to achieve ultimate mastery.[32] Even when *détente* was at its height in 1972–4, the KGB continued the habit of referring to the US as the 'Main Adversary' and doubled the number of officers active in the US.[33] A vestigial predisposition too to see Britain as fundamentally hostile plus a totalitarian system's 'necessity to know' meant that the British Embassy in Moscow continued to be excessively spied upon with even junior clerks having their own 40 page KGB dossier. In this respect there was no 'new' Cold War at all but simply the 'old' Cold War fought by other means. *Détente* did, none the less, at least offer the West some prospect of victory by erosion, as opposed to the alternatives of perpetual confrontation or the non-existent triumph following a nuclear nightmare. The corollary of the subversion of the Soviet system via *détente* was, however, a vision which some in the Foreign Office seemed to have had difficulty with. 'I have never', commented one senior official, 'been convinced that instability within the Soviet empire would necessarily work out to the advantage of the West: and I have never thought that attempts actively to promote instability added up to a prudent long term policy for the West.'[34] A similar failure of imagination was also to trouble Margaret Thatcher once the Soviet system began to show clear signs of collapsing.

It was, however, the election of a new American President in November 1980, Ronald Reagan, rather than Thatcher's own electoral victory the previous year, which provided the catalyst for hiked up East-West tension. Reagan's unreconstructed Cold Warrior bravado and his increase in military spending by almost 10 per cent convinced Yuri Andropov, then Head of the KGB, that the Americans would risk a pre-emptive nuclear strike. In May 1981 Andropov instituted a concerted intelligence operation (Operation RYAN) to provide forewarning of an attack. This involved monitoring activities in Britain, regarded as the Americans' most faithful ally, including any unusual night-time activity in government offices and military installations. Soviet foreboding reached a climax during a NATO exercise in November 1983 which Moscow seems to have seriously believed was intended as a cover for a first strike by the West. Less apocalyptically, the KGB also made inept attempts to influence the British General Election of that year against Thatcher.[35] The fact of the matter is that during her first term of office, Thatcher's attention was not dominated by the Soviet threat. She had a range of distractions – Britain's poor economic performance, conflict with the EEC over Britain's budget contributions, Ireland, Rhodesia and then the Falklands – which ensured that, whilst there was plenty of sound and fury hurled against the dangers of Soviet Communism, rhetoric had a higher profile than policy. For example, denunciation of the invasion of Afghanistan was loud though action against it was muted. After the declaration of martial law in Poland in December 1981, itself a further sign of the Soviet Union's disenchantment with the disconcerting spin-offs of *détente*, she successfully opposed – alongside other Western European leaders – President Reagan's plan to include technology for a gas pipeline from Siberia to the West within a tranche of sanctions to demonstrate displeasure with the USSR. Here was an indication that the Prime Minister drew the line at political points-scoring against totalitarian Communism if it was at the expense of self-inflicted economic damage. It is important not to underplay Thatcher's zeal to avoid permitting the Soviet Union to steal a lead via the SS-20 deployment, though there was often an interconnection between economic and strategic considerations behind her actions. The decision in December 1979 to permit the Americans to station Cruise missiles in England and to go along with the American devised 'zero option' – removal of SS-20s, no Cruise (or Pershing short-range missiles) in Western Europe – was, as was the Trident decision, such a case. With the Vulcan, the last in the line of the V-bombers, in need of replacement if there was to be a realistic notion of a gradation in response to attack before Polaris was used, it seemed a good bargain to buy extra Cruise missiles on top of those required by NATO to serve as a stop-gap until an alternative to the Vulcan had been produced. In sum, during Thatcher's first Government 'Britain was in no sense an initiator, still less an architect, of Western policy in the way that the Attlee government had been with respect to the first cold war in the late 1940s.'[36]

Following her decisive electoral victory in June 1983, Thatcher's foreign policy initiatives took on a somewhat less belligerent tone towards the Soviet Union and, seemingly, a greater international significance. Though her own claims to have been a prime mover in the events which were to bring about the collapse of the Soviet system in Eastern Europe and the end of the Cold War itself are exaggerated, her influence with President Reagan provided the semblance of Britain as an intermediary between East and West in a way which Churchill, Eden, Macmillan and Wilson might each have envied. Even Thatcher's modest part in these events is a testimony to her extraordinary personality. Following his successful visit to London in December 1984, she had the confidence of Mikhail Gorbachev, the rising personality in the Soviet Union. Characteristically, she judged this to be Gorbachev's good fortune rather than her own. She 'spotted him', we are told, 'because I was searching for someone like him' who would be prepared to challenge the system through which he had risen. (His main domestic rival, Grigory Romanov, notwithstanding the appealing historical symmetry of his surname, was apparently rejected by Thatcher because of his cavalier treatment of priceless Hermitage glassware.)[37] More prosaically, she appears to have been persuaded by some of her political associates that a softer approach to the Soviet Union might help take the steam out of significant domestic opposition to the deployment of Cruise missiles and exploit the already evident indications of Moscow's loosening grip on its European satellites. The Moscow Embassy too had discovered that meetings with Gorbachev were qualitatively different from anything they had experienced before in their dealings with the USSR.

But Thatcher's change of direction and her influence on the dramatic shift in the Cold War which was about to unfold were more apparent than real. In the last resort, Thatcher did not have the temperament of a go-between. Her feet were firmly in the Atlanticist camp and until the unification of Germany had altered the political geography of Europe, she remained suspicious of Soviet wedge-driving.[38] That Gorbachev was acceptable to Thatcher was, no doubt, some recommendation to Reagan and may have assisted the thaw in Soviet-American relations from 1985. On the other hand, the President's own anti-Soviet verbosity had never precluded negotiation and, like the Prime Minister, he adopted a more accommodating approach to Moscow even before Gorbachev had been installed as General Secretary in March 1985.[39] In this climate, Gorbachev was quite capable of making his own *entré* into Washington circles and more so after

June 1985 when the approachable Eduard Shevardnadze replaced the
stone-faced Andrei Gromyko as Foreign Minister. On a more particular matter, Thatcher was able to communicate Soviet, and her own,
anxieties over Reagan's Strategic Defence Initiative (SDI) which Gorbachev had expressed whilst in London. In the President's mind, the
SDI would end the nuclear threat by the development of a laser anti-
ballistic system in space. Considering herself 'in my element' with
the scientific concepts involved and having an understanding to enable the 'right policy decisions to be made' which 'laid back generalists
from the Foreign Office' and 'the ministerial muddlers in charge of
them' could not be relied upon to grasp, Thatcher supported SDI.
She provided a balance between the views of the Western Europeans
and the Russians that it would fearfully tear down the nuclear deterrent which had helped preserve peace for 40 years and Reagan, who
saw SDI as the preliminary to the abolition of nuclear weapons. She
did not believe that lasers in space could provide a perfect defence.
What it would do would be to enhance the American's 'second strike'
position and, therefore, the deterrent itself. On top of this, 'science is
unstoppable' and therefore 'we had to be the first to get it.'[40]

In any case, Reagan demonstrated an obstinate reluctance to abandon his pet project and at his first meeting with Gorbachev at Geneva
in November 1985, Reagan attempted to deflect Soviet concern over
SDI with assurances that it was entirely defensive. More demonstrably, a year later at Reykjavik when both leaders appeared ready to
eradicate nuclear weapons, the moment totally evaporated when Reagan refused to bargain away SDI. Despite the President's return to
resoluteness, Thatcher's commitment to *détente*, always tissue-slim,
had begun to waver. To her, Reykjavik was a Soviet trap for the Americans set by offering sweeping concessions in the deployment of
strategic nuclear weapons in the hope of bringing an effective end to
SDI. Gorbachev was, no doubt, fearful of the strategic advantage which
SDI would give to the West. But he was also motivated by a desperate
need to reduce defence expenditure in order to tackle severe economic dislocation in the USSR and to eliminate the prohibitively
expensive cost of the Soviet's own space weapon programme. Grati-
fied by Reagan's refusal to go along with this, she was nevertheless
disturbed by the apparent willingness of the two leaders to abolish all
nuclear weapons – though Reagan's incoherent sticking point was an
absolute refusal to abandon the development of SDI which would provide the defence against the weapons he seemed prepared to outlaw.

To Thatcher's keener eye, total abolition would expose Europe to the twin hazard of Soviet predominance in conventional forces and also put Britain at risk of losing Trident. To counter both possibilities she felt compelled to dash to Washington to remonstrate with the President. The satisfactory outcome she put down to her influence upon Reagan which, according to her own account, Gorbachev acknowledged too.[41] But, unsurprisingly, Thatcher was not alone in her remonstrance. Even before being got at by the British Prime Minister, some of Reagan's senior advisers, including the chairman of the Joint Chiefs of Staff had already advised that the offer to eliminate all nuclear weapons was too dangerous to be repeated.[42] Thatcher's warnings may have had some impact, but the heed that the Americans took of British, and the other Western Europeans would have seemed the more impressive had their likely objections been taken into account before the Reykjavik discussions took an abolitionist turn. Though a disappointing performance for many at the time, Reykjavik proved to be a breakthrough. In succeeding talks, which were never far from the danger of breakdown, SDI and notions of total abolition of nuclear weapons were surreptitiously dropped permitting agreement to be reached over the reduction of intermediate-range weapons and the signing of an Intermediate Nuclear Force (INF) Treaty in December 1987. This, the most significant disarmament agreement for over 50 years, legislating for the removal of American Cruise and Pershing missiles and Soviet IRBMs – the so called 'zero option', was a source of some concern to the Western Europeans, including Thatcher, who looked askance at its potential for decoupling the defence of Europe from that of the USA.

Adulation and warm words from Reagan ( and to a lesser degree from Gorbachev) gave the impression, not least perhaps to the Prime Minister herself, that British ability to change the direction of policy in Washington was greater than was the case. Suggestions that Britain under Thatcher might become part of an international 'troika' now look decidedly excessive.[43] Inevitably, once Reagan and Gorbachev had begun to deal with each other directly (as Macmillan had discovered a quarter of a century earlier after Eisenhower and Khruschev had first met) Britain's input began to decline. From 1989, when Bush replaced Reagan as President, the trans-Atlantic link between London and Washington, and therefore British influence on Cold War events, weakened. By this time, Moscow's grip on its Eastern European satellites had perceptibly relaxed as the will to retain them evaporated and they increasingly seemed to be a drag on the economic revitalisation of the USSR itself. In contrast to the majority of her NATO allies, who began to contemplate a 'third zero' to eliminate short-range missiles (which would complement the INF Treaty and a 'second zero' reduction of lower class weapons which Gorbachev had since thrown in), Thatcher asserted the need for the West to keep up its guard by updating its short-range nuclear forces based in Germany. This rapidly became an illogical position as those Eastern European states targeted by such weapons slipped away from Moscow's control. By the late summer of 1989, Poland had a non-Communist government and Hungary a reformist regime which had opened its frontier with Austria, which provided an emigration route to the West for increasing numbers of East Germans. Thatcher, insisting that the Cold War would 'last until 2000', had lost the plot.[44]

In November a reconstituted East German Government opened the control points in the Wall. In this situation, not only did Britain revert in American eyes to just another European country but, as the GDR disintegrated and the Berlin Wall fell, Germany reappeared as the most significant state on the Continent. To Thatcher's dismay, Bush was already publicly referring to America and Germany as 'partners in leadership'. In a kind of parallel to her aspiration to introduce 'Thatcherism' into the European Community via the Single Market which, too late, she recognised had opened the gates to those who sought greater political unity, her initial flirtation with Gorbachev and *détente* and the ramifications of this – possibly strategic advantage to the Soviets, certainly the disconcerting crumbling of the existing order – caused her to backpedal. The common denominator between the two reactions was the haunting presence of Germany. A united Germany, which looked increasingly likely as the Wall was pulled down in November 1989, would probably dominate a European Community (EC) which seemed bent on moving towards a federal Europe. Through a federal EC Germany would dominate Europe. The Foreign Office was banned from even discussing the possibility. Others' deliberations were less easy to supress. Though she tried to alert Bush and President Mitterrand to the German danger (armed somewhat superfluously with a handbag full of maps to instruct the French President on Germany's volatile past) and persuade them to slow the process down, they showed little interest. Indeed, in the last stages of the drama neither they, nor Gorbachev, had much control over events. The initiative was seized by the West German Chancellor, Helmut

Kohl, who, after the emotional scenes in Berlin of November 1989, began to push for unification. On 3 October, 1990, this came about and the Cold War ended where it had begun, in Germany. Fittingly, Margaret Thatcher's final appearance as Prime Minister was at the Paris CSCE – part of a process of East-West dialogue upon which her predecessors had embarked so grudgingly in the 1970s – which on 21 November, 1990, officially announced that the Cold War was over.

# CONCLUSIONS

At the time when Gorbachev was being cultivated by the British, Thatcher visited Hungary (1984) and the Soviet Union (1986). Both were to rapturous popular acclaim leaving her with an impression of a palpable thirst for Western-style liberty and, less accurately, that in Eastern Europe she – with Reagan – 'personified' these freedoms.[1] The reality was that Britain's part either in producing or preventing the final *dénouement* was peripheral. Thatcher's inspirational role was surely no more significant than, say, Pope John Paul II's and it was principally Gorbachev who forced the pace to which everyone else had to respond. What drove Gorbachev was the chaos of the Soviet economy which he recognised he had to attend to before the whole system imploded. This was not, as Thatcher implies in her memoirs, a circumstance imposed from without by the costs of matching SDI. Gorbachev was unfortunate in succeeding the sclerotic leadership of the later Brezhnev, Andropov and Chernenko at a time when the language of the USA was exceptionally strident. But really what troubled him were long standing, inherent structural defects in the economy which had been acknowledged by some within the Soviet system 20 years before Gorbachev came to power. These were capable of being masked or controlled until they collided with arguably the greatest of all the revolutions of the twentieth century – that in information technology and computing – which the USSR could not produce with sufficient sophistication to match the requirements of a late twentieth-century economy and anyway, threatened to open up a system whose very *modus operandi* was secrecy.[2] In the final analysis, the Soviet State was destroyed not by NATO or the arsenals of the West, but by the computer chip.

Gorbachev did not envision the end of Soviet Communism, but rather that restructuring would engender a new vitality to the system.

The failure of this to materialise in the Eastern satellites, coupled with the inadequacy of his economic reforms inside the USSR, sapped his authority at home and in December 1991, just over a year after Germany had become a united state again, the Soviet Union became a historical term. The speed and shock of this collapse suggests that no Western Government anticipated this turn of events, still less, worked systematically towards it by aiming to outspend the Soviet Union. Most Western leaders, Thatcher included, suspected that Gorbachev was engaged in a skilful process of dividing the West and that his failure would be followed by a hard-line regime. Neither the diplomatic nor the intelligence services were helpful in framing a picture in such unprecedented circumstances. There were signs to be seen from the 1970s of the widening gap in science and technology between the Soviet Union and the West, but the mind-set of the times conditioned most supposed expert opinion to see threats and not opportunities. It was preferable to continue to see the USSR as solid because it was easier to make policy that way. The Cold War was part of the international scenery and few could imagine and, indeed, hardly liked to contemplate the destabilised world which might replace it. Balancing the interests of East and West had become part of the, potentially lethal, game of diplomacy.

The Cold War ended as it had begun and as it had largely been 'fought', that is in significant perplexity on the part of the West about Moscow's intentions and capabilities at any particular juncture. Indeed, a remarkable constant of the Cold War is – despite supposedly sophisticated and, certainly expensive, intelligence systems – how often decisions were taken from a point of more or less ignorance and how major developments in the conflict frequently took the Western combatants by surprise. As attitudes towards the Soviet Union began to harden inside the Foreign Office around March 1946 for instance, the JIC admitted that they had hardly any solid information on conditions inside the USSR and none at all on the purposes of the leadership. The same was true as British policy in occupied Germany crucially began to stiffen. Moreover, British knowledge of Soviet weapons development was so imperfect that estimates on the detonation of a Russian atom bomb were out by five years. Given that an important thrust in the early postwar expansion of the intelligence corps had been the fear of a surprise attack, a 'nuclear Pearl Harbor', this is pretty damning.[3] Korea was another shock. Not only were the British and the other Western Powers taken unawares, they remained uncertain throughout that conflict about who had instigated it and what were the motives. Not much changed. In August 1991, after the Cold War had officially ended, columns of tanks moving through the streets of the Soviet capital suggested to the Moscow Embassy that an attempted coup against Gorbachev might be brewing, although British intelligence failed to predict it. There was no spectacular code-breaking success to match the Enigma triumph during the Second World War, though 'Operation Gold', a joint MI6/CIA enterprise which plugged into the Soviet military headquarters in Berlin via tunnels from the American sector, may have come close. But the venture was revealed to the Russians by an agent working within the British side of the operation. This was George Blake, who was himself uncovered on the evidence of a Soviet bloc defector and was duly arrested, but embarrassingly escaped from Wormwood Scrubbs in 1966, only to turn up in Moscow.

There were some famous successes. A joint British/Commonwealth/ American cryptanalysis programme helped uncover the British atom spy, Klaus Fuchs and the Foreign Office mole, Donald Maclean. The damage caused by the work of such agents remains speculative. It is worth noting that the presence of the Soviet agent Kim Philby as Head of the Soviet section of MI6 between 1944 and 1946 did not prevent a distinct hardening of attitude towards the Russians in sections of Whitehall during this period. As for Fuchs, he was able to pass on valuable atomic information between 1941 and 1948, though the assistance this gave to the Russians in the manufacture of their first atom bomb was probably minimal. Perhaps, as Margaret Gowing implies, Fuchs's activities were, on the whole, beneficial in that they made the world a safer place once the Soviets had achieved nuclear parity.[4] What we do know is that the uncovering of such espionage provided self-inflicted damage to the West by breeding years of distrust between the two major Western Allies over the supposed leakiness of British security and attempts to correct this image merely fed an existing British governmental obsession with secrecy.

The discovery of Soviet missiles in Cuba may be taken as another triumph for Western intelligence, particularly of aerial surveillance. Here too the West was assisted by a lucky break. In the late 1950s Oleg Penkovsky, a General in Soviet military intelligence, agreed to work for the British secret services and it was his smuggled information which helped the Kennedy Administration accurately to decipher what U-2 planes had photographed. Aerial reconnaissance, an essential factor in understanding the capabilities (and intentions) of the Communist bloc, should have meant that there was less to fear and therefore feasibly have reduced both pressure and heat. But the process of obtaining such intelligence could slip, possibly with intent, into dangerously provocative probing of the enemy's radar and defence systems.[5] At the same time, the imperfect results of intelligence acquisition and analysis could and did allow scope for those so inclined to judge the very absence of evidence as indication of the Soviet's artfulness in concealing it. This highlights an associated problem with undercover work of any kind; that is the danger of believing that what is secret is necessarily true. A more particular example of this proclivity is provided in a revealing exchange in November 1945 between Stalin and Wladyslaw Gomulka, the Head of the Polish Communist Party. Stalin accused the British Intelligence Service of the assassination of General Sikorski, the wartime leader of the exiled Poles in London, as well as attempts on the lives of Marshal Tito and Molotov. The truth or otherwise of such claims seems less interesting than Stalin's assertion that the 'rascals and ruthless murderers' within British intelligence 'usually invite you to their country to find out what your weak spots are through either drunkenness or women. Whenever they can, they blackmail the chosen victim and try to recruit people.' This, of course, is a neurotic mirror-image of what was generally taken in the West to be the classic *modus operandi* of the KGB.[6] A sceptic might be tempted to suggest that a good deal of the panoply of intelligence gathering produced little more than a series of stand-offs and shifted the essential direction of the Cold War hardly at all. Except that much remains undisclosed and the definitively clandestine nature of its operation means that its full significance will probably always remain hidden to historians.

By the time of the Cuban success, Britain's voice in the conduct of the Cold War had weakened. It had, in any case, been articulated from the beginning in a predominantly diffident tone. Though they had often been the first to draw lines and to give shape to the Cold War, engagement had rarely been given with enthusiasm and once in the lists, the predominant British inclination was to parley. (Something of the exception to this being, perversely, during the period of détente in the 1970s when most others seemed willing to do so.) That Britain did not naturally produce Cold Warriors was because she had too much to lose. This was partly to do with Britain's obvious vulnerability should war come. On the other hand, though the likelihood of the UK as a target was increased by harbouring American atomic weapons the reaction of successive Governments to having further exposed Britain's position was to construct or purchase more costly and sophisticated armaments of their own. The official view formed quite early on, however, was that existing nuclear weapons were a brake on full-scale military activity and that global war would not erupt as part of a Soviet plan, but through terrible accident or miscalculation. Nevertheless, a whole theory of British deterrence was elaborated, though it was always recognised that this would be inferior to that which the USA could mobilise and that alone it would not be capable of checking the Russians. More than this, Britain's economic and technological deficiencies meant that because of the delays in V-bomber production, they were beaten to the draw by Soviet atomic developments to the extent that between 1954 and the end of the decade a British deterrent did not exist. By the time the V-bombers, were operational they were outmoded by the development of the IRBM. Difficulties in producing a British missile then led to another gap in the deterrent between 1965 and 1969 until Polaris was available from the Americans.[7] This suggests that vulnerability was less a consideration for policy-makers than was often asserted and that at root, the deterrent was not so much about protection as the need for a symbol of Britain's Great Power status and an affirmation that it intended to retain this rank. After all, in relation to her Western European neighbours, Britain's debilitation at the end of the Second World War was relative and the chances of a return to prosperity appeared robust. Overcoming what were regarded as temporary difficulties remained the sought-after grail for much of the period. Thus, the decision to build a British atomic bomb started from the assumption that Britain was one of the Big Three and that her standing demanded that she be a member of the atomic club.

There was another reason why Britain was a somewhat reticent Cold Warrior. As Paul Kennedy has written of the 1930s, Britain 'was now a cautious, rather introspective power hoping for a peaceful life, a restoration of prosperity and the preservation of the *status quo.*'[8] How much more so in 1945. As in the decade before, however, Britain's world-wide responsibilities and interests made this an impossible aspiration. These were bound to rub against the cautious probings of a suspicious, insecure but essentially ideological state which made it irreconcilably hostile in the long run. British responses, at first in the Near East and then in Europe were, notably in Germany, sometimes provocatively premature, though the danger doubtless seemed real at the time and, indeed, was so in the longer term. In the dazzling glare of hindsight it has been said that 'the Soviet system could never have won the Cold War. To do that, it would have needed at some point to have opted for Hot War.'[9] Not so. Between 1945 and 1948 all the Russians had to do was push at weak spots around the territorial core which they controlled and see whether they would be stopped. A good deal of the credit for the failure of these tactical explorations must go to the British decision to stand firm. Behind this tough approach, reluctance elicited the hope of accommodation. As Bevin expressed it at the time of the Berlin blockade, 'one of our great tasks [is] to try to bring about understanding as to how the two countries with their different systems can live together.'[10]

One alternative would have been for the British to have abdicated their position as a world player. But this was never an option and on the infrequent occasions when the possibility was raised, it was done so only to be dismissed. It is, after all, a rarity for a major Power to consign itself to history – the Soviet Union itself providing such an unusual exception. In the final analysis, British policy-formers and -makers were the products of a society with a fixation for rank. In much the same way that they would disdain identification as a third-(or even second-) class brain, British leaders deplored the possibility that their country might become what was so often dismissively termed a 'minor power'; 'just another Luxembourg'; 'another Netherlands' as Bevin and Macmillan respectively expressed it. Instead, they opted for meeting the challenge at first in the Near East and then in Europe and beyond by standing square, holding what they had (and even informally had) and hopefully sending out signals to Moscow that on this basis, some mutually acceptable arrangement could be found. In this way Britain helped shape the contours of the Cold War not just in terms of strategic geography, but also in its language and concepts; containment, globalism, deterrence and *détente* were already part of the thinking of British planners and politicians before being appropriated by the Americans.

Britain, indeed, believed that she had much to teach her transatlantic partner. It would be mistaken to see Britain's engagement in the Cold War as stemming from the determination of a worn-out Power either to make a fighting retreat or to subordinate itself to the mightier Anglo-Saxon state. Exhausted and apprehensive for the future, certainly. But victory over the Axis Powers had augmented the self-confidence of a nation long accustomed to governing much of the world, and which they continued to do. Economically and militarily they might be temporarily down, but they were not out. America's prosperity would sustain them until they were back on their feet. The developing Cold War turned what was intended to be a temporary dalliance with Washington into a dependant's habit. Britain's own technological endeavours, which allowed them entry into the atomic circle, were overwhelmed in an arms race which made continuing subscriptions to this exclusive club supportable only with American donations. Paradoxically, what was intended to be the token of Britain's top-table status became a further drain on a frequently faltering economy and, though there were many who claimed to see it otherwise, a manifestation of British subordination.

The Cold War also diverted the British from another avenue. This was a European role. Their determination to share the contest against Soviet Communism with the United States added another set of blinkers to their attitude to European co-operation. The pass was sold in 1949 when, after a frustrated shot at independence in the shape of Bevin's 'Western Union', the Labour Government linked British defence intimately with the United States, moulding a junior partnership which was to last for the remainder of the century. This did not, however, mark the conclusion of Britain's contribution to the Cold War. For much of the period they continued to have sufficient global real estate to be impossible to ignore making them highly important, if not always compatible, collaborators with the USA in the process of containing Communism. They also took it upon themselves to attempt to restore the formal dialogue between the Powers which had dried up at the end of the 1940s. Indeed, the British frequently coveted the role of intermediary between the Superpowers and possibly of being the broker of a final settlement, as a means of enhancing their esteem and also with the intention that, as the mature Power, they might divert their more excitable partner from unfortunate decisions. There were notable achievements. The Geneva Conference of 1954 and, possibly, Macmillan's part in the embryonic beginnings of nuclear disarmament nine years later. These were sufficiently successful undertakings as a middleman to encourage Wilson and Thatcher, Premiers of a more obviously enfeebled and less confident Britain, to try to continue the process. It may be that those earlier British efforts held the germ of the *détente* of the 1960s and 1970s. This is impossible to judge with any certainty and the truth is that the Americans proved to be not especially susceptible to British influence over major matters. They were not, for instance, enticed by the British in 1949 to guarantee the defence of Western Europe. They had drawn their own conclusions based on their own interests and acted accordingly. Similarly, discourse with the Soviets was resisted by the Americans until the early 1960s when Washington deemed it appropriate and then, unless it suited the Americans to do otherwise, the British tended to be cut out. In the meantime, Britain continued to play its allotted cards in the Cold War game with the zeal of one for whom even being allowed at the table was prize enough and to be proffered the glimpse of undefinable reward. Yet for Britain, as for all those participating in it, the Cold War was, to paraphrase Yeats's verdict on life, a long preparation for nothing.

# NOTES

## Introduction

1.  Geoffrey Warner, 'The Study of Cold War Origins', *Diplomacy and State-craft*, 1:2, 1990, p. 14.
2.  J. Kent (ed.), *British Documents on the End of Empire* (BDEEP), *Egypt and the Defence of the Middle East, I*, p. xxxvi. Some corrective to this view may be found in S. L. Carruthers, 'A Red Under Every Bed?: Anti-Communist Propaganda and Britain's Response to Colonial Insurgency', *Contemporary Record*, 9:2, 1995.
3.  D. C. Watt, 'Rethinking the Cold War: A Letter to a British Historian', *The Political Quarterly*, 49:4, 1978; B. Zeeman, 'Britain and the Cold War: An Alternative Approach. The Treaty of Dunkirk Example', *European History Quarterly*, 16:3, 1986.

## 1 Combat Reconnaissance, 1945–46

1.  Public Record Office (PRO), FO 371 31525, U742/742/70.
2.  PRO, CAB 66/30, WP(42)516, 8 November, 1942.
3.  FO 371 40696, U5407/180/70, May, 1944.
4.  FO 371 C1866/146/18. Minute by Oliver Harvey 12 August, 1944.
5.  FO 371 40725, U8625/180/70.
6.  *Documents on British Policy Overseas* (DBPO), *1/1, The Conference at Potsdam, 1945*, Sir A. Clark Kerr to Eden, 10 July, 1945, p. 147.
7.  *Ibid.*, Memorandum by Sir O. Sergeant, 'Stocktaking after VE-Day', 11 July, 1945, p.187.
8.  PRO, FO 800/302, Inverchapel Papers Vol. 5, record of meeting between Churchill and Stalin at the Kremlin, October, 1944. Churchill was supported by General Sir Ian Jacob, Military Assistant Secretary to the War Cabinet, who had accompanied the Prime Minister to Moscow. Liddell Hart Papers, King's College, London, 1/1944/1.
9.  J. Charmley, *Churchill's Grand Alliance: The Anglo-American Special Relationship 1940-57* (London: Hodder & Stoughton, 1995), p. 127.
10. Halifax Microfilm, Churchill College, Cambridge, A4 410.19.5, note

197

by Halifax, 15 September, 1952.

11. *Daily Telegraph*, 1 October, 1998. There are also indications that, during the war, Stalin believed Churchill capable of using the Germans against him. See C. Andrew, 'Anglo-American-Soviet Intelligence Relations' in A. Lane and H. Temperley (eds), *The Rise and Fall of the Grand Alliance 1941–45* (London: Macmillan, 1995), p. 127.

12. See John Baylis, *The Diplomacy of Pragmatism: Britain and the Formation of NATO, 1942–1949* (London: Macmillan, 1993), pp. 19–36.

13. FO 371, 6793/748/70; COS(44)248.

14. CAB 87/66, Armistice and Post-war Committee, 20 July, 1944.

15. FO 371, 40725, U8625/180/70; FO 371, 40741A, U6793/748/70.

16. FO 371, 40741 A, U6793/748/70.

17. FO 800/302, Inverchapel Papers Vol. 5, 187/24/44, Warner to Sir Archibald Clark-Kerr, 15 May, 1944.

18. Hugh Dalton Diary, London School of Economics, Vol. 31, 9 November, 1944.

19. J. Saville, *The Politics of Continuity: British Foreign Policy and the Labour Government 1945–46* (London: Verso, 1993), p.57.

20. *Foreign Relations of the United States (FRUS), 1945 (II)*, p. 558, Sargent to US Ambassador in London, 5 October, 1945. Sargent was to become Permanent Under-Secretary in the Foreign Office in 1946.

21. Ibid., Record of meeting between Churchill and Stalin at the Kremlin, 9 October, 1944.

22. A. M. Filitov, 'Problems of Post-War Construction in Soviet Foreign Policy Conceptions during World War II', in F. Gori and S. Pons (eds.), *The Soviet Union and Europe in the Cold War, 1943–53* (London: Macmillan, 1996), pp. 3–22.

23. I. Clark and N. J. Wheeler, *The British Origins of Nuclear Strategy 1945–1955* (Oxford: Clarendon Press, 1989), p. 42.

24. FO 371, 43336, N6177/183/38, 4 October, 1944.

25. A. Gorst, '"We Must Cut Our Coat According to Our Cloth": The Making of British Defence Policy, 1945–48', in R. J. Aldrich (ed.), *British Intelligence, Strategy and the Cold War 1945–51* (London: Routledge, 1992), p. 146.

26. See e.g. Bevin Papers, Churchill College, Cambridge, BEVN 3/2E, Bevin to Eden 8 December, 1942; PRO, FO 954/22B, Eden Papers, PWP/45/59 Attlee to Eden 18 July, 1945.

27. Jean Van der Poel (ed.), *Selections from the Smuts Papers, Vol. VII*, (Cambridge: CUP, 1973), p. 6, Attlee to Smuts, 31 August, 1945.

28. M. Gowing, *Independence and Deterrence, Vol. 1* (London: Macmillan, 1974), p. 80.

29. Cripps Papers, Nuffield College, Oxford, Speech at Newcastle, 23 September, 1945.

30. Allan Bullock, *Ernest Bevin: Foreign Secretary* (London: Heinemann, 1983), p. 186; DBPO I/II, p. 525.

31. CAB 132/2, DO(46)40, 13 March, 1946.

32. CAB 132/2, DO (45) 4, 8 August, 1945; FO 371, 50920, conversation between Bevin and Molotov, 1 October, 1945.

33. Minute by Brimelow, 29 October, 1945, cited in M. Kitchen, 'British Policy Towards the Soviet Union, 1945–1948', in G. Gorodetsky (ed.), *Soviet Foreign Policy, 1917–1991: A Retrospective* (London: Frank Cass, 1994), p. 114.

34. CAB 128(7); CM(46)1, 1 January, 1946.

35. Dalton Diary, Vol. 34, 1946, 22 March, 1946.

36. Quoted in Saville, op. cit., p.63.

37. I. Clark and N. J. Wheeler, op. cit., p. 82.

38. DBPO, I/II, p.484.

39. DBPO, I/VI, p. 188.

40. S. Greenwood, 'Frank Roberts and the "Other" Long Telegram: The View from the British Embassy in Moscow, March 1946', *Journal of Contemporary History*, Vol. 25, 1990; R. Smith, 'Ernest Bevin, British Officials and British Soviet Policy, 1945–47', in A. Deighton (ed.), *Britain and the First Cold War* (London: Macmillan, 1990), p. 37.

41. DBPO, I/VI, JIC Report, 1 March, 1946, pp. 297–301.

42. FO 371, N5169/5169/38, memorandum by Christopher Warner, 'The Soviet Campaign Against This Country And Our Response To It', 2 April, 1946.

43. V. O. Pechatnov, 'The Big Three After World War II, New Documents on Soviet Thinking about Post War Relations with the United States and Great Britain', *Cold War International History Project* (CWIHP), Woodrow Wilson Centre, Washington DC, Working Paper 13.

44. Surveys of this material are in William C. Wohlforth, 'New Evidence on Moscow's Cold War' and V. Zubok, 'Stalin's Plans and Russian Archives' in *Diplomatic History*, 21:2, (Spring 1997). See also R.C. Raack, 'Stalin Plans his Post-War Germany', *Journal of Contemporary History*, Vol. 28, (1993).

45. J. van der Poel, *op. cit.*, p. 6, Attlee to Smuts, 31 August, 1945.

46. A. Cairncross, *The Price of War*, (Oxford: Oxford University Press, 1986), p. 99.

47. J. Farquharson, 'From Unity to Division: What Prompted Britain to Change its Policy in Germany in 1946?', *European History Quarterly*, Vol. 26, 1996.

48. FO 371, C4633/14/18, 13 April, 1946.

49. See G. Warner, 'The Study of Cold War Origins', *Diplomacy and Statecraft*, 1:3, 1990.

50. S. Greenwood, *The Alternative Alliance: Anglo-French Relations Before the Coming of NATO, 1944–48*, (London: Minerva, 1996), p. 95.

51. Ibid., pp. 88 and 90.

52. FO 181/990/2, Report of meeting in the Kremlin, 17 October, 1944. See also A. Deighton, *The Impossible Peace: Britain, the Division of Germany and the Origins of the Cold War* (Oxford: Clarendon Press, 1990), pp. 63–4.

53. S. Greenwood, op. cit., p. 142.

54. CAB 128(5); CM(46)11, 4 February, 1946.

55. FO 371, C2188/14/18, 18 February, 1946.

56. FO 371, C1480/131/18, 9 February, 1946.

57. Oliver Harvey Papers, British Library, London, 56402, Vol. XXIV, diary entry 25 March, 1946.
58. FO 371, UR5561/17/851, 27 March, 1946.
59. FO 371, C3997/131/18.
60. CAB 128(5); CM(36)46, 17April, 1946; CAB 129(8); CP(46)139, COS(46)105(0).
61. FO 371, C5123/131/18; CAB 129(9), CP(46)186; C. Kennedy-Pipe, *Stalin's Cold War: Soviet Strategies in Europe, 1943–1956* (Manchester: Manchester University Press, 1995), p. 97.
62. J. Farquharson, op. cit.
63. See A. Bullock, op. cit., p. 268.
64. CAB 129(8), CP(46)139; FO 800, 272, Sargent Papers, CFC/46/1.
65. A. Deighton, op. cit., p. 78.
66. CAB 129(9), CP(46)156, 11 March, 1946; CAB 128(5), CM(46)48, 16 May, 1946; FO 371, C6643/131/18; FO 371, C8643/131/18.
67. J. Farquharson, op. cit., p. 110; Greenwood, op. cit., p. 206.
68. CAB 129(9), CP(46)186, 3 May, 1946.
69. CAB 128(6), CM(46)68, 15 July, 1946; Greenwood, op. cit., p. 209.
70. CAB 129(15),CP(46)461, 3 December, 1946.
71. J. Farquharson, op. cit., p.108.
72. Cited in A. Deighton, 'The "Frozen Front", the Labour Government, the Division of Germany and the Origins of the Cold War, 1945–7', *International Affairs*, 63:3, 1987, p. 453.
73. FO 800, 272 Sargent Papers, Vol. 1, Cfc/47/4, Bevin to Attlee, 16 April, 1947.
74. W. Loth, 'Stalin's Plans for Post-War Germany', in F. Gori and S. Pons (eds), op. cit.; R.C. Raack, op. cit.; and V. Zubok, op. cit.
75. FO 371, C3997/131/18, 3 April, 1946.
76. CAB 134, 595 ORC(46)6, 21 March, 1946. Statement by Dalton.
77. Cited in R. Smith, op. cit., A. Deighton (ed.), *First Cold War*.
78. A. Bullock, op. cit., p. 90.
79. Dalton Diary, Vol. 35, 17 January, 1947; CAB 128(9), CM(47)15, 3 February, 1947.
80. Quoted in M. Blackwell, *Clinging to Grandeur: British Attitudes and Foreign Policy in the Aftermath of the Second World War* (Westport, Connecticut: Greenwood Press, 1993), p. 70.
81. H. Nicolson, *Diaries and Letters, 1945–62*, (London: Collins, 1968), p.76, diary entry, 6 September, 1946.
82. R. Smith and J. Zametica, 'The Cold Warrior: Clement Attlee reconsidered, 1945–7', *International Affairs*, 6:2, 1985.
83. Quoted in ibid.
84. Dalton Diary, Vol. 34, 22 March, 1946.
85. Quoted in R. Smith and J. Zametica, op. cit.
86. PRO, FO 930/488; P449/1/907.
87. R. Merrick, 'The Russia Committee of the British Foreign Office and the Cold War, 1946–47', *Journal of Contemporary History*, Vol. 20, 1985, p. 461.
88. R. Smith, op. cit., in Deighton (ed.), *First Cold War* .

89. See R. Ovendale, *The English-Speaking Alliance: Britain, the United States, the Dominions and the Cold War 1945–51* (London: Allen & Unwin, 1985), pp. 48–52 and J. Saville, op. cit., pp. 135–143.

90. R. Smith, op. cit., in Deighton (ed.) *First Cold War*.

91. Cited in A. Bullock, op. cit., p. 351.

92. S. Greenwood, 'The Third Force in the late 1940s', in B. Brivati and H. Jones (eds.), *From Reconstruction to Integration: Britain and Europe Since 1945* (London, 1993), pp. 59–70.

93. Halifax Microfilm, 410, 4.11. Halifax to Churchill, 3 August, 1945.

94. DBPO, I/II, p. 480.

95. CAB 131(2), DO(46)40, 13 March, 1946.

96. CAB 129(8), CP(46)139, 15 April, 1946.

97. See S. Greenwood, *Britain and European Co-operation Since 1945* (Oxford; Blackwell, 1992), chapters 2 and 3.

## 2 Caught Up in Cold War, 1947–49

1. R. Edmonds, *Setting the Mould: The United States and Britain 1945–1950* (Oxford: Clarendon Press, 1986), p. 168.

2. D. Holloway, *Stalin and the Bomb* (Yale: Yale University Press, 1994), p. 257.

3. V. Zubok and C. Pleshakov, *Inside the Kremlin's Cold War: From Stalin to Khrushchev* (Harvard: Harvard University Press, 1996), p. 39.

4. V. Zubok and C. Pleshakov, 'The Soviet Union' in D. Reynolds (ed.) *The Origins of the Cold War in Europe: International Perspectives* (Yale: Yale University Press, 1994), p. 60.

5. M. P. Leffler, *A Preponderance of Power: National Security, the Truman Administration and the Cold War* (Stanford: Stanford University Press, 1992), chs 1–3.

6. Ibid., p. 99.

7. J. Kent, *British Imperial Strategy and the Origins of the Cold War 1944–49* (Leicester: Leicester University Press, 1993), p. 88.

8. FO 800 272, Sargent Papers, vol. 1, Bevin to Attlee, 16 March, 1947.

9. Pierson Dixon Papers, letter from Gladwyn Jebb to Dixon, 13 March, 1947.

10. Pierson Dixon Diary, 24 February and 21 February, 1947.

11. M. J. Hogan, *The Marshall Plan: America, Britain and the Reconstruction of Western Europe, 1947–1952* (Cambridge: Cambridge University Press, 1987), p. 87.

12. FO 371, C8643/131/18, 23 July, 1946.

13. CAB 128(6); CM(46)100, 25 November, 1946.

14. CAB 128(6); CM(46)68, 15 July, 1946.

15. Hugh Dalton Diary, vol. 35, entry for 17 January, 1947.

16. W. C. Cromwell, 'The Marshall Plan, Britain and the Cold War', *Review of International Studies*, 8:4, 1982.

17. Pierson Dixon Papers, diary entry 17 July, 1947.

18. Cited in G. Roberts, 'Moscow and the Marshall Plan: Politics, Ideology and the Onset of the Cold War, 1947', *Europe-Asia Studies*, 46:8, 1994. Stalin seems to have used this analogy on several occasions around this time.

19. S. Parrish and M. Narinsky, *New Evidence on the Soviet Rejection of the Marshall Plan: Two Reports*, CWIHP, Washington, 1994, p. 41.

20. FO 371, UE 4108/413/53, Bevin to Washington Embassy, 18 October, 1946.

21. S. Parrish, op. cit., p. 23.

22. Ibid., pp. 35–7.

23. Cited in Cromwell, op. cit.

24. F. Williams, *Ernest Bevin* (London: Hutchinson, 1952), p. 265; and I. McDonald, *A Man of the Times* (London: Hamish Hamilton, 1976), p. 114.

25. M. Narinsky, op. cit., pp. 45–6.

26. Pierson Dixon Papers. Account of Paris discussions, 27 June, 1947.

27. M. J. Hogan, op. cit., p. 89.

28. FO 371, N10709/1380/38, Roberts to Warner, 16 September, 1947.

29. P. G. Boyle, 'The British Foreign Office and American Foreign Policy, 1947–48', *Journal of American Studies*, 16:3, 1982, pp. 378–84.

30. FO 371, 67673/Z8579/G, 27 September, 1947.

31. Cited in M. J. Hogan, op. cit., p. 111.

32. B. Pimlott (ed.) *The Political Diary of Hugh Dalton 1918–40* (London: 1986), entry for 15 October, 1948 p. 443.

33. FRUS, 1947, II (Washington, 1972), pp. 815–17.

34. Attlee, Robin Hankey (Head of the Northern Department of the FO) and Christopher Mayhew (Minister at the FO) may each have had a hand in influencing Bevin's famous speech. The overall content, however, was clearly Bevin's own. See V. Rothwell, 'Robin Hankey', in J. Zametica (ed.), *British Officials and Foreign Policy 1945–50* (Leicester: Leicester University Press, 1990), p. 170; and C. Mayhew, *Time to Explain* (London: Hutchinson, 1987), pp. 112–13.

35. On Bevin's supposed evasion see M. Dockrill, 'British Attitudes Towards France as a Military Ally', *Diplomacy and Statecraft*, 1:1, 1990, p. 50 and p. 67.

36. S. Greenwood, 'Return to Dunkirk: The Origins of the Anglo-French Treaty of March, 1947', *Journal of Strategic Studies*, vol. 6, 1983.

37. Cited in M. J. Hogan, op. cit., p. 113. See also J. Kent and J. W. Young, 'British Policy Overseas: The "Third Force" and the Origins of NATO – in Search of a New Perspective', in B. Heuser and R. O'Neill (eds), *Securing Peace in Europe, 1945–62* (London: Macmillan, 1992), pp. 49–50. This article also contains a helpful review of historical interpretations of Britain's Third Force idea.

38. CAB 128/12, CM(48)2, 8 January, 1948; CAB 129/023, CP(48)6, CP(48)7, CP(48)8.

39. Cited in W. Scott Lucas and C. J. Morris, 'A Very British Crusade: The Information Research Department and the Beginning of the Cold War', in Aldrich (ed.), op. cit., p. 91.

40. E. Barker, *The British Between the Superpowers, 1945–50* (London: Macmillan, 1983), p. 104.
41. CAB 128/11; CM(48)2; CAB 129/23; CM(48)8, 8 January, 1948.
42. P. Weiler, *British Labour and the Cold War* (Stanford: Stanford University Press, 1988), pp. 207–13.
43. G. Warner, 'From "Ally" to Enemy: Britain's Relations with the Soviet Union, 1941–48', in F. Gori and S. Pons (eds.), op. cit., p. 306.
44. V. Rothwell, op. cit., p. 173.
45. CAB 129/023; CP(48)7, 5 January, 1948.
46. CAB 128/11; CM(47)3, 15 January, 1947.
47. Cited in J. Kent and J. W. Young, 'The "Western Union" Concept and British Defence Policy, 1947–48', Aldrich (ed.), op. cit., p. 173. See also pp. 177–8.
48. FO 371, 667674, conversation between Bevin and Marshall, 17 December, 1947.
49. Cited in J. Baylis, op. cit., p. 65.
50. J. Kent and J. W. Young, in Aldrich (ed.), op. cit., p. 171.
51. M. Leffler, op. cit., p. 203.
52. See J. Baylis, op. cit., p. 73.
53. J. Charmley, op.cit., pp. 233–39.
54. Ibid., p. 70.
55. Ibid., pp. 85–7.
56. J. Kent and J. W. Young, in Aldrich (ed.), op. cit., pp. 174 and 182.
57. N. Petersen, 'Who Pulled Whom and How Much? Britain, the United States and the Making of the North Atlantic Treaty', *Millenium; Journal of International Studies*, 11:2, 1982, p. 99.
58. J. Kent, op. cit., p. 168.
59. E. Mark, 'The War Scare of 1946 and Its Consequences', *Diplomatic History*, 21:3, 1997.
60. Cited in D. C. Watt, 'British Military Perceptions of the Soviet Union as a Strategic Threat, 1945–50', in J. Becker and F. Knipping (eds), *Power in Europe? Great Britain, France, Italy and Germany in a Postwar World, 1945–50* (Berlin: de Gruyter, 1986), p. 333.
61. FO 371, 70490, C2319/3/18.
62. R. Pearce (ed), *Patrick Gordon Walker: Political Diaries, 1932–71* (London: Historian's Press, 1991), 28 June, 1948, p. 180.
63. A. Shlaim, 'Britain, the Berlin Blockade and the Cold War', *International Affairs*, 60:1, 1983–84. See also R. Edmonds, op. cit., 179.
64. CAB 130/38, GEN 240/1, 24 June, 1948.
65. I. McDonald, op. cit., p. 111.
66. A. Bullock, op. cit., p. 581.
67. J. Kent, op. cit., p. 184.
68. FO 371, 73057/Z3412/G, 17 April, 1948.
69. M. J. Hogan, op. cit., pp. 115–19.
70. Ibid., pp. 239–40.
71. J. Baylis, op. cit., p. 123 and p. 72. Rather differently, some, such as Alan Milward, suggest that Bevin's interest in economic co-ordination with the French had never been serious and that he abandoned even

this low level of interest with the Brussels Treaty. Such a view no longer fits the evidence. A. S. Milward, *The Reconstruction of Western Europe, 1945–51* (London: Methuen, 1984), pp. 235, 248.

72.   J. Kent, op. cit., p. 186.
73.   Cited in N. Petersen, op. cit., p. 108.
74.   M. J. Hogan, op. cit., p. 180.
75.   FO 371, 76384/45405/W3114, PUSC(22), March, 1949.
76.   E. Barker, op. cit., p. 108.
77.   W. Scott Lucas and C. J. Morris in Aldrich (ed.), op. cit., p. 105.
78.   W. K. Wark, 'Coming in from the Cold: British Propaganda and Red Army Defectors, 1945–1952,' *The International History Review*, IX:I, 1987, p. 51 also L. Smith, 'Covert British Propaganda: The Information Research Department, 1947–77', *Millenium*, 9:1, 1980.
79.   A. Danchev, *Oliver Franks: Founding Father* (Oxford: Clarendon Press, 1993), p. 107.
80.   J. Kent, 'Bevin's Imperialism and the Idea of Euro-Africa, 1945–49' in Dockrill and Young, p. 66; J. W. Young, *France, the Cold War and the Western Alliance, 1944–1949* (Leicester: Leicester University Press, 1990), p. 169.
81.   FO 371, 73109/Z9292/G, 26 October, 1948.

## 3  Empire Without Clothes, 1945–51

1.    PRO, CAB 81/94, JIC(46)28 22 May, 1946.
2.    CAB 128/1, CM28(45)6, 4 October, 1945.
3.    CAB 81/133, JIC(46)70, 23 September, 1946.
4.    CAB 129/2, CP(45)174, 17 September, 1945.
5.    R. Hyam (ed.), *British Documents on the End of Empire* (BDEEP): *The Labour Government and the End of Empire 1945–51, Part III* (London: HMSO, 1992), p. 222, Dixon to Bevin, 9 December, 1946.
6.    CAB 81/132, JIC(46)1, 1 March, 1946; CAB 81/133, JIC(46)64 6 July, 1946.
7.    CAB 81/133, JIC(46)70, 23 September, 1946; FO 930/488, 29 May, 1946.
8.    CAB 128/11, CM6(47)3, 15 January, 1947.
9.    FO 371 69193, 12 March, 1948; DEFE 4/8, COS 144 (47) 1, 21 November, 1947, cited in BDEEP, Egypt, Part I, pp. 251–2. See also, P. Weiler, *Ernest Bevin* (Manchester: Manchester University Press, 1993), p. 169.
10.   W. K. Wark, 'Development Diplomacy: Sir John Troutbeck and the British Middle East Office, 1947–50', in J. Zametica (ed.), *British Officials and British Foreign Policy, 1945–50* (Leicester: Leicester University Press, 1990).
11.   BDEEP, Egypt, pt. I, pp. lv–lvi.
12.   CAB 129/2, CP(45)174, 17 September, 1945.
13.   J. Kent (ed.), BDEEP, Egypt, pt I, p. lix.
14.   CAB 131/9, DO(50)45, 7 June, 1950.

15. Historical Branch of the Foreign and Commonwealth Office, Occasional Papers No. 5, April 1992, p. 13.

16. T. Remme, *Britain and Regional Cooperation in South-East Asia, 1945–49* (London: Routledge, 1995), pp. 57–8.

17. Ibid., p. 123.

18. R. Ovendale, *The English Speaking Alliance: Britain, the United States, the Dominions and the Cold War, 1945–51* (London: Unwin, 1985), pp. 151–2; T. Kaplan, 'Britain's Asian Cold War: Malaya', in A. Deighton (ed.), *First Cold War*, pp. 212–13.

19. FO 371, F8338/1075/61G, 24 May, 1949.

20. T. Remme, op. cit., pp. 140–3.

21. CAB 131/9, DO(50)45, 7 June, 1950.

22. T. Kaplan, op. cit., p. 216; S. L. Carruthers, op. cit., p. 302.

23. R. Ovendale, op. cit., pp. 171–2; A. J. Rotter, *The Path to Vietnam: Origins of the American Commitment to South-East Asia* (Ithaca: Cornell University Press), ch. 3.

24. DBPO, II/II, p. 271, Bevin to Acheson, 9 May, 1950.

25. FO 371, W3114/G, PUSC(51), Final Report by the Permanent Under-Secretary's Committee on 'Anglo-American Relations: Present and Future', 24 August, 1949.

26. T. Remme, op. cit., p. 196.

27. R. J. Aldrich, 'British Strategy and the End of Empire: South Asia, 1945–51' in R. J. Aldrich (ed.), op. cit.

28. A. J. Rotter, op. cit., pp. 152–3.

29. R. Ovendale, op. cit., p. 166.

30. R. Ovendale, 'Britain and the Cold War in Asia', in R. Ovendale (ed.), *The Foreign Policy of the British Labour Governments* (Leicester: Leicester University Press, 1984), p. 142.

31. A. J. Rotter, op. cit., p. 163.

32. Ibid., p. 119.

33. PRO, DEFE 4/31, COS 70(50)4, 2 May, 1950, cited in Hyam, op. cit.

34. K. Harris, *Attlee* (London: Weidenfeld and Nicolson, 1982), p. 456.

35. DBPO, II/IV, p. 4, minute by P. Dixon, 26 June, 1950; 12, p. 32, letter from Sir A. Gascoigne (Tokyo), 5 July, 1950.

36. Ibid., 8, p. 18, despatch from Sir D. Kelly, 30 June, 1950.

37. E. Bajanov, 'Assessing the Politics of the Korean War, 1949–51', CWIHP Bulletin, issues 6–7, Winter 1995/96, p. 87.

38. DBPO, II/IV, p. 5, despatch from Sir O. Franks (Washington), 27 June, 1950.

39. Ibid., 2i, pp. 2–4.

40. CAB 128/18, CM42(50)3, 4 July, 1950.

41. CAB 128/18, CM(50)50, 25 July, 1950; M. L. Dockrill, 'The Foreign Office, Anglo-American Relations and the Korean War, June 1950–June 1951', *International Affairs*, 26:3, 1986, p. 460.

42. DBPO, II/IV, pp. 76–8, despatch by Sir O. Franks, 23 July, 1950.

43. Ibid., 35, p. 100, Bevin to Franks, 11 August, 1950.

44. Ibid., 17, pp. 46–9.

45. CAB 128/18, CM(50)55, 4 September, 1950; DBPO, II/IV, 35, pp. 99–

102, Bevin to Franks, 11 August, 1950.

46. DBPO, II/IV, pp. 210–12, Bevin to Franks, 22 November, 1950.
47. P. G. Boyle, 'Oliver Franks and the Washington Embassy, 1948–52', in J. Zametica (ed.), *British Officials*, p. 202.
48. DBPO, II/IV, p. 171.
49. E. Bajanov, op. cit., p. 89.
50. CAB 128/18, CM(50) 78, 29 November, 1950.
51. DBPO, II/IV, p. 238, Bevin to Franks, 4 December, 1950.
52. Ibid., 81, p. 223.
53. I. Clark and N. J. Wheeler, op. cit., pp. 137–9.
54. DBPO, II/IV, p. 235.
55. Ibid., p. 249; p. 311.
56. Ibid., p. 239.
57. Ibid., p. 257, Attlee to Bevin, 10 December, 1950.
58. Ibid., p. 275, minute by Shuckburgh, 28 December, 1950.
59. B. Pimlott (ed.), *Dalton Diary*, op. cit., 21 December, 1950, p. 495.
60. DBPO, II/IV, p. 250, minute by Sir P. Dixon, 8 December, 1950.
61. Minute by Strang, 3 January, 1951, cited in Dockrill, *Korean War*, p. 468.
62. DBPO, II/IV, p. 288.
63. Ibid., p. 323–4, FO to Franks, 23 January, 1951.
64. P. M. Williams (ed.), *The Diary of Hugh Gaitskell, 1945–56* (London: Cape, 1983), 2 February, 1951, p. 233.
65. DBPO, II/IV, p. 343–4, minute by Pierson Dixon, 28 January, 1951.
66. Ibid., pp. 52–62, FO memorandum, 13 July, 1950.
67. DBPO, II/II, 56, p. 209, Dening to Strang, 3 May, 1950.
68. DBPO, II/IV, pp. 375–6, Commonwealth Relations Office to Canberra, 13 March, 1951.
69. Ibid., pp. 389–94, Younger to Jebb, 31 March, 1951; p. 351, memorandum by Scott, 1 February, 1951.
70. CAB 128/18, CM(50)79, 11 November, 1950.
71. PREM 8/1439, Bevin to Attlee, 12 January, 1951.
72. A. Cairncross (ed.), *The Robert Hall Diaries, 1947–53* (London: Unwin Hyman, 1989), p. 156, diary entry, 30 April, 1951; p. 119, diary entry, 26 June, 1950.
73. DBPO, II/III, p. 382, CoS draft report, 15 December, 1950.
74. Ibid., pp. 111–18, Franks to Bevin, 27 September, 1950.
75. Ibid., p. 4, 23 August, 1950.
76. B. Pimlott (ed.), *Dalton Diary*, op. cit., 21 December, 1950, p. 495; R. Pearce (ed.) Gordon Walker Diaries, 1 November, 1950, p. 191; T. Shaw, 'The Information Research Department of the British Foreign Office and the Korean War', *Journal of Contemporary History*, 34:2, 1999.
77. DEFE 6/14, JP(50) 90 (Final), 1 July, 1950.
78. M. Leffler, op. cit., pp. 384 and 401.
79. P. Hennessy, *Never Again: Britain 1945–1951* (London: Cape, 1993), p. 415.

## 4  Innovators, 1950–56

1.  PUSC(51)16, 17 January, 1952. Cited in J. Young (ed.), 'The British Foreign Office and Cold War Fighting in the Early 1950s: PUSC(51)16 and the 1952 "Sore Spots" Memorandum', *University of Leicester Discussion Papers in Politics, No. P95/2*. The PUSC's was not very different from one Soviet projection of the postwar world made in 1944. See above p. 12.
2.  FRUS, 1952–54, II, 7 October, 1953, pp. 514–34.
3.  CAB 131/12, D(52)26, 17 June, 1952.
4.  PREM 11/323 15 November, 1952.
5.  J. Young, 'Cold War Fighting', op. cit.
6.  CAB 129/53, C(52)202, 18 June, 1952.
7.  CAB 129/48, C(51)1, 31 October, 1951.
8.  Harold Macmillan Diary, Bodleian Library, Oxford, 27 September, 1952; 27 January, 1952.
9.  CAB 131/12, D(52)41, 29 September, 1952; D(52)45, 31 October, 1952; CAB 129/55, C(52)320, 3 October, 1952.
10. V. Rothwell, 'Britain and the First Cold War', in R. Crockatt and S. Smith (eds), *The Cold War Past and Present* (London: Unwin Hyman, 1987), p. 67. On Britain's supposed use of Cold War rhetoric to gain American support for traditional British interests in the Middle East, see W. Scott Lucas, 'The Path to Suez: Britain and the Struggle for the Middle East, 1953–56' in A. Deighton (ed.), *First Cold War*, op. cit., p. 254.
11. E. Shuckburgh, *Descent to Suez: Diaries 1951–56* (London: Weidenfeld and Nicolson, 1986), p. 59, diary entry, 24 November, 1952. Shuckburgh was Eden's Private Secretary.
12. A. Adamthwaite, 'The Foreign Office and Policy Making', in J. W. Young (ed.), *The Foreign Policy of Churchill's Peacetime Administration, 1951–55* (Leicester: Leicester University Press, 1988), p. 10.
13. CAB 131/12, D(52)26, 'Defence Policy and Global Strategy', 17 June, 1952.
14. J. Baylis and A. Macmillan, 'The British Global Strategy Paper of 1952', *Journal of Strategic Studies*, 16:2, June 1993.
15. See e.g. A. M. Johnston, 'Mr. Slessor Goes to Washington: The Influence of the British Global Strategy Paper on the Eisenhower New Look', *Diplomatic History*, 22:3, Summer 1998.
16. I. Clark and N. J. Wheeler, op. cit., pp. 165–9.
17. Ibid., p. 217.
18. Macmillan Diary, 22 February, 1953; 23 July, 1954.
19. CAB 131/12, D(51)3, October 1951; D(52)2, 19 March, 1952.
20. E. Shuckburgh, op. cit., p. 54, diary entry, 19 November, 1952.
21. P. Lowe, 'The Significance of the Korean War in Anglo-American Relations, 1950–53, in M. Dockrill and J. W. Young ( eds), op. cit., p. 145.
22. Lord Moran, *Winston Churchill: The Struggle for Survival* (London: Constable, 1966), p. 355, 5 January, 1952.
23. CAB 129/54, C(52)267, 28 July, 1952.

24. D. Goldsworthy (ed.), *British Documents on the End of Empire* (BDEEP), series A, vol. 3, pt 1 (London: HMSO, 1994), p. 44.
25. Moran, op. cit., p. 367, 17 January, 1952.
26. See e.g. BDEEP, A/3, p. xxxiii and J. Charmley, *Grand Alliance*, op. cit., p. 269.
27. BDEEP, A/3, p. 9 and p. 44; Macmillan Diary, 28 January, 1952; 29 April, 1952; E. Shuckburgh, op. cit., p. 63, 2 December, 1952.
28. BDEEP, A/3, p. 129.
29. CAB 129/53, C(52)202.
30. D. R. Devereux, 'Britain and the Failure of Collective Defence in the Middle East, 1948–53', in A. Deighton (ed.), *First Cold War.*
31. CAB 129/59, C(53)65, 16 February, 1953; CAB 129/56, C(52)269, 27 October, 1952.
32. E. Shuckburgh, op. cit., p. 76, diary entry, 30 January, 1953.
33. BDEEP, A/3, p. 122, Churchill to Eden, 15 January, 1953; p. 135, Cabinet note by Macmillan, 14 October, 1955.
34. CAB 131/13, D(53)45.
35. National Archives, Washington, RG59, Box 2770, 611.41/6–1553, Livingstone Merchant to Dulles, 15 June, 1953. I am grateful to Dr Kevin Ruane for drawing my attention to this document.
36. B. Holden Reid, 'The "Northern Tier" and the Baghdad Pact', in J. W. Young (ed.), *Churchill's Peacetime Administration*; W. Scott Lucas, 'The Path to Suez: Britain and the Struggle for the Middle East, 1953–56', in A. Deighton (ed.), *First Cold War.*
37. Macmillan Diary, 30 July, 1952.
38. Ibid., 23 December, 1952.
39. Ibid., 20 August, 1952.
40. PREM 11/323, 15 November, 1952.
41. B. Holden Reid, op. cit., p. 169.
42. PREM 11/49, report from Franks, 1 August, 1952; Ewbank to Hunt, 20 August, 1952.
43. On the EDC, see S. Greenwood, *European Co-operation* ch 5 and S. Greenwood, *Britain and European Integration Since the Second World War* (Manchester: Manchester University Press, 1996), ch 2.
44. PREM 11/49. Report by Franks, 1 August, 1952.
45. K. Ruane, 'Anthony Eden, British Diplomacy and the Origins of the Geneva Conference of 1954', *The Historical Journal*, 37:1, 1994.
46. P. G. Boyle (ed.), *The Churchill-Eisenhower Correspondence, 1953–55* (Chapel Hill: University of North Carolina Press, 1990), p. 137.
47. Macmillan Diary, 12 April, 1954.
48. K. Ruane, 'Containing America: Aspects of British Foreign Policy and the Cold War in Southeast Asia, 1951–54', *Diplomacy and Statecraft*, 7, 1996.
49. K. Ruane, 'Geneva Conference', pp. 168–9.
50. K. Ruane, 'Geneva Conference', p. 168.
51. CAB 129/68, C(54)155; record of emergency Cabinet meetings, 25 April, 1954.
52. K. Ruane, 'Containing America', pp. 164–6.

53. J. Cable, *The Geneva Conference of 1954 on Indochina* (Macmillan: London, 1986), pp. 56–60.

54. E. Shuckburgh, op. cit., p. 172, 24 April, 1954.

55. CAB 129/68, C(54)155.

56. Macmillan Diary, 25 April, 1954.

57. Ibid., 6 June, 1954.

58. E. Shuckburgh, op. cit., p. 175–6, 25 April, 1954.

59. I. McDonald, op. cit., p. 137; E. Shuckburgh, op. cit., p. 172, 24 April, 1954.

60. J. Cable, op. cit., p.51.

61. I. McDonald, op. cit., p. 136.

62. E. Shuckburgh, op. cit., p. 174, 25 April, 1954; p. 198, 9 May, 1954.

63. I. McDonald, op. cit., p. 138; K. Ruane, *War and Revolution in Vietnam, 1930–75* (London: University College London Press, 1998), pp. 35–6.

64. Macmillan Diary, 22 May, 1954.

65. Ibid., 26 October; 31 October, 1952.

66. Ibid., 24 August, 1954.

67. A. Deighton, 'Britain and the Cold War, 1945–55: An Overview', in Brivati and Jones, op. cit., p. 12.

68. Macmillan Diary, 19 August, 1954.

69. Ibid., 3 September, 1954.

70. S. Dockrill, 'Britain and the Settlement of the West German Rearmament Question in 1954', in M. Dockrill and J. W. Young, op. cit., p. 167.

71. P.-H. Spaak, *The Continuing Battle* (London: Weidenfeld and Nicolson, 1971), p. 188; Macmillan Diary, 24 October, 1954; S. Greenwood, *European Cooperation*, p. 54.

72. J. W. Young, *Winston Churchill's Last Campaign: Britain and the Cold War, 1951–55* (Oxford: Clarendon Press, 1996), p. 292; D. Dutton, op. cit., pp. 304–5.

73. Macmillan Diary, 27 September, 1954; Avon Papers (Birmingham University), Eden Diary, 15 September, 1954. B. R. Duchin, 'The "Agonizing Reappraisal": Eisenhower, Dulles and the European Defense Community', *Diplomatic History*, 16, 1992. Similar claims have been made for Eden's success at the Geneva Conference. See K. Ruane, *War and Revolution*, p. 36.

74. Macmillan Diary, 24 October, 1954.

75. Avon Papers, Eden Diary, 17 September, 1954.

76. S. Dockrill, op. cit., p. 157.

77. Moran, op.cit., p. 558, 24 June, 1954.

78. M. Gilbert, 'From Yalta to Bermuda and Beyond: In Search of Peace with the Soviet Union', in J. W. Muller (ed.), *Churchill as Peacemaker* (Cambridge: Cambridge University Press, 1997), p. 326.

79. J. W. Young, *Last Campaign*, p. 29.

80. FO 371/103660/C 1016/32, 19 May, 1953.

81. E. Shuckburgh, op. cit., pp. 82–5, 1 and 2 April, 1953.

82. Macmillan Diary, 4 August, 1953.

83. Ibid., 12 May; 19 August, 1953.

84. Ibid., 14 February, 1954.
85. Y. Smirnov and V. Zubok, 'Nuclear Weapons After Stalin's Death: Moscow Enters the H-Bomb Age', *CWIHP Electronic Bulletin*, b4a14.
86. Macmillan Diary, 10 July, 1954.
87. Ibid., 4 August, 1953.
88. .Ibid., 10 July, 1954. For an American view of Churchill's declining powers see, FRUS, 1952–54, vol. vi, p. 1099.
89. J. Colville, *The Fringes of Power: 10 Downing Street Diaries* (Hodder and Stoughton: London, 1985), p. 683.
90. Macmillan Diary, 10 July, 1954.
91. FRUS, 1952–54, vol. vi, p. 1111.
92. J. W. Young, *Last Campaign*, pp. 281–2.
93. Macmillan Diary, 10 July, 1954.
94. Unpublished Shuckburgh Diaries, 5 and 6 July, 1954.
95. Ibid., 12 July, 1954.
96. Ibid., 14 July, 1954.
97. Macmillan Diary, 10 July, 1954.
98. Moran, op. cit., p. 590, 12 August, 1954.
99. J. W. Young, *Last Campaign*, pp. 325–6.
100. Ibid. p. 317.
101. Macmillan Diary, 21 October, 1954.
102. J. Colville, op. cit., p. 680, October 1953.
103. J. Richter, 'Reexamining Soviet Policy Towards Germany During the Beria Interregnum', CWIHP, Working Paper 3: V. M. Zubok, 'Soviet Intelligence and the Cold War: The "Small" Committee of Information, 1952–53', CWIHP, Working Paper 4.
104. J. Colville, op. cit., p.683, diary entry for 4 December, 1953.
105. Macmillan Diary, 31 July, 1954.
106. Cited in K. Ruane, 'Containing America', p. 169.
107. DEFE 6/51, JP(58)110, 22 August, 1958; DEFE 5/82, COS(58), 12 March, 1958.
108. E. Shuckburgh, op. cit., p. 187, 2 May, 1954.

## 5 Dedicated to *Détente*, 1956–63

1. Macmillan Diary, 15 September and 3 October, 1956. Emphasis in original.
2. Arthur Mann Papers, Bodleian Library, Oxford, Eden to Mann, 5 May, 1958.
3. Macmillan Diary, 25 September, 1956.
4. DEFE 4/87, JP(56)71, 28 May, 1956; FO 371/ 118676, February, 1956.
5. Arthur Mann Papers, Eden to Mann, 3 December, 1956.
6. D. Dutton, *Anthony Eden: A Life and Reputation* (London: Arnold, 1997), pp. 368–72.
7. J. Charmley, op. cit., p. 328 and p. 342.
8. Macmillan Diary, 2 May, 1953; 6 May, 1953.

9.  FO 371, 126082, Caccia to Foreign Office, 1 January, 1957, cited in M. Dockrill, 'Restoring the "special relationship": The Bermuda and Washington Conferences, 1957', in D. Richardson and G. Stone ( eds), *Decisions and Diplomacy: Essays in Twentieth-Century International History* (London: Routledge, 1995), p. 207.

10.  W. Clark, *From Three Worlds* (London: Sidgwick and Jackson, 1986), p. 211; Y. Smirnov and V. Zubok, op. cit.

11.  Comments by Lord Strang in 1963, cited in A. Adamthwaite, 'Suez Revisited', in M. Dockrill and J. W. Young (eds), op. cit., p. 242.

12.  D. Dutton, op. cit., p. 390.

13.  Arthur Mann Papers, Eden to Mann, 31 December, 1957.

14.  CAB 134, 1929, 'Future Policy Study 1960–70', 24 February, 1960.

15.  Lord Beloff, 'The Crisis and its Consequences for the British Conservative Party', in William Roger Louis and R. Owen (eds), *Suez 1956: The Crisis and its Consequences* (Oxford: Clarendon Press, 1989), p. 334.

16.  N. Ashton, 'Macmillan and the Middle East', in R. Aldous and S. Lee (eds), *Harold Macmillan and Britain's World Role* (London: Macmillan, 1996), p. 53.

17.  N. J. Ashton, '"A Great New Venture" ? – Anglo-American Cooperation in the Middle East and the Response to the Iraqi Revolution July 1958', *Diplomacy and Statecraft*, 4:1, March 1993.

18.  Ibid. For a different perspective, see R. Ovendale, 'Great Britain and the Anglo-American Invasion of Jordan and Lebanon in 1958', *International History Review*, 16:2, May, 1994.

19.  Arthur Mann Papers, Eden to Mann, 15 December, 1958; A. Horne, *Macmillan, 1957–1986* (London: Macmillan, 1989), p. 98.

20.  PREM 11/1138, note by Eden, 28 December, 1956.

21.  CAB 129/84, CP(57)6, 5 January, 1957.

22.  CAB 128/30/2, CM(57)3 dated 9 January, discussed 8 January, 1957.

23.  PREM 11/1841, Selwyn Lloyd to Macmillan, 28 May, 1957.

24.  Macmillan Diary, 9 March and 7 May, 1957.

25.  CAB 134/1315, PR(56)11, note by Eden, 15 June, 1956.

26.  E. Shuckburgh, op. cit., p. 335, 20 February, 1956. The view is not Shuckburgh's own, but allegedly that of Foreign Office colleagues.

27.  S. J. Ball, 'Macmillan and British Defence Policy', in Aldous and Lee (eds), op. cit.

28.  FRUS, 1955–57, vol. XXVII.

29.  M. S. Navias, '"Vested Interests and Vanished Dreams": Duncan Sandys, the Chiefs of Staff and the 1957 White Paper', in P. Smith (ed.), *Government and the Armed Forces in Britain, 1856–1990* (London: Hambledon Press, 1996), p. 223.

30.  A. Horne, op. cit., p. 46.

31.  PRO, FO 371, 126683, AU/1501/28, Washington to the Foreign Office, 28 January, 1957.

32.  Macmillan Diary, 12 May, 1957.

33.  Cited in I. Clark, *Nuclear Diplomacy and the Special Relationship: Britain's Deterrent and America, 1957–62* (Oxford: Clarendon Press, 1994), p. 122.

34.  Ibid., 23 October, 1957.

35.  FRUS, 1955–57, vol. XXVII, 309, p. 794, Livingston Merchant, US Ambassador to Canada, to Dulles, 19 October, 1957.

36.  I. Clark, op. cit., p. 77.

37.  FRUS, 1955–57, vol. XXVII, pp. 790–96.

38.  FO 371/ 132330, SC(58)8, 27 January, 1958.

39.  FRUS, 1955–57, vol. XXVII, p. 776, Macmillan to Eisenhower, 12 June, 1957.

40.  PREM 11/449, Selwyn Lloyd to Churchill, 22 June, 1953.

41.  K. Schake, 'The Berlin Crises of 1948–49 and 1958–62', in B. Heuser and R. O'Neill (eds), *Securing Peace in Europe, 1945–62* (London: Macmillan, 1992), p. 67; 'New Evidence on the Berlin Crisis 1958–62,' CWIHP, Bulletin II, 1998, p. 202.

42.  D. R. Thorpe, *Selwyn Lloyd* (London: Cape, 1989), p. 287.

43.  Macmillan Diary, 5 January, 1959.

44.  R. Aldous, '"A Family Affair": Macmillan and the Art of Personal Diplomacy', in R. Aldous and S. Lee (eds), op. cit., p. 16.

45.  FRUS, 1961–63, vol. XIII, Bruce to State Department, 12 December, 1961, p. 1045.

46.  R. Lamb, *The Macmillan Years: The Emerging Truth* (London: John Murray, 1995), p. 329.

47.  Ibid., p. 326.

48.  J. P. S. Gearson, *Harold Macmillan and the Berlin Wall Crisis, 1958–62: The Limits of Interest and Force* (London: Macmillan, 1998), pp. 190–8.

49.  Macmillan Diary, 19 December, 1958.

50.  FRUS, 1955–57, vol. XXVII, p. 808, Washington Conference, October 23, 1957.

51.  H. Macmillan, *Riding the Storm, 1956–59* (London: Macmillan, 1971), p. 588–9. This was outlined to Dulles on 4 February, 1959. See also comments to Khrushchev, ibid., p. 626.

52.  J. Turner, *Macmillan* (London: Longman, 1994), p. 147. The invitation to Khrushchev seems to have been the result of a bureaucratic error rather than a deliberate change of policy. CWIHP, Bulletin II, 1998.

53.  R. J. Aldrich, *Espionage, Security and Intelligence in Britain, 1945–70* (Manchester: Manchester University Press, 1998), pp. 87–90, 101–6; P. Lashmar, *Spy Flights in the Cold War* (Stroud, Glos.: Sutton, 1996).

54.  A. Horne, op. cit., p. 231 and p. 233.

55.  FO 371/13451, 6 November, 1958.

56.  CAB 134/1820, EQ(60)27, 25 May, 1960.

57.  O. Bange, 'Grand Designs and the Diplomatic Breakdown', in G. Wilkes (ed.), *Britain's Failure to Enter the European Community 1961–63* (London: Frank Cass, 1997), p. 197.

58.  H. Macmillan, *Pointing the Way 1959–61* (London: Macmillan, 1972), p. 253.

59.  I. Clark, op. cit., pp. 299, 316–7, 325–37.

60.  H. Macmillan, *At the End of the Day 1961–63* (London: Macmillan, 1973), p. 361–2.

61.  FRUS, 1961–63, vol. XIII, p. 1090.

62.  P. G. Boyle, 'The British Government's View of the Cuban Missile Cri-

sis', *Contemporary Record*, 10:3, 1996; L. Scott, 'Close to the Brink? Britain and the Cuban Missile Crisis', in ibid., 5:3, 1991.

63. E. R. May and P. D. Zelikow, *The Kennedy Tapes: Inside the White House During the Cuban Missile Crisis* (Cambridge, Mass.: Harvard University Press, 1997), p. 692.

64. H. Macmillan, *At the End of the Day*, p. 361–2.

65. A. Horne, op. cit., p. 437.

66. Cited in J. L. Gaddis, *We Now Know: Rethinking Cold War History* (Oxford: Clarendon Press, 1998), p. 264.

67. FRUS, 1961–63, vol. XIII, American Mission to NATO to State Department, 18 December, 1961, p. 1052.

68. Cited in R. Lamb, op. cit., p. 303.

69. S. Zuckerman, *Monkeys, Men and Missiles: An Autobiography, 1946–88* (London: Collins, 1988), p. 254.

70. R. H. Paterson, *Britain's Nuclear Deterrent* (London: Frank Cass, 1997), p. 22.

71. PREM 11/4230, Julian Amery to Macmillan, 27 December, 1962.

72. A. Horne, op. cit., p. 447.

73. H. Evans, op. cit., p. 285; J. Turner, op. cit., pp. 172–3; R. Lamb, op. cit., p. 373; C. J. Bartlett, *The Special Relationship* (Longman: London, 1992), p. 97.

74. K. Pyne, 'Art or Article?: The Need for and Nature of the British Hydrogen Bomb, 1954–58', *Contemporary Record*, 9:3, 1995, pp. 574–9; I. Clark, op. cit., p. 210.

75. FRUS, 1955–57, vol. XXVII, p. 769.

76. I. Clark, op. cit., p. 108.

77. R. Lowe, review of R. Lamb, op. cit., *Contemporary British History*, 10:2, 1996 , p. 239.

78. B. White, *Britain, Détente and Changing East-West Relations* (London: Routledge, 1992), p. 105.

79. R. Crockatt, *The Fifty Years War: The United States and the Soviet Union in World Politics, 1941–1991* (London: Routledge, 1995), p. 157.

80. Ibid., p. 158.

## 6 Defeating Themselves, 1964–91

1. FRUS, 1955–57, vol. XXVII, Macmillan to Eisenhower, 10 October, 1957, p. 785.

2. PREM 11/3325, Macmillan memorandum, composed 29 December, 1960 to 3 January, 1961.

3. J. Kent (ed.), BDEEP, B/4, pt 1, p. xciv.

4. PREM 11/4791, memorandum by J. O. Wright (Personal Secretary) to Home, 26 March, 1964.

5. R. Crossman, *The Diaries of a Cabinet Minister, Vol. 1* (London: Cape, 1975), p. 95, 11 December, 1964.

6. PREM 13/104, record of Washington talks, 7 December, 1964. Eight-

een months earlier McNamara had urged Gordon Walker that 'it was important that [Britain] should stay in the Indian Ocean. [The US] didn't want to be gendarmes of the whole world', R. Pearce (ed.), *Gordon Walker Diaries*, op. cit., 31 May, 1963, p. 290.

7. PREM 13/004, Wilson to Australian and New Zealand Prime Ministers, 14 December, 1964.
8. B. Reed and G. Williams, *Denis Healey and the Policies of Power* (London: Cape, 1971), p. 173.
9. PREM 13/104.
10. B. White, op. cit., p. 119.
11. PREM 13/692, Washington Embassy to Foreign Office, 1 December, 1964.
12. R. Steininger, '"The Americans are in a Hopeless Position": Great Britain and the War in Vietnam, 1964–65', *Diplomacy and Statecraft*, 8:3, November, 1997.
13. R. Pearce (ed.), *Gordon Walker Diaries*, op. cit., pp. 302–6.
14. See e.g. G. Brown, *In My Way* (London: Gollancz, 1971), pp. 142–7.
15. A. P. Dobson, *Anglo-American Relations in the Twentieth Century* (London: Routledge, 1995), pp. 132–7.
16. J. Darwin, *Britain and Decolonisation: The Retreat from Empire in the Postwar World* (London: Macmillan, 1988), pp. 294–8.
17. R. Crossman, *The Diaries of a Cabinet Minister, Vol. 2* (London: Cape, 1976), p. 646–7, 12 January, 1968.
18. PREM 13/103, 2 December, 1964.
19. DBPO, III/I, Moscow Embassy to the Foreign Office, 30 September, 1968, p. 77–9.
20. H. Kissinger, *White House Years* (Boston, Massachusetts: Little Brown, 1979), p. 421.
21. DBPO, III/I, FCO minute, 22 July, 1970, p. 248; Cabinet conclusions, 11 December, 1969, p. 199.
22. Ibid., Joint Intelligence Committee (A) Paper, 14 September, 1972, p. 517; see also JIC(A) report, 15 December, 1969, pp. 200–5.
23. Ibid., Sir Thomas Brimelow to Moscow Embassy, 14 August, 1970, pp. 257–8.
24. B. White, op. cit., p. 135.
25. The debate is covered in DBPO, III/I, Douglas-Home to Wilson, 1 December, 1970, p. 287; Wilson to Douglas-Home, 8 February, 1971, p. 298; Wilson to Douglas-Home, 10 August, 1971, p. 366.
26. Ibid., p. 377.
27. DBPO, III/II, Wiggin to Brimelow, 14 March, 1972, p. 19; Killick to Preston, 12 August, 1975, p. 447.
28. D. Healey, *The Time of My Life* (London: Michael Joseph, 1989), p. 309–10.
29. DBPO, III/II, p. 456; J. Callaghan, *Time and Chance* (London: Collins, 1987), pp. 552–7.
30. B. White, op. cit., pp. 136–40.
31. DBPO, III/II, Killick to Tickell, 4 August, 1972. p. 497.
32 .J. P. D. Dunbabin, *The Cold War: The Great Powers and Their Allies* (Lon-

don: Longman, 1994), pp. 310–11; S. J. Ball, *The Cold War: An International History 1947–1991* (London: Arnold, 1998), p. 150.

33.   C. Andrew and O. Gordievsky, *KGB: The Inside Story* (London: Hodder and Stoughton, 1990), p. 450.

34.   DBPO, III/I, minute by Sir T. Brimelow, August 1971, p. 369.

35.   C. Andrew and O. Gordievsky, op. cit., pp. 488–9, 493, 495–6, 502–3.

36.   B. White, op. cit., p. 143.

37.   M. Thatcher, *The Downing Street Years* (London: Harper Collins, 1993), p. 452.

38.   M. Thatcher, op. cit. p. 238.

39.   R. Crockatt, op. cit., p. 307.

40.   M. Thatcher, op. cit., pp. 463–6.

41.   Ibid., pp. 474 and 482.

42.   D. Oberdorfer, *The Turn: How the Cold War Came to an End* (London: Cape, 1992), p. 207–8.

43.   P. Sharp, *Thatcher's Diplomacy: The Revival of British Foreign Policy* (London: Macmillan, 1997), p. 200.

44.   Ibid., p. 215.

## Conclusion

1.   M. Thatcher, op. cit., p. 485.

2.   S. J. Ball, op. cit., p. 148.

3.   R. J. Aldrich, *Espionage, Security*, pp. 1–3, 76.

4.   M. Gowing, II, op.cit., p.150.

5.   Lashmar, op. cit., p. 169.

6.   A. Werblan, 'The Conversation Between Wladyslaw Gomulka and Josef Stalin on 14 November 1945', CWIHP, Bulletin II, 1998, p. 136.

7.   R. H. Paterson, op. cit., p. 167.

8.   P. Kennedy, *The Realities Behind Diplomacy: Background Influences on British External Policy, 1865–1980* (London: Allen and Unwin, 1981), p. 276.

9.   Niall Ferguson, *The Independent*, 10 October, 1998.

10.   Cited in E. Barker, op. cit., p. 185.

# SELECT BIBLIOGRAPHY

## Official Sources

1. Great Britain

*a) Public Record Office, Kew*

| | |
|---|---|
| CAB 81 | Joint Intelligence Staff Committee |
| CAB 128 and 129 | Cabinet minutes and memoranda |
| CAB 131 | Defence Committee |
| CAB 130 and 134 | *ad hoc* Cabinet Committees |
| DEFE 4 and 5 | Chiefs of Staff minutes and memoranda |
| DEFE 6 | Joint Planning Staff reports |
| FO 371 | Foreign Office general correspondence |
| FO 800 | Foreign Office private papers collections |
| PREM 11 and 13 | Prime Minister's Office |

b)  *Documents on British Policy Overseas* (HMSO, London, various volumes).
*British Documents on the End of Empire* (HMSO, London, various volumes).

2. United States

*Foreign Relations of the United States* (Washington, volumes regularly published).

## Private Papers Collections

Ernest Bevin, Churchill College, Cambridge.
Stafford Cripps Papers, Nuffield College, Oxford.
Hugh Dalton diary, London School of Economics.
Pierson Dixon, by permission of Mr Piers Dixon.
Anthony Eden Papers, Public Record Office, Kew (FO 954).
Lord Halifax, Churchill College, Cambridge.
Oliver Harvey Papers, British Library.
Inverchapel Papers, Public Record Office, Kew (FO 800).
Liddell Hart Papers, King's College, London.

Harold Macmillan diary, Bodleian Library, Oxford.
Arthur Mann Papers, Bodleian Library, Oxford.
Sargent Papers, Public Record Office, Kew (FO 800).

## Memoirs and Diaries

Please note that unless otherwise stated the place of publication is London.

Acheson, D., *Present at the Creation* (1970).
Boyle, P. G., *The Churchill-Eisenhower Correspondence, 1953–5* (Chapel Hill, NC, 1990).
Brown, G., *In My Way* (1971).
Cable, J., *The Geneva Conference of 1954 on Indochina* (1988).
Cairncross, A., (ed.), *The Robert Hall Diaries, 1947–53* (1989).
Callaghan, J., *Time and Chance* (1987).
Clark, W., *From Three Worlds* (1986).
Colville, J., *The Fringes of Power: 10 Downing Street Diaries* (1985).
Crossman, R., *The Diaries of a Cabinet Minister, I and II* (1975/6).
Healey, D., *The Time of My Life* (1989).
Kissinger, H., *White House Years* (Boston, Mass., 1979).
Macdonald, I., *Man of the Times* (1976).
Macmillan, H., *Tides of Fortune, 1945–55* (1969).
    *Riding the Storm, 1956–59* (1971).
    *Pointing the Way, 1959–61* (1972).
    *At the End of the Day, 1961–63* (1973).
Mayhew, C., *Time to Explain*, (1987).
Moran, Lord, *Winston Churchill: The Struggle for Survival* (1966).
Morgan, J. (ed.), *The Backbench Diaries of Richard Crossman* (1981).
Nicolson, H., *Diaries and Letters, 1945–62* (1968).
Pearce, R. (ed.), *Patrick Gordon Walker: Political Diaries, 1932–1971* (1991).
Pimlott, B. (ed.), *The Political Diary of Hugh Dalton, 1918–40, 1945–60* (1986).
Shuckburgh, E., *Descent to Suez: Diaries, 1951–6* (1985).
Thatcher, M., *The Downing Street Years* (1993).
Van der Poel, J. (ed.), *Selections from the Smuts Papers, VII* (Cambridge, 1973).
Williams, P. M. (ed.), *The Diary of Hugh Gaitskell, 1945–56* (1983).
Zuckerman, S., *Monkeys, Men and Missiles: An Autobiography* (1988).

## Secondary Works

Aldous, R., and Lee, S. (eds), *Harold Macmillan and Britain's World Role* (1996).
Aldrich, R. J. (ed.), *British Intelligence Strategy and the Cold War, 1945–51* (1992).
Aldrich, R. J., *Espionage, Security and Intelligence in Britain, 1945–70* (Manchester, 1998).
Aldrich, R. J., and Hopkins, M. F. (eds), *Intelligence, Defence and Diplomacy:*

*British Policy in the Post–War World* (1994).

Andrew, C., and Gordievsky, O., *The KGB: The Inside Story* (1990).

Barker, E., *The British Between the Superpowers, 1945–50* (1983).

Bartlett, C. J., *The Special Relationship: A Political History of Anglo-American Relations Since 1945* (1992).

Baylis, J., *The Diplomacy of Pragmatism: Britain and the Formation of NATO, 1942–4* (1993).

Becker, J., and Knipping, F., *Power in Europe? Great Britain, France, Italy and Germany in a Postwar World, 1945–50* (Berlin, 1986).

Brivati, B., and Jones, H. (eds), *From Reconstruction to Integration: Britain and Europe Since 1945* (1993).

Bullock, A., *Ernest Bevin: Foreign Secretary, 1945–51* (1983).

Cairncross, A., *The Price of War* (Oxford, 1986).

Charmley, J., *Churchill's Grand Alliance: The Anglo-American Special Relationship, 1940–57* (1995).

Danchev, A., *Oliver Franks: Founding Father* (Oxford, 1993).

Clark, I., *Nuclear Diplomacy and the Special Relationship* (Oxford, 1994).

Clark, I., and Wheeler, N. J., *The British Origins of Nuclear Strategy, 1945–55* (Oxford, 1989).

Crockatt, R., *The Fifty Years War: The United States and the Soviet Union in World Politics, 1941–91* (1995).

Deighton, A., *The Impossible Peace: Britain, the Division of Germany and the Origins of the Cold War* (Oxford, 1990).

Deighton, A. (ed.), *Britain and the First Cold War* (1990).

Dobson, A. P., *Anglo-American Relations in the Twentieth Century* (1995).

Dockrill, M., and Young, J. W. (eds), *British Foreign Policy, 1945–56* (1989).

Dutton, D., *Anthony Eden: A Life and Reputation* (1997).

Edmonds, R., *Setting the Mould: The United States and Britain, 1945–50* (Oxford, 1986).

Gaddis, J. L., *We Now Know: Rethinking Cold War History* (Oxford, 1998).

Gearson, J. P. S., *Harold Macmillan and the Berlin Wall Crisis, 1958–62* (1998).

Gori, F., and Pons, S. (eds), *The Soviet Union and Europe in the Cold War, 1943–53* (1996).

Gorodetsky, G. (ed.), *Soviet Foreign Policy, 1917–1991: A Retrospective* (1994).

Gowing, M., *Independence and Deterrence: Britain and Atomic Energy 1945–92*, I and II (1974).

Greenwood, S., *Britain and European Cooperation Since 1945* (Oxford, 1992).
*Britain and European Integration Since the Second World War* (Manchester, 1996).
*The Alternative Alliance: Anglo-French Relations Before the Coming of NATO, 1944–48* (1996).

Harris, K., *Attlee* (1982).

Hennessy, P., *Never Again: Britain 1945–51* (1993).

Heuser, B., and O'Neill, R. (eds), *Securing Peace in Europe, 1945–62* (1992).

Hogan, M. J., *The Marshall Plan: America, Britain and the Reconstruction of Western Europe, 1947–52* (Cambridge, 1987).

Holloway, D., *Stalin and the Bomb* (New Haven, Conn., 1994).

Horne, A., *Harold Macmillan*, I and II (1988/9).

Kennedy-Pipe, C., *Stalin's Cold War: Soviet Strategies in Europe, 1943–56* (Manchester, 1995).

Kent, J., *British Imperial Strategy and the Origins of the Cold War, 1944–49* (Leicester, 1993).

Lamb, R., *The Macmillan Years: The Emerging Truth* (1995).

Lane, A., and Temperley, H. (eds), *The Rise and Fall of the Grand Alliance, 1941–45* (1995).

Leffler, M. P., *A Preponderance of Power: National Security, the Truman Administration and the Cold War* (Stanford, Calif., 1992).

Louis, William R., and Owen, R. (eds), *Suez 1956: The Crisis and its Consequences* (Oxford, 1989).

May, E. R., and Zelikow, P. D. (eds), *The Kennedy Tapes: Inside the White House During the Cuban Missile Crisis* (Cambridge, Mass., 1997).

Muller, J. W. (ed.), *Churchill as Peacemaker* (Cambridge, 1997).

Naimark, N. M., *The Russians in Germany: A History of the Soviet Zone of Occupation, 1945–49* (Cambridge, Mass., 1995).

Oberdorfer, D., *The Turn: How the Cold War Came to an End* (1992).

Ovendale, R., *The English-Speaking Alliance: Britain, the United States, the Dominions and the Cold War, 1945–51* (1985).

Ovendale, R. (ed.), *The Foreign Policy of the British Labour Governments* (Leicester, 1984).

Reynolds, D. (ed.), *The Origins of the Cold War in Europe: International Perspectives* (Yale, Conn., 1994).

Richardson, D., and Stone, G. (eds), *Decisions and Diplomacy: Essays in Twentieth-Century International History* (1995).

Rotter, A. J., *The Path to Vietnam: Origins of the American Commitment to South-East Asia* (Ithaca, NY, 1987).

Ruane, K., *War and Revolution in Vietnam, 1930–75* (1998).

Saville, J., *The Politics of Continuity: British Foreign Policy and the Labour Government, 1945–46* (1993).

Sharp, P., *Thatcher's Diplomacy: The Revival of British Foreign Policy* (1997).

Smith, P. (ed.), *Government and the Armed Forces in Britain, 1856–1990* (1996).

Thorpe, D. R., *Selwyn Lloyd* (1989).

Turner, J., *Macmillan* (1994).

Weiler, P., *British Labour and the Cold War* (Stanford, Calif, 1988).
 *Ernest Bevin* (Manchester, 1993).

White, B., *Britain, Detente and Changing East-West Relations* (1992).

Wilkes, G. (ed.), *Britain's Failure to Enter the European Community, 1961–63* (1997).

Young, J. W. (ed.), *The Foreign Policy of Churchill's Peacetime Administration* (1988).
 *France, the Cold War and the Western Alliance, 1944–49* (Leicester, 1990).
 *Winston Churchill's Last Campaign: Britain and the Cold War, 1951–55* (Oxford, 1996).

Zametica, J. (ed.), *British Officials and Foreign Policy, 1945–50* (Leicester, 1990).

Zubok, V., and Pleshakov, C., *Inside the Kremlin's Cold War: From Stalin to Khrushchev* (Harvard, Mass., 1994).

## Articles

Baylis, J., and Macmillan, A., 'The British Global Strategy Paper of 1952', *Journal of Strategic Studies*, 16:2 (June 1993).

Boyle, P., 'The British Foreign Office and American Foreign Policy, 1947–48', *Journal of American Studies*, 16:3 (1982).

'The British Government's View of the Cuban Missile Crisis', *Contemporary Record*, 10:3 (1996).

Carruthers, S. L., 'A Red Under Every Bed?: Anti-Communist Propaganda and Britain's Response to Colonial Insurgency', *Contemporary Record*, 9:2 (1995).

Cromwell, W. C., 'The Marshall Plan, Britain and the Cold War', *Review of International Studies*, 8:4 (1982).

Deighton, A., 'The Frozen Front: The Labour Government and the Origins of the Cold War, 1945–47', *International Affairs*, 63:3 (1987).

Dockrill, M., 'The Foreign Office, Anglo-American Relations and the Korean War, June 1950-June 1951', *International Affairs*, 26:3 (1986).

Duchin, B. R., 'The "Agonizing Reappraisal": Eisenhower, Dulles and the European Defense Community', *Diplomatic History*, vol. 16 (1996).

Farquharson, J., 'From Unity to Division: What Prompted Britain to Change its Policy in Germany in 1946?', *European History Quarterly*, vol. 26 (1996).

Greenwood, S., 'Frank Roberts and the "Other" Long Telegram: The View from the British Embassy in Moscow, March 1946', *Journal of Contemporary History*, vol. 20 (1990).

'Return to Dunkirk: The Origins of the Anglo-French Treaty of March, 1947', *Journal of Strategic Studies*, vol. 6 (1983).

Johnston, A. M., 'Mr. Slessor Goes to Washington: The Influence of the British Global Strategy Paper on the Eisenhower "New Look"', *Journal of Strategic Studies*, 22:3 (1998).

Mark, E., 'The War Scare of 1946 and Its Consequences', *Diplomatic History*, 21:3 (1997).

Merrick, R., 'The Russia Committee of the British Foreign Office and the Cold War', *Journal of Contemporary History*, vol. 20 (1985).

Petersen, N., 'Who Pulled Whom and How Much? Britain, the United States and the Making of the North Atlantic Treaty', *Millenium: Journal of International Studies*, 11:2 (1982).

Pechatnov, V. O., 'The Big Three After World War II: New Documents on Soviet Thinking About Postwar Relations with the United States and Great Britain', *Cold War International History Project* (CWIHP), Working Paper 13 (Woodrow Wilson Center, Washington).

Pyne, K., 'Art or Article? The Need for and Nature of the British Hydrogen Bomb, 1954–58', *Contemporary Record*, 9:3 (1995).

Raack, R. C., 'Stalin Plans His Postwar Germany', *Journal of Contemporary History*, vol. 28 (1993).

Roberts, G., 'Moscow and the Marshall Plan: Politics, Ideology and the Onset of the Cold War', *Europe-Asia Studies*, 46:8 (1994).

Ruane, K., 'Anthony Eden, British Diplomacy and the Origins of the Geneva Conference of 1954', *Historical Journal*, 37:1 (March, 1994).

'Refusing to Pay the Price: British Foreign Policy and the Pursuit of Victory in Vietnam, 1952–4', *English Historical Review*, vol. CX (1995).

'Containing America: Aspects of British Foreign Policy and the Cold War in Southeast Asia, 1951–54', *Diplomacy and Statecraft*, vol. 7 (1996).

Scott, L., 'Close to the Brink? Britain and the Cuban Missile Crisis', *Contemporary Record*, 5:3 (1991).

Shaw, T., 'The Information Research Department of the British Foreign Office and the Korean War', *Journal of Contemporary History*, 34:2, 1999.

Shlaim, A., 'Britain, the Berlin Blockade and the Cold War', *International Affairs*, 60:1 (1983/4).

Smirnov, Y., and Zubok, V., 'Nuclear Weapons After Stalin's Death: Moscow Enters the H-Bomb Age', CWIHP, Bulletin 4.

Smith, L., 'Covert British Propaganda: The Information Research Department: 1944–77', *Millennium: Journal of International Studies*, 9:1 (1980).

Smith, R., and Zemetica, J., 'The Cold Warrior: Clement Attlee Reconsidered, 1945–7', *International Affairs*, 6:2 (1985).

Wark, W. K., 'Coming in from the Cold: British Propaganda and Red Army Defectors, 1945–1952', *International History Review*, IX:I (1987).

Warner, G., 'The Study of Cold War Origins', *Diplomacy and Statecraft*, 1:3 (1990).

Wohlforth, W. C., 'New Evidence on Moscow's Cold War', *Diplomatic History*, 2:2 (1997).

Young, J. W., 'The British Foreign Office and Cold War Fighting in the Early 1950s: PUSC(51)16 and the 1952 "Sore Spots" Memorandum', *University of Leicester Discussion Papers in Politics*, P95/2.

Zubok, V., 'Soviet Intelligence and the "Small" Committee of Information, 1952–3', *CWIHP*, Working Paper 4.

# INDEX

223